The Lions of Carentan

The Lions of Carentan
Fallschirmjäger Regiment 6, 1943–1945

Volker Griesser

Translated by Mara Taylor

CASEMATE PUBLISHERS
Philadelphia & Newbury

Published in the United States of America in 2011 by
CASEMATE
908 Darby Road, Havertown, PA 19083

and in the United Kingdom by
CASEMATE
17 Cheap Street, Newbury, Berkshire, RG14 5DD

© 2011 VS-BOOKS Torsten Verhülsdonk.
Originally Published in Germany as *Die Löwen von Carentan—
Das Fallschirmjäger-Regiment 6, 1943–45* / VS-BOOKS 2007

ISBN 978-1-61200-006-0

Cataloging-in-publication data is available from the Library of
Congress and from the British Library.

Printed and bound in the United States of America.

10 9 8 7 6 5 4 3 2 1

For a complete list of Casemate titles, please contact

United States of America:
Casemate Publishers
Telephone (610) 853-9131, Fax (610) 853-9146
E-mail casemate@casematepublishing.com
Website www.casematepublishing.com

United Kingdom:
Casemate-UK
Telephone (01635) 231091, Fax (01635) 41619
E-mail casemate-uk@casematepublishing.co.uk
Website www.casematepublishing.co.uk

CONTENTS

Preface

The Fallschirmjäger (paratroopers) were the elite arm of the German Wehrmacht (Armed Forces). Hermann Göring assumed control of the Luftwaffe (Air Force) in 1935, and the Fallschirmjäger were created from a combination of his personal paramilitary regiment and volunteer parachutists. Their subsequent outstanding achievements in World War II were based upon two major factors: voluntary enlistment in the Fallschirm Division, and outstanding modern and demanding military training. None rivaled them in ability and motivation; they were respected within the German forces and feared by their opponents.

A new generation of German paras grew out of their early victories. Even when, during the course of the war, training had to be shortened and specialized equipment became scarce, the example of the battle-tried Fallschirmjäger and the aura that surrounded them swept up many young volunteers, and fighting spirit often compensated for logistical problems.

Much general history has been already written about the origins of the Fallschirmjäger and their deployment in World War II; the prevalence of material makes another such history unnecessary here. This project instead grew from a personal interest in documenting, as seamlessly as possible and from the scant existing information, the history of the 6th Fallschirmjäger Regiment (FJR 6). It is not intended to recapitulate once more the global circumstances of the time; these have been portrayed often enough, usually from the point of view of the Allies. Rather, the goal of this work is to illuminate the part that FJR 6 played in the events of the war, seen from their own unique perspective.

This work aims to capture the authentic nature of Fallschirmjäger service, as former members of the regiment describe in their own words what they experienced. In this way, the reader is provided with a wealth of new information. The photographs included here all stem from private collections of the former comrades and the author. Most of these pictures have not been published before in an English-language publication and are introduced here for the first time. The physical quality of the photographs is not always of the highest standard; the reader should consider, however, the circumstances over 60 years ago under which they were created. Yet they enable the reader to look into the faces of the men who were constantly fighting on the front lines, their faces etched with exhaustion, pain and sorrow, but also with hope, assurance, and bold courage. In contrast to the photographs from the propaganda companies, here we see the true face of the German Fallschirmjäger.

Furthermore, this account is based on numerous primary sources: official corps, division and regimental orders; battle reports; war daybooks; as well as personal documents such as diaries and other handwritten records. I have drawn on this material to provide the reader with a complete picture of FJR 6's term of service.

During my first meeting with Alexander Uhlig, the head of the Fellowship of the 6th Fallschirmjäger Regiment veterans group, it became clear to me that my research should have commenced decades earlier in order to be able to capture more eyewitness material. Indeed, the news reached me during writing that a further former member of 6 FJR had been called to the great hunting ground in the sky. The list of comrades who were not able to participate in the Fellowship meeting in autumn 2002, because of health or other reasons, was unfortunately longer that the list of actual participants. Yet all those present displayed much enthusiasm when Alexander Uhlig announced the beginning of this project. In the course of the evening as well as in the following weeks and months, I received many reports, personal documents and photos; they extended invitations to me and bestowed me with so much support that I can only describe it as the 'true spirit of the Fallschirmjäger'. This chronicle could never have been realized without the active assistance of the comrades of the FJR 6, and I owe them my earnest thanks.

This book is therefore dedicated to the men of FJR 6, the Lions of Carentan.

VOLKER GRIESSER
Oberpleis

CHAPTER ONE

The Initial Organization, 1943

The history of FJR 6 began on 13 February 1943, with the creation of the 2nd Fallschirmjäger Division (2 FJD). Major Egon Liebach took command of the newly organized regiment. An experienced paratrooper and troop leader, he had already taken part in the battle of Crete in May 1941, and his headquarters lay in Vannes in the French Bretagne. The 2nd Battalion, FJR 6 (II./FJR 6), was created from the former 4th Battalion, Sturmregiment (Assault Regiment). The personnel the 1st and 3rd Battalions came from the veterans of the famous Ramcke Brigade (named after General Hermann-Bernhard 'Gerhard' Ramcke) – the trial battalion of the XI Fliegerkorps (Air Corps) – and the 100th Luftwaffen-Jäger-Batallion z.b.V. (Luftwaffe Rifle Battalion for Special Use). Other men included those fresh from jump training /parachute school. Some of these Fallschirmjäger were old hands at soldiering, and had volunteered for the paras following service on the Eastern Front. This diverse mixture of individuals would quickly form into a hard-hitting troop.

Major Liebach could, to a great extent, count on the battle experience of his 'old warriors'. Field exercises and close combat quickly become the focus of training for FJR 6, and the example set by the veterans guided the younger soldiers. Despite the fact that all members of the regiment were graduates of the parachute schools, they

FJR 6's jump training was not neglected in 1943. Due to their capability to conduct air landings via parachute drops and military gliders, the regiment was one of the few that could be deployed for airborne assaults without considerable restructuring.

Three men, seen in the first hours of the creation of FJR 6, pose in Bretagne for a souvenir picture.

received further instruction in combat parachute deployment. In addition, they were trained in operations from military gliders, including a novel dive-glider.

Such training prepared FJR 6 for carrying out a broad range of air assault missions. The regiment also received considerable firepower; heavy companies were equipped with 7.5cm recoilless guns in addition to mortars and heavy machine guns. In terms of strength, the rifle squads consisted of 12 men, instead of nine, and the additional paratroopers built a second machine-gun troop in their squad. At this point in time, the 2nd Battalion was still stationed in Mourmelon, serving as an instruction battalion for the ground-fighting school of the Luftwaffe.

The 2nd Battalion received a leading role in a major exercise: an air assault on the Mourmelon airfield itself. Dietrich Brehde, at the time an Oberleutnant and platoon leader in the 6th Company, here describes the mission:

According to the starting position, a Fallschirmjäger Battalion, represented by a company, was responsible for taking the Mourmelon airfield from the air. Beforehand, a howitzer battery that controlled the airfield from a firing position near the Ferme de Buy, an abandoned farmstead, was supposed to be taken out by a surprise attack. For this, a platoon of gliders with drogue parachutes would land directly in the confined space of the firing range and neutralize the artillery.

The personnel of the artillery school also located at Mourmelon played the 'enemy'. The artillerymen were unaware of how the attack would take place. Because they were dealing with Fallschirmjäger, they naturally were counting on a parachute jump.

The Fallschirmjäger launched their attack from Reims, and the platoon that was to assault the artillery position with gliders decamped early in Mourmelon in order to be able to depart on time. They arrived so early in Reims that the platoon leader decided to stop over at the soldiers' rest centre. Just after he and his men had entered the centre and sat down, a chubby Heeres-Oberst [army colonel] stormed over in a raging fury, verbally attacking the unsuspecting lieutenant; he asked him if he was the leader of this commando, from which unit he came, and to present his pay book. Such a disgrace had never happened to him, the Oberst, in his whole life, he claimed. He was so worked up that it took a while before the Leutnant could even begin to understand what he was going on about.

On their trip though the city, a few of the 'heavenly dogs', as they were called, in the last car had made a game out of throwing detonators from practice hand grenades onto the sidewalk; they had exploded with a loud rattle, terrifying the passersby. They had been so wrapped up in having fun that they had missed the fact that the German commanding officer of the station in Reims, namely this Oberst, had been among the civilians; along with the French, he had been forced to take to his heels in the face of the cracking detonators. After the Leutnant had identified himself and understood the full particulars of the situation, he apologized for the misdeeds of his men and tried to spark the Oberst's interest in the upcoming exercise. He told him about the dive-gliders with the drogue parachutes and explained that the young soldiers, who otherwise were kept on a tight leash, wanted to blow off some steam before this complicated operation. The Oberst thought at first that the Leutnant was pulling his leg about the dive and the drogue parachutes, and he forbade him from making such jokes. He calmed down only after seeing a written training document. Finally the Fallschirmjäger and the Oberst parted ways on friendly terms, and if time hadn't been pressing, the senior officer probably would have bought them another drink.

At the airfield there was no more waiting. The three gliders were towed up to over 2,000m altitude and released. Silently they volplaned towards their objective. In each plane, 12 men sat astride a bench, one behind the other. The sidewalls [of the glider] were constructed so that they could be thrown off in the landing, so that all the men could jump out of the plane at the same

Two Fallschirmjäger pose for the camera in a quiet moment. They are wearing the second model olive-green coveralls with built-in trouser legs. The man on the left has a bandolier for 20 clips (each with five shots of ammunition) for his Karabiner 98k rifle. According to regulations, he is wearing his gasmask across his chest in the canvas bag issued for Fallschirmjäger. (His comrade is wearing his gasmask bag in the same way.) In order to avoid injuries when jumping, and especially during landing, the conventional gasmask canister was not issued to Fallschirmjäger. Both men have Luger pistols worn in holsters on the front left of their waist belts.

time. The Leutnant flew with the 'chain leader' in the middle plane, the other 'chain dogs' followed on the left and right...

Soon the goal became identifiable, even from this great height. The buildings were as big as coffee beans from this distance, and the landing zone in front was not bigger than a 10 Pfennig stamp. Maintaining height, the aircraft glided silently forward over the objective. Then finally the chain leader pressed the control stick far forward, and the plane shot sharply down; both 'chain dogs' followed close behind. The air current began to roar; the whole plane trembled, and the fragile wings shuddered suspiciously under the pressure. The ground began to rush ever closer, and they could make out the weapons in firing range and an audience across the street.

The pilot was yanking and yanking on the lever, but nothing was happening. He pulled the plane out of the dive without the drogue parachute; that manoeuvre pushed the men hard against the bench. Like an arrow, the large glider shot under a power line towards a long stretch of stables; it lost the ends of both wings against light posts. With a lurch, the pilot ripped the plane to the left into a tight hole between the buildings, in order to avoid a front-on collision with the stable wall. In the process, the wings were completely torn off, and, in a cloud of brick and mortar dust and roofing tiles, the body of the plane crashed sideways into a wall of a neighbouring building.

The Fallschirmjäger unbuckled themselves in lighting speed and jumped with a hurrah out against the concerned artillerymen, who were rushing to help them with first aid kits. Instead, they were pelted with practice hand grenades and taken prisoner. The drogue parachutes of the two chain dogs also did not open, and they made an equally dangerous crash landing that knocked over a freestanding toilet, which thankfully had nobody in it.

On the 'commanders hill', over a thousand observers, including three generals, could watch this part of the exercise from close by. They were all impressed with the lightning speed of the attack, because no one, neither the observers nor the artillery, nor even the personnel in charge, had noticed the approach of the three machines out of the sun, before they had careened into firing position like lightning from the sky.

The happiest part of the whole thing was that there were no serious injuries; the failure of the three drogue parachutes could easily have lead to a catastrophe. The fact that the exercise occurred without losses was entirely thanks to the presence of mind and the flying abilities of the three pilots. After the spectacular prelude, the exercise played out according to plan. An attack by the dive-bombers followed, with practice bombs dropped on the enemy position, then the parachute jump of a company on the landing field of Mourmelon. All in all, a nice success for the battalion. But one topic was the subject of much discussion over the next few days: the crash landing of the gliders near the Ferme de Buy.

The troop never figured out why the drogue parachutes failed on all three machines, after they had always functioned perfectly in the pre-exercise training. It can hardly have been a coincidence.

After the landing in gliders during an exercise, the Fallschirmjäger move without delay to attack the army's artillery position. Major Liebach placed great value on training that was as close to reality as possible. He took his assignment as the senior training supervisor of his regiment very seriously. Every phase of FJR 6's manoeuvres was analyzed thoroughly and discussed with the officers and NCOs. Liebach's supervisors and subordinates viewed him as a brave and methodical leader.

On 27 May 1943, FJR 6 was transferred with 2 FJD to southern France, near Combe-St Gervais, Vallabrix and Goudargues. II./FJR 6, had already moved into quarters, establishing themselves at the end of April on the troop drill ground La Courtine near Clermont-Ferrand. They also took on the role of the instruction battalion.

Despite their transfer, owing to an expected invasion by the Allies in southern France, as the strategic reserve of the Oberkommando der Wehrmacht (OKW; Supreme Command of the Armed Forces), the troops' training was continued with high intensity. Combat practice and jump duty still occupied a big chunk of the available time, so that Major Liebach could still justifiably claim to have under him one of the best-trained and most hard-hitting units within the Fallschirmjäger.

When the Allies landed in Sicily on 9 July 1943, the division stayed in the south of France with all the units under it. Only the selected top commanding officers knew that the battalion stood ready in case Italy were to change sides due to the Allied invasion. On the night of 26 July, however, FJR 6 received orders to prepare to march – Mussolini had been deposed the day before and replaced by Marshal Pietro Badoglio. Despite Badoglio's assurance that Italy would remain an ally to Germany, the OKW had decided to relocate the whole of 2 FJD to Rome to cover German backs in southern Italy and Sicily.

In true Fallschirmjäger tradition, much was demanded of the officers, so cigarette breaks were seldom taken. This Oberleutnant is wearing the second model of the coveralls in the Splittertarn (a German military camouflage pattern) of the Luftwaffe, and the first model of combat boots with side laces. His garrison cap has a border of silver braiding that was typical for officers; his rank is identified by the insignia sewed onto his upper sleeve.

A machine-gunner finds time after an exercise to have his picture taken in combat uniform. He has fitted his steel helmet with a camouflage cover and is also wearing knee protectors, to cushion the knees during parachute landings. On his belt he has the accessories pouch for the MG34 machine gun, as well as a P38 pistol in a soft case. The breechblock of the MG34 is protected against dirt and damage with a canvas covering.

This rifleman of FJR 6, wearing full combat gear, has coloured marking tape around the camouflage cover of his steel helmet to differentiate between the parties on the airfield assault exercise. Many of the Fallschirmjäger received a pair of marching boots, so they could spare their jump boots by wearing them only for jump duty and missions. Later, when jump boots could only be issued sparingly, the standard footgear for Fallschirmjäger became a mixture of jump boots, marching boots or traditional ankle-high lace-up boots.

Fallschirmjäger prepare for their relocation to Italy, loading up a JU 52 transport aircraft. The Fallschirmjäger packed their own parachutes, and similarly these men do not allow anyone else to lay a hand on the drop containers used for deploying weapons, ammunition and other supplies. The special assignments of the Fallschirmjäger and their elite status meant they preferred to rely on themselves.

Before the paras' departure to Italy, the subordinate commanders receive instructions from their officers. The concept of 'advanced leadership' was common within the Fallschirmjäger. A high degree of responsibility was demanded of subordinate commanders, whether commissioned and non-commissioned, in tactical leadership and battlefield logistics. The caste-like system that was still widespread in other places was practically unknown in the Fallschirmjäger divisions, and the divide between officers and non-commissioned officers (NCOs) was less prominent than in the older branches of service.

These two men, who would later definitively shape FJR 6, were deployed in 1943 to the headquarters of 2 FJD: on the left is Major Friedrich August Freiherr von der Heydte as chief of staff, and on the right Hauptmann Rolf Mager as his executive officer. Major von der Heydte took over the regiment in January 1944 and Hauptmann Mager commanded the 2nd Battalion. The regiments of FJD 2 received the sand-coloured uniforms of the Luftwaffe that were designed for the tropics; the alternative heavy wool uniforms were only suited to the summery Italian weather to a limited extent.

CHAPTER TWO

Deployment in Italy, 1943

On 26 July 1943, the 1st and 3rd Battalions of FJR 6 arrived at Istres airport near Marseille and from there flew to the temporary Pratica di Mare airport, to the southwest of Rome. The 2nd Battalion left France on the 26th, flying from Avignon to Foggia. Major Liebach had received orders to release the 2nd Battalion temporarily to the command of the XI Air Corps; it moved into a bivouac shelter in the olive groves near Manfredonia, while the other battalions camped in the dried-out swamps around Pratica di Mare.

On arrival in Italy, the men of FJR 6 had no immediate campaigns, only individual small exercises, so they spent their free time mostly pursuing athletic activities, like swimming at the Ostia beach. The 1st Battalion organized a track-and-field competition for the regiments of 2 FJD at the nearby barracks. The world record holder for the 800m dash, Oberfeldwebel Rudolf Harbig from the 2nd Battalion, completed the 4 <x> 100m relay single-handedly. Meanwhile, the 3rd Battalion ran a singing competition in Ostia's amphitheatre, and the kitchen crews held a contest in the 2nd Battalion camp to determine which mobile canteen

Immediately after arriving in Italy, the regiments of 2 FJD began to set up camp. Here a member of the signal communications platoon strings a telephone line high up in a tree.

produced the most delicious meals.

The 2nd Battalion, however, was also covertly preparing for a secret mission, of which only a few were aware, including Major Gericke, the battalion commander. The forced disarmament of Italian forces, Operation *Alaric*, was an essential part of German strategy in Italy. Eliminating the Italian Army headquarters was also a primary objective, and the 2nd Battalion had already been chosen, through their relocation to Italy, for this particular task.

Regimental commander Major Liebach congratulates the world-record holding athlete, Oberfeldwebel Rudolf Harbig, for his impressive athletic achievement in a relay.

This photo shows Rudolf Harbig in uniform during the arrival at the train station Gare du Nord in Paris, France.

Despite the fact that Rome and the surrounding areas were blocked for German troops, Major Gericke undertook a reconnaissance of the zone of operation around Monterotondo, the seat of the Italian headquarters. He personally travelled in a jeep towards Monterotondo, and through various acts of subterfuge he penetrated the inner circles of Italian defences, all while taking notes for the mission in his head. A later fly-over in a German liaison aircraft confirmed his notations and brought additional information.

On 8 September 1943, at 1945hrs, Italian radio announced Italy's capitulation by Marshal Badoglio and right away, at 2000hrs and launched by the codeword *Walpurgisnacht* (Walpurgis Night), German forces began the fight for Rome. Because several officers of 2 FJD had been tapping into enemy broadcasts, actions could be taken right away against the Italians.

In a surprise attack Major von der Heydte, the Ia (operations officer) of 2 FJD, and a group of Fallschirmjäger of the 2nd Battalion, FJR 6, apprehended the commander of the Italian coastal division. The general was in the middle of dictating orders for the capture of General Ramcke and Major von der Heydte. Left leaderless, the Italian troops stationed in the vicinity of the German camp around Pratica di Mare were quickly taken prisoner and disarmed.

While off-duty hours were used to play sports, swim and relax, the Fallschirmjäger spent most of their time around Pratica di Mare getting acclimatized and training. Here a squad of II./FJR 6 can be seen handling a drop container after a training session.

Despite the fine weather and the signorinas, the Fallschirmjäger stayed sharp regarding training. In preparation for the capture of Rome, FJR 6 here practices exercises in house-to-house fighting, far away from the curious eyes of the Italians. These soldiers are practising entering a house from the back using a ladder. Under the direction of an Obergefreiter, the soldier at the front experiments with the right angle for placing the scaling ladder.

When General Ramcke became suddenly ill, Oberstleutnant Meder-Eggebrecht took over control of the division and Major von der Heydte led the combat group for the capture of Rome on 9 September. The 2nd Fallschirmjäger Artillery Regiment (FJAR 2), as well as other divisional troops, reinforced FJR 6's 1st and 3rd Battalions during the mission. They pushed forward along the Via Ostiense. The Italian armoured corps 'Roma', whose vehicle fleet included German-made heavy tanks, resisted the regiment with determination. The Italians transformed the fortress-like buildings in the southwestern part of the city into practically impregnable bulwarks, forcing the regiment to take down the defensive works one by one.

While Major Liebach is conferring with officers and the mayor of Pratica di Mare, his escort keeps a professional distance, yet remains watchful of what is happening in the area.

The 3rd Battalion remained in front of one of these fortresses, waiting for artillery support; Major von der Heydte, in the scout car that served as his command vehicle, joined a Major Pelz and personally directed the attack on the building with a 10.5cm *Leichtgeschütz* (recoilless gun). After breaking through the Italian resistance, the Germans advanced further along the Via Ostiense.

Because the deployment to Italy occurred quickly and by surprise, this Fallschirmjäger's wedding – which had been scheduled to take place in Germany – had to be cancelled at short notice. Instead, he is married by proxy.

In order to do the occasion justice, the setting for the wedding was arranged accordingly. Oberjäger Gerd Kubassa was the groom.

In the early-morning hours of 9 September, the men of II./FJR 6, carried out the last preparations for their special mission, so that they could fly out from Foggia at 0630hrs. Dietrich Brehde described the mission:

During the battle for Rome, Major Liebach's regimental command post was kept as mobile as possible. A motorcycle sidecar, and a few motorcyclist serving as combat messengers, were sufficient for the Major, and allowed him to stay close to the fighting and lead his men effectively. This photo shows Major Liebach in the middle of the picture, issuing commands.

At 0630hrs the battalion set out in the following order: headquarters with the signal communication platoon, 5th, 6th, 7th and 8th Companies. The threatening engines and full-throttle starts of the aircraft kicked up enough dust to obscure the rising sun and reduce visibility on the ground.

Just as the aircraft were rolling up to the starting point, one of the pilots braked hard; a small human form came running, waving at the starting plane. The machine stopped, and a panting Obergefreiter appeared at the door, yelling 'Take me with you, take me with you!' His comrades pulled him in, and the plane started without further delay. Only once they were in the air were they able to figure out what was going on with the Obergefreiter, a rugged old hand, who had been in Crete and Russia. His outfit was as unusual as his whole entrance: he was dressed in nothing but a paratrooper suit and combat boots from which his naked, hairy thighs were sticking out. In other words, he lacked a helmet, waist belt, pants and above all a weapon! At least he had schlepped along a parachute.

What had happened? The schnapps from the victualer the previous night hadn't been to everyone's taste, so this Obergefreiter had happily volunteered to take portions of schnapps off his comrades' hands. The result was such a solid state of inebriation that he had wanted to sleep it off in hiding. Of course, he was missing during the alarm the next morning, but his group had not had time for further investigation. The roaring of the engines had woken him up. In his haste, he thought

At certain points, the men of FJR 6 met strong resistance from well-armed Italian troops and partisans. Here two Fallschirmjäger take cover from enemy snipers' harassing fire behind a half-track vehicle.

In the fighting along the Via Ostiense, which included breaking pockets of enemy resistance, the anti-tank defence units took on a special role. Their anti-tank guns prove to be a practical means for clearing out Italian positions with direct fire, and also for effectively countering those Italians who were armed with German tanks.

only of the items necessary for jumping, namely combat boots, a jump suit and a parachute from the equipment tent. He hadn't even remembered a weapon! Now, his comrades equipped him with a pistol and some hand grenades; he'd have to find himself a weapon below. His colleagues impressed upon him that he absolutely could not let himself be captured in this getup; he would bring shame to the name Fallschirmjäger if he were caught without trousers!

The troops would now have to prove in battle what they had practised and tested in Mourmelon. They would now all jump with weapons. Some companies were prepared with bursting charges and even anti-tank mines fitted with hand grenade detonators, in order to destroy the enemies on the ground. Those who carried automatic pistols were supposed to shoot as soon as possible while descending in the parachute.

At 0825hrs, the paras approached Monterotondo and the enemy immediately fired on them. It was like a bad joke, that German-made 8.8cm anti-aircraft artillery

Shortly before the start of the Monterotondo operation, the Fallschirmjäger of the 2nd Battalion put on their chutes. Because this mission was supposed to have the advantage of a surprise attack, the men jump already geared up for battle. They check the secure fit of each other's equipment.

on the ground was firing at Germans – the guns were a present from Hitler to his friend, the 'Duce'. The 6th and 7th Companies missed their landing space by up to 4km. Some of the battalion staff also flew past the planned landing zone. Only the battalion commander with part of the staff and the signals communication platoon

Under the oversight of their Feldwebel, Hauptmann Gericke's men board a transport aircraft.

Upon reaching the jump zone, each man checks the fit of his helmet one last time in order to prevent it shifting during the jump. The pictures shows clearly that Fallschirmjäger could carry out jumps without special protective cases for their weapons.

landed correctly, after the commander himself instructed the pilot. Yet he was left on his own with only a few men, because the 7th Company, which was supposed to jump with the battalion staff, had flown farther on. The farmstead that they had planned to use as the battalion's command post proved to be a fire-direction centre occupied by the Italians. The Fallschirmjäger took three officers and seven squads prisoner after briefly exchanging fire.

While some of the battalion staff organized an all-round defence of the command post, the remaining parts of the signals communication platoon tried, at first unsuccessfully, to get in contact with the other companies. The 5th Company landed under heavy anti-aircraft and infantry fire, but they missed their landing point only marginally. They cleared out a cantonment, a tent camp and some field positions, and took 180 prisoners in the process. They also destroyed three anti-aircraft guns. The garden plots by the sports ground were swarming with armed soldiers, who had been very trigger-happy at first, but, as soon as they were directly attacked, offered little resistance. The whole area appeared to be full of troops.

The leader of the 1st Platoon guided an Italian 1st lieutenant, whom he was

After landing at the enemy headquarters, the Fallschirmjäger gather and proceed to the attack. They realize that their best chance for success against the larger numbers of Italians is a determined advance.

holding at gunpoint, and a portion of his men around a minefield on the closest path to the fort. In double time they climbed uphill; a few nests of resistance were quickly cleared out. But above, on the tree-lined avenue that led to the fort, they became stranded. In front of a bunker-like roadblock, submachine-gun fire sparked along the whole length of the street; there was no way through. The platoon swerved to the right, and circumvented the roadblock by going through gardens and backyards. The houses near the fort were occupied by the enemy troops, and the Fallschirmjäger had to fight their way through. The Italian 1st lieutenant, a communications officer, followed them obediently, although one could see the horror on his face when his comrades were overrun in close combat. At the front section of the fort– a huge, centuries-old building that was built out of massive blocks of stone – stood a terraced garden, whose slope tended towards the street and was partially supported by walls. A few old trees stood between them.

Both gates were closed, and heavy fire streamed out of the fort's tower and out of the many open windows along its broad front section. Right away, our soldiers suffered casualties, and the Fallschirmjäger had to search for cover on the slope and behind the trees. They sent the Italian officer ahead with a white flag, demanding that the enemy surrender. But those inside refused to consider it; the Italian officer was shot at, and had to take himself with his white flag to safety as quickly as possible. The Fallschirmjäger also could not reach the gates

An Oberjäger, most likely acting as squad leader, is passing on orders to his men. This photo illustrates the comfortable and well-loved tropical uniform worn by the Fallschirmjäger during the battle of Rome. Note that his rank is displayed on blue-grey shoulder straps, however, not on the tropical straps.

from the side. As soon as anyone reached the wall, hand grenades and demolition charges would hail down from the tower and windows. For the time being, the platoon had to limit themselves to exchanging fire with the enemy and picking them off with sharpshooters, as they waited for reinforcements.

The 2nd Platoon of the 5th Company also had to overpower enemy positions immediately on landing, in order to gain any kind of foothold. Then they attacked and took out a strongpoint whose occupants were armed with anti-tank artillery and submachine guns. Near the hospital the resistance grew stronger; the platoon now had two dead. The platoon leader decided to surround the enemy from the west. After heavy exchanges of fire, the platoon broke through to the street and in that way

The Italians doggedly defended the fort in Monterotondo. The men of the 2nd Battalion here approach under covering fire, and suffer serious losses when storming the well-fortified location.

covered the right wing of the 5th Company.

The 6th Company, like the 7th Company and The 6th Company, like the 7th Company and part of the staff, disembarked too late and landed about 4km northwest of Monterotondo. The company jumped into intense enemy fire, and one transport aircraft fell burning to the ground. An explosion ripped apart one paratrooper in the air, most probably due to a demolition charge detonating. Some of the company were flown over the Tiber River, where many men landed in the water and drowned. Some of the men in the transport aircraft witnessed this; a few machines flew over again and inflatable boats were dropped down, so that those who had landed on the other side of the river could cross and link up with their company. The area in which the company had landed offered little cover, and sat under heavy anti-aircraft and infantry fire. Monterotondo could not be seen from the position, and there were no clear points of reference for orientation. Finally, the company managed to push forward to the train station, advancing with those from the battalion's staff who had similarly been dropped in the wrong area. There a troop transport had just arrived. The soldiers on the transport were disarmed, and an ammunitions wagon was blown up. As they advanced further towards the fortress objective, the company then became entangled in house-to-house fighting.

The 7th Company found themselves between the railway tracks and the Tiber. Apparently the 6th and 7th Companies had crossed each other during the approach, so that a change of sides had taken place. The 7th Company also lost two men in the Tiber; in heavy paratrooper gear, even the best swimmer

A sharpshooter of the 2nd Battalion gives his comrades covering fire, while another group works towards the fort.

stood no chance if he fell into the water. Those who had landed on the other side of the Tiber crossed the river by using the air-dropped inflatable boats, and linked up with their company. As they assembled, the company was under heavy fire from factory grounds near a fork in the road. They succeeded in reaching the main street that ran north–south to the west of the city. The company leader sent the 3rd Platoon back to the west as reserve protection, and attacked the enemy in the factory grounds with the 1st and 2nd Platoons. As in the city and indeed the whole area, this area was also swarming with Italian troops. It appeared, however, that those who had challenged the Fallschirmjäger so hard during the landing were not as steady on their feet when directly attacked. Twenty officers and about 200 men surrendered to the Fallschirmjäger's considerably smaller numbers.

As they advanced towards the city, the company came up against bunker-like large emplacements occupied by the Italians, and which the company could hardly take by force. A negotiator sent ahead achieved their surrender through clever discussion, and the company could now push forward towards the fort, their original combat objective. But they had lost valuable time. The 2nd Platoon advanced through the southern part of the city, while the company leader with the Command Platoon and the 1st Platoon preceded through the ravine to the south of the city and the 3rd Platoon pushed forward along the edge of the city towards the fort.

In the battle of Rome, every suitable building was turned into a little fortress by the Italian defenders. The paratroopers make good use of the PaK 40 anti-tank gun to crack nests of resistance, but also to beat back the counterattacks by Italian units, which were partly equipped with German-made tanks.

The 8th Company landed as planned and secured its intended east position. While the company pushed forward through the cluster of houses around the hospital, the company leader and some of the company captured and put out of commission a naval radio station, which had not been identified as such earlier. A swift seizure of the building thus prevented the transmission of radio messages. About 200 naval personnel, including ten officers, were taken prisoner after brief resistance. In the cloister, there were around 300 men and 11 officers. The large number of prisoners began to be a problem for all the German companies; no one had reckoned on handling so many captive enemy. As events unfolded, the companies took ever more prisoners, including a colonel and his aide-de-camp. Of two large-calibre guns captured, one could be made ready for action and used against the enemy, who was increasingly pressing forward from the east. In clearing the houses on either side of the Monterotondo–Mentana road, the paras took further prisoners and secured vehicles and other material.

The situation in front of the fort had not changed much by midday. The rest of the 1st Platoon, 5th Company, had gathered. In their approach through the gardens and houses, the 1st Platoon had encountered heavily armed and numerically superior opponents lurking everywhere in the houses and cellars. The platoon leader in the

A mortar crew poses with their support weapon. Called the 'artillery of the common soldier', mortars were very effective when handled by an experienced team. Leaning against the wall in the background are two FG42 automatic rifles, 1st Model. Although not produced in huge quantities, a handful of these weapons made their way into the hands of FJR 6 men, mostly to officers and high-ranking NCOs.

front garden of the fort was forced to establish his positions increasingly further back.

Some of the 8th Company had reached the fort and brought a recoilless gun into position. The 7.5cm shells, however, did little except impress the enemy shooters in the windows – such a light calibre could do no real damage to the giant structure. Yet soldiers of the 5th Company had brought a captured light mortar into position, whose high-angle trajectory made it possible to shoot into the castle's courtyard. Shell after shell detonated in the closed-in area, making life extremely uncomfortable for those inside. Nevertheless, all attempts to reach the entrance remained fruitless, given the concentrated fire coming from the fort.

Around 1500hrs, the aide to the battalion commander appeared at the castle and informed the Fallschirmjäger there about the situation. The other companies had fought their way through, and were close by; shortly they would arrive in a focused, combined attack. Even before this plan was set in motion, the 2nd Platoon, 5th Company, reached the northeast corner of the fort; across from them, coming from the southwest, the commander of the 7th Company, with some of his men, pushed from the left into the circle besieging the fort. 'Yes, are you still alive!' he hollered to the leader of the 1st Platoon, waving his submachine gun.

Without planning, but as if on command, the Fallschirmjäger now bombarded the fort windows and tower with such heavy fire that the defenders had to take cover. Under the protection of this fire, several men of 5th Company pressed close to the wall and snuck from the right towards the fortress portal. The Leutnant of 2nd Platoon and his men planted a 3kg charge on the main gate; an Oberjäger of the 1st Platoon simultaneously attached a 1kg charge to the side gate. As quickly as they had approached, the three vanished as deftly as weasels, including the Leutnant with his stately height of 1.9m.

Almost simultaneously, the two cutting charges detonated, splitting the heavy planks of the gates. With a hurrah, the Fallschirmjäger stormed the portal, shooting at the wall of windows. At that moment, a white flag appeared at the gate, pushed on a stick through the destroyed gate. The gate was opened, and the two platoon leaders of the 5th Company and the aide to the battalion commander were the first to enter the castle. An old Italian captain, probably the commander of the headquarters, came towards them and offered them a proper surrender. But the Fallschirmjäger had no time for that. While one platoon leader, the commander of the 7th Company and some others concerned themselves with taking prisoners, the two other officers ran with the Italian captain up the stairs to the tower. They let the Italians themselves lower their flag and raise the white flag of surrender. Meanwhile, an aerial surveillance sign was obtained, and at around 1530hrs it was raised as a German flag over the fort. The effect of this action, designed as an assembly point signal and a means of orientation for the German troops, was astounding. Even before the three had returned from the tower, the fort came under heavy artillery fire. Tanks and artillery began to shoot on the captured headquarters from the surrounding heights.

The MG34 was an effective support weapon for the Fallschirmjäger. This machine gun is engaging an enemy position.

But this massive construction could take quite a lot of punishment. Defended by a Fallschirmjäger battalion, it would not be easy to retake.

Below, on the ground floor of the tower, lay a pile of dead soldiers. They had fallen between the battlements and tumbled down when hit by the German sharpshooters. The Italian captain pulled a sheet over the corpses and crossed himself – they were probably his men. Because the flag above the fort was visible from all around, the battalion met up there quickly. The castle was given over again formally to the battalion commander. A check of the captured officers made it clear that Badoglio was no longer to be found in Monterotondo. Together with the king and the royal family, he was on his way to his new buddies, the Allies. Many military leaders also fled with him into exile.

In Monterotondo, the pressure on the city increased from the east, and the battalion had to pull back its positions to close to the fort. More and more troops arrived that had been scattered, and fought their way through from the outer edges of the city to the fort. The biggest problem in defending the fort was the many prisoners. More than 2,000 Italian soldiers, including about 100 officers, had to be watched and cared for in the longer term. In addition, there were numerous civil employees and workers, who could not be let free for security reasons. It turned out that a subterranean tunnel led outside from the rambling cellars, ending near the church. Just in the nick of time, the 3rd platoon of the 5th Company prevented a group of officers from breaking out in this way.

Street fighting in Rome required precise coordination between the units involved. Here squad leaders are receiving a situation report.

II./FJR 6, lacked any radio contact with 2 FJD headquarters or other elements of their own regiment; there was no information to be had about the situation in and around Rome. While they had fulfilled their own mission – occupying and capturing the Italian high command headquarters (although Marshal Badoglio eluded the action) – but the situation still remained critical for the battalion due to the surrounding superior Italian forces. The success of the operation relied not only on their own endurance in defensive combat, but also on the rest of the division's progress in occupying Rome.

Major Gericke knew that his men simply had to bide their time. He sent his aide under the protection of a flag of truce to the Italians, demanding their unconditional surrender while exaggerating the size of the German force. During the negotiations, the aide came to the conclusion that the enemy had at least 250 tanks. Because of his superiority in numbers, the Italian commander turned down surrender, but accepted a cessation of hostilities for the duration of the negotiations. The argument that 2,500 captured Italian men were now under the barrels of their own weapons in the fort seemed worth a ceasefire.

Because the aide did not return, nor did a message from the Italians arrive, Major Gericke sent an Oberfähnrich with two volunteers and an Italian captain as a second attempt. They, however, were held up at an Italian regiment's command post, and were unable to push forward to the aide. From the discussions of the Italians, however, they figured out that the aide has fulfilled his assignment in division headquarters and was carrying out negotiations. The Oberfähnrich then decided make the best of the opportunity – at 0200hrs, they succeeded in breaking out of the regiment's command post and shortly thereafter made it back to their own troop. Under the protection of the ceasefire negotiated by the aide, the men of the II./FJR 6, were able to look after their own wounded and fallen men, and to retrieve their parachutes and other equipment.

Meanwhile, the other units of 2 FJD succeeded in taking and securing the exhibition area of San Paolo fuori le Mura. Recon patrols of the 1st and 3rd Battalions of FJR 6 stayed close to the enemy during the night of 10 September. They were able to bring Major von der Heydte valuable information about the strength of the Italian troops and the presence of black-shirted divisions that were armed with German weapons as a 'Führer-Gift'. Despite their superior numbers, the Italians did not attempt to seize the initiative during the night, probably because of the lack of orders from Monterotondo. So von der Heydte's men had a quiet night.

At the break of dawn, the 1st and 3rd Battalions continued their attack on both sides

During street fighting, the Fallschirmjäger companies here divide up into assault groups to break the enemy's resistance in house-to-house fighting. This group prepares for a rush crossing of the intersection. The Fallschirmjäger in the foreground is securing the back and flank. In the heat of the Italian late summer, the Fallschirmjäger fight in short-sleeves and with light combat gear. Even their bread bags and canteens are not worn for street fighting. Because the machine gun is the group's primary weapon, most of the Fallschirmjäger carry boxes of belted machine-gun ammunition, in addition to their own gear.

of the Via Ostiense. The electric currents of the trolley that ran through the area prevented the effective use of radio equipment, so both battalions proceeded toward the city centre independently of each other, according to their combat mission.

With no radio contact, Major von der Heydte decided to get a picture of the situation for himself, and he took his scout car on a recon tour, or as he recalls in his memoirs, 'sitting on the tower and eating grapes – without a weapon'. He soon met not only the men from FJR 6, but also an Italian tank unit, well armed with German Panzer IV tanks, headed towards the Coliseum. From the rooftops and windows of the surrounding houses, the Italian civilians (partisans) opened fire on the Fallschirmjäger. Major von der Heydte was himself caught in the fire:

> The scout car that I was sitting on, stopped immediately. I jumped down, the scout car drove back. Alone and unarmed I was on the Via Ostiense – not quite a comfortable feeling. The only wish that I had was: 'Get away from the street!' As if sent by God, a house door to the right of me stood open. I gathered all my courage and jumped towards the open door and into the house, and received a shock: in the corridor stood a platoon of Italian infantry men under direction of a young Leutnant. Then I had more luck than sense: the Italian lieutenant held his hands up and his men hurried to do the same. It was the one time during the whole war that I personally took prisoners.

A troop of 2nd Company took the prisoners off his hands minutes later, so Major von der Heydte could coordinate his seven battalions again. The 1st and 3rd Battalions of FJR 6 received the mission to advance from Porta di Sao Paolo by the Viale Aventino to the Coliseum, which they were to take and secure.

An Italian officer plus other soldiers came out of the Porta di Sao Paolo waving a

A Fallschirmjäger patrol brings in captured Italians. The Italians weren't resisting strongly everywhere – threatening them with weapons was often enough to make them surrender without firing a shot.

white flag. The officer tried to formulate conditions for the surrender of his formation, the Grenadier Division 'Sardegna', but in the face of Major von der Heydte's decisive demeanour and the firepower of both FJR 6 battalions , the officer wisely declared the unconditional surrender of his division.

While the other five battalions trailed behind to collect the prisoners, the 1st and 3d Battalions of FJR 6 carried forwards the attack on the Coliseum. When Major von der Heydte entered the Coliseum with his scout car and set up his command post on the uppermost tribune, he found the area already secured by both battalions of the Fallschirmjäger regiment, according to their combat mission. A message that the 3rd Panzergrenadier Division had opened the second frontline against Rome's defenders from the north, reached von der Heydte in the Coliseum. His informants also reported that near Tivoli the Italian tank division 'Centauro' stood ready for battle on the right flank of 2 FJD. This Italian division was also well equipped with German vehicles and could, in the worst-case scenario, seriously hinder the operation, if not cause its failure. Because, however, the central train station at this time was being attacked by his Fallschirmjäger, Major von der Heydte decided to demand that the Italian leadership surrender.

Under the protection of a white flag, von der Heydte drove to the commander-in-chief of Rome, Count Carlo Calvi, a brother-in-law of the king and who was known to him as honest and trustworthy. In his memoirs, he described the situation:

Count Calvi sat alone in his room and tried to explain to me that he was functioning as a representative of the king, while the leadership of the combined divisions in Rome –including the two tank and two motorized divisions – lay in the hands of General Carboni. Calvi stressed that up until now only a quarter of the city was in German hands. A continuation of the fight in Rome would be possible, but would signal the end of Rome. Therefore – and not because he had been beaten – he was ready to surrender the city to the Germans and demobilize the forces that had been assigned to Rome's defence. The capitulation of the city would occur right away. The fight for Rome would be finished by 0600hrs. We concentrated then on allocating forces to those points that were less strategically important to us, such as a guard at the Vatican.

The capitulation agreement was written out on a piece of paper from my message pad; then Calvi and I signed it. In the moment of signing it, it occurred to me that there was a possibility that the Italians, who had higher numbers than us, would use the withdrawal of the Germans to plan a strategically decisive attack on German troops. I let Calvi know about my concerns. He tried to assuage them by giving me his 'word of honour as an Italian general'. I had to answer him that up until three days ago the word of honour of an Italian general would have been enough for every German officer, but after the events of the last three days, the word of honour of an Italian general had lost its value for a German. When Calvi heard my answer –

Italian prisoners are disarmed, and taken to the main train station to be processed.

the whole discussion had taken place in French – he broke out in tears. I was pretty clueless about what to do. What is one supposed to do with a crying general! Finally, I suggested that we overlook our rank and appointment and instead commit ourselves from one aristocrat to another. The honour of our families was enough of a guarantee for me. Calvi stood up and offered his hand. The first treaty concerning the surrender of Rome was thus, in a sense, sealed with a handshake.

Calvi and I kept our word. After 0600hrs the 7th Battalion of the 2nd Fallschirmjäger Division left the city. The Italian divisions surrendered their weapons to German command. The number of German troops had been steadily increasing since midday. Meanwhile, the combat-strong parts of the 3rd Panzergrenadier Division and the armoured units of the 26th Panzer Division had pushed forward – or better said, marched – into Rome. During the night I learned that the King of Italy as well as his top command and the newly formed Cabinet of Rome had fled the city without leaving clear instructions to the commanding generals about the defence of Rome.

The 1st and 3rd Battalions of FJR 6 began to disarm the surrendering Italian groups. Most of the Italians were sent home on the spot; others declared themselves ready to take on the fight with the Germans against the Allies or to offer work service.

The news of Rome's capitulation did not reach Monterotondo right away; despite the agreed ceasefire, the unarmed recovery parties of the 2nd Battalion were repeatedly

This photo shows a group of FJR 6 troopers guarding the German Embassy after the end of the battle for Rome. Despite appearances, the men are not wearing camouflaged jump smocks – a brief rain shower caused the dark spots on their uniforms.

fired upon by the Italian troops, so that the battalion still had losses to report in Monterotondo even after the surrender of the Italians in Rome. The battalion's dead were buried in the local cemetery and on 11 September the battalion relocated to Tivoli. There they were ordered to disarm the Italian tank division 'Centauro' and to secure their weapons and vehicles. Dietrich Brehde recalls:

> ... German weapons and German vehicles of the most modern make... The soldiers of the 2nd Battalion couldn't believe their eyes. The 5th Company, responsible for collecting the anti-aircraft artillery, took from the Italians factory-new 8.8cm anti-aircraft guns, heavy half-track tractor units by Henschel and barely driven off-road bucket-seat cars, Kfz 12 and Kfz 15. But what really caught the Fallschirmjägers' eye was the MG42! This was the legendary new German machine gun that was known to have as good as no stoppages when firing, and which the Russians supposedly designated an 'electric machine gun' because of its enormously quick rate of fire.

The Italian troops around Rome were anything but poorly armed and ill-disciplined. The Fallschirmjäger are here sorting through the captured weapons and equipment to pick up additional machine guns, submachine guns and add vehicles to their motor pool.

The Fallschirmjäger, who were still equipped with the good, but much more delicate, MG34 that had got them into some tight spots in Russia, now saw their chance. With an 8.8cm anti-aircraft gun they couldn't do much, and a heavy Henschel tractor unit similarly did them no good. But they were after the MG42! They dusted them and some vehicles off. This 'clearance sale' in Tivoli went unnoticed! The other companies had similar experiences, and the battalion ended this mission once again fully motorized and well armed.

Originally, II./FJR 6 was scheduled to carry out Mussolini's rescue mission out of the Sport Hotel Campo Imperatore on Gran Sasso. Yet due to the Fallschirmjäger instruction battalion being equipped with the new Fallschirmjägergewehr 42 (FG42) assault rifle, and to the first successfully completed mission in Monterotondo, the battalion was sent towards the sea to secure the coast after the 'Centauro' mission in Tivoli. The instruction battalion took over freeing Mussolini. In the next few days, the battalion developed a special appreciation for the Castle Torre Astura, the supposed home of an Italian actor, the contents of which would have been an honour for any museum. Above all they liked the bathroom with a water heater and a view to the ocean. The Leutnant staying in the castle gladly allowed his comrades to use this for only a small payment to cover expenses.

Only a few days later the 2nd Battalion relocated to Frascati. Major Gericke kept them from idling with numerous training

This Oberjäger finds time to sightsee in Rome and to pose for a souvenir photo. He is wearing Luftwaffe uniform with the sand-coloured side cap. The Fallschirmjäger marksmanship badge and the jump boots identify him as a paratrooper. Having fought in Crete, he wears the Crete cuff title on his upper left sleeve.

A motorcycle patrol of FJR 6 takes a British soldier prisoner; the soldier had been let go by the Italians near Anzio.

exercises, although he still left the Fallschirmjäger enough free time to help the local population with the wine harvest. They were dealing here with an especially good drop of wi3h had become impassable for trucks due to constant American artillery fire and Allied bombing. Under cover of night, on 3 November, III./FJR 6 took their position on the Cesima Massif and immediately began to prepare for an all-around defence, because the Americans had almost completely surrounded the mountain. Major Pelz sent out assault troops, whose reports confirmed the situation around Monte Cesima.

Nevertheless, the battalion advanced the next morning according to plan; they were able to break through the ring of besiegers and take and secure Elevation 484. Thus into the late hours of the evening, III./FJR 6 held the southernmost positions of the German Army in Italy completely on their own. Because the Americans advanced powerfully on the position, the battalion relocated around midnight back to Elevation 620, in order to prevent being encircled.

Supported by some of the 3rd Panzergrenadier Division, III./FJR 6 fell in on 5 November to an attack on Monte Cesima. They were faced with heavily armoured American units and air raids. On the afternoon of 5 November, the enemy seized the initiative and led a counterattack on Elevation 687, but this was fought off by the rearguard of III./FJR 6. A flanking attack by the Americans on Elevation 689 was similarly fruitless, but the battalion suffered heavily losses from all the counterattacks. III./FJR 6 was subsequently thrown into battle at focal points of the Reinhard Position,

After the successful operation in Monterotondo, Major Walter Gericke, commander of II./FJR 6, hands out medals and promotions to those Fallschirmjäger who distinguished themselves during the battle.

then on 9 November on Monte Rotondo and later near St Pietro Infine. With the end of the American offensive, III./FJR 6 relocated on 16 November to Rome, and then in the first half of December to Roccaraso. The operations in the Reinhard Position cost the battalion over half its manpower.

As III./FJR 6 was serving in a 'fire-fighter' role on the Volturno Front, 2 FJD was preparing for relocation from Italy to Russia. This move also affected FJR 6. While the 1st Battalion was sent to Russia with the division, the regimental staff and the 2nd and 3rd Battalions stayed in Italy. On 12 November 1943, the men of I./FJR 6 under Hauptmann Finzel boarded the train to Nuremberg at the Chisui train station. In Nuremberg the men received uniforms and equipment suitable for winter, and prepared the wagons for the ride into the Russian winter.

The 2nd Battalion was separated out from FJR 6 and laid the foundations of the newly formed FJR 11, part of of 4 FJD. Thus, FJR 6 was not only fighting on two fronts at this time, but also was doing so with considerably less men.

Already in the last ten days of November, III./FJR 6, reinforced by the regimental staff and the 13th as well as the 14th Company, found themselves once again at the heart of the fighting, this time on the Adria Front. At the beginning of December, the German positions on the Ortona–Canosa–Arielli–Orsogna line were under heavy enemy fire, and some of the British 8th Army had gained ground near Arielli. So the reinforced

The 3rd battalion relocates to the positions on Monte Cesima. A group of NCOs heads up the column of men and pack animals. They are armed with MP40s and carry an important piece of equipment around their necks – binoculars. The pack animals relieve the Fallschirmjäger of the weight of their heavy weapons for the march.

Assault troops of the 3rd Battalion near St Pietro Infine. The Fallschirmjäger held the southernmost positions of the German line against massive US attacks. Despite the attempt to distribute additional automatic weapons to the Fallschirmjäger regiments, most were armed with the Karabiner 98k bolt-action rifle. Submachine guns were reserved for the officers and the NCOs. The MG42s recovered in Rome were immediately divided up amongst the group and complemented the older MG34s.

The 3rd Battalion stands on the Reinhard Line and resists a powerful US attack, suffering heavy losses in the process. These two Fallschirmjäger use the break in fighting to rest – the exhaustion of combat is evident on the soldier's faces.

III./FJR 6 received orders to lead a counterattack in order to repel the advances and restore the old line of battle.

The counterattack began in the early hours of 16 December, supported by elements of 26th Panzer Regiment, with the plan of clearing out the area from Arielli to Orsogna. Due to heavy Allied artillery fire, however, the attack ran aground in the cemetery at Orsogna. A decisive counterattack by the British finally quashed the objective of the operation, and the battalion once again sustained heavy losses to show. On the morning of 17 December, the flanking 9th Panzergrenadier Regiment were thrown back by the Allies, but III./FJR 6 maintained close contact with the army unit and relieved their 2nd Battalion of their position.

As it turned out, the British attack near Orsogna did not succeed, so the enemy prepared a new offensive, preceded by massive artillery fire and air raids. Moving up behind heavy shelling, the British led an attack on 23 December, succeeded only partially, and had once again to break away from the defensive line of the Fallschirmjäger.

Over Christmas the weapons fell silent in this part of the front. For the New Year, III./FJR 6 relocated to Florence, and from there to French Bretagne, where the battalion formed the basis for the the new FJR 8 under Major Liebach.

This young Fallschirmjäger NCO has obviously lost the right pin on his helmet so he has had to field-repair the chinstrap. He is carrying his folded blanket under the backstrap of his webbing, and the butt of a flare pistol can be seen protruding from the pocket of his jump smock, under his magazine pouches.

In Nuremberg, railway wagons are prepared for deployment into the Russian winter. The Fallschirmjäger exchange their tropical uniforms for wool combat trousers and pilots' shirts, and use a rest stop as an opportunity to clean their weapons.

After the lightning-quick relocation to the Adria Front, the 3rd Battalion find themselves once again on a combat mission. They use short breaks in the battle to get ammunition and rations.

Fallschirmjäger position an MG34 on the Adria Front near Orsogna. The heavy machine guns were used for flank protection, and because of their great range and devastating crossfire, they were much feared by the enemy. Despite the planned introduction of the MG42 as the standard machine gun for the army, Luftwaffe and Waffen-SS, many Fallschirmjäger regiments used the MG34 until the end of the war, because the production of MG42s could not meet frontline demands.

The positions of the III./FJR 6 on the Adria Front were anything but heavily fortified or well constructed. Often the Fallschirmjäger have nothing more than a quickly dug trench, whose excavated material was thrown up as breastwork. The scene in this position near Orsogna is typical of life in the trenches during a pause in firing. The group leader scans the area with his binoculars; his men use the time to catch a break, to eat and to repair the position.

CHAPTER THREE

Deployment in Russia, 1943

After the massive redistribution of personnel for the formation of new Fallschirmjäger regiments, FJR 6 consisted of only a sole battalion. I./FJR 6 arrived at the Shitomar train station in Russia in the late evening hours of 28 November 1943. The Fallschirmjäger spent a few hours of peace in a local bombed-out school, which partially protected them from the snowing cold and the drafts. Eugen Griesser, Oberjäger at the time, remembers: 'Like sheep, we huddled together in the corner of a classroom – everyone wrapped up in his blanket and shelter quarter – so that we could keep each other warm. There were no more school benches to burn; others before us had used them as fuel. So we stayed

A typical view of the Soviet Union presents itself to the Fallschirmjäger during their relocation to Russia.

For most of the Fallschirmjäger under Hauptmann Finzel's command, war in Russia was a completely new experience. The icy cold and the seemingly endless horizons make a strong impression on the men. While his comrades bunk in Shitomir, this Oberjäger gathers first impressions of the area. The soldiers of I./FJR 6 are well equipped with quilted snow camouflage suits.

For those on patrol, good camouflage was essential to survival, because dark uniforms showed up all too clearly against the white snow. These Fallschirmjäger are wearing the long snow camouflage coats that had a good obscuring effect and also provided additional warm outer layers. Hand grenades are stuck in their belts, at the ready.

up freezing all night.'

The next morning, the battalion marched on foot to Potaschnja, northwest of the city of Kotscherowo. They arrived on 1 December and took up position as reserves.

On St Nicholas Day, 6 December, Operation *Advent* began. Supported by a Panzer team from the 2nd SS-Panzer Division, I./FJR 6 formed Battlegroup 'Finzel', and took the lead for the division. The goal was to capture the area around Radomyschl. The battalion were able to take and secure the open land quickly, but the Russians offered strong resistance under cover of a local forest. Nests of machine guns and sharpshooters prevented the German advance. In forest fighting, the SS-Panzer division offered little help. The 1st Battalion Fallschirmjäger took over artillery support and continued the attack. A battery of Nebelwerfer (rocket launchers; lit. 'fog thrower') effectively supported the forest clearance, so that the first para section could, according to plan, occupy a kolkhoz (a collective farm) near Garboroff. The units of 2 FJD had trouble advancing beyond their sectors, so Battlegroup 'Finzel' was on its own. The area's landscape did not allow for the tanks' further advance, so the battalion prepared for an all-around defence in the kolkhoz.

Now the Russians attacked repeatedly and in increasing strength, but the cluster of houses stayed in the hands of the Fallschirmjäger. The other battalions, however, were unable to establish communications with the combat troop, so Hauptmann Finzel

In their advance towards Garboroff, the Fallschirmjäger of Battlegroup 'Finzel' meet enemy tanks, which the SS Panzers can incapacitate with direct fire. The burnt-out wrecks serve as good cover for the advancing men. Here a Fallschirmjäger of I./FJR 6 opens fire on the enemy with his submachine gun; his comrade is prepared to advance in a rush.

received the order to wait out the night and then lead the combat troop back to their own lines.

Strengthened by the SS-Panzer troops, III./FJR 6 renewed their attack on Jelnitsch and Radomyschl on 8 December, while German armoured units held Pilipowitschi and Borschtschew on the flanks. The Russians stubbornly defended the edge of the Jelnitsch area, so that the forward edge of the German attack intermittently ground to a halt.

Between the dense trees, the men could often only make out the outlines of the well-camouflaged enemy; it was easy to fall into an ambush. They chased the fleeing enemy, even if it meant having to leave the secure cover of a tank.

Fallschirmjäger of I./FJR 6 return from their deployment on the Eastern Front. On top of their clothing, the men only wear weapons and ammunition; their canteens are worn under their jackets, in order to use body heat to prevent their drinking water from freezing. For the same reasons, their rations are kept in the pockets of their uniforms. The Fallschirmjäger in the right foreground is carrying a canvas pack for six submachine-gun magazines.

The 1st Battalion takes part in the capture of the village of Jelnitsch. Despite the Russians' stolid resistance, the Fallschirmjäger succeed in taking the location and in setting up a defence. The men received warm clothing in Nuremberg and are therefore well-equipped for the Russian winter.

After they had finally pushed the defenders out of their positions, the attack was carried forward and the location was taken. The battlegroup set up a defensive line here that encircled the pocket of Radomyschl.

According to orders from XXXXII Corps on 9 December, the whole division was relocated to Kirowograd in order to block a Russian offensive, all battalions moving in an 'air march' from Shitomir. I./FJR 6 followed in vehicles as cover for the heavy equipment.

By 16 December, the battalions of 2 FJD had occupied their new positions and reported themselves ready for battle. I./FJR 6 made up the division's reserve once again.

Surprisingly, the Russian positions in the Nowgorodka sector proved to be heavily occupied, so the 11th Panzer Division's attack was abandoned after half of its tanks were lost to anti-tank artillery. To support them, I./FJR 6 advanced and were able to occupy the ridge of the hill south of the city. To push things forward, FJR 7 moved to

occupy the heights southwest of Rybtschina. Both units carried out a coordinated attack and cleared the edges of Nowgorodka. The battle came down to bitter close combat, in which every foot of ground was hotly contested. With support from some of the released the 11th Panzer Division, the Fallschirmjäger went on to clear western Nowgorodka of the enemy and secure the immediate area. With the arrival of the other battalions, the paras were able to take Nowgorodka by 23 December. The enemy's heavy resistance led to severe casualties in the battalions. Because the 11th Panzer Division was relieved from the front, 2 FJD took over the sector on the evening of 23 December. I./FJR 6 occupied Elevation 159.9.

Christmas proved to be a restless period, as the Russians made several attempts to break through the front. The

While the rest of 2 FJD relocated to Kirowograd via air, the 1st Battalion had to fight their way through ice and snow with baggage and heavy equipment. The recon patrols were provided with skies when possible, so they could move faster through the snow.

The 1st Battalion occupies the hill south of the hotly contested city of Nowgorodka. This patrol is determining the strength of the regrouping enemy.

These Fallschirmjäger-occupied elevations are well fortified with trenches and bunkers. Despite their massive superiority in men and materials, the Russians were often unable to throw the Fallschirmjäger out of their positions.

Fallschirmjäger were consistently able to push back the enemy, due to the fact that the forays were not well supported by tanks. On 27 December, several Russian battalions arrived to attack Elevations 167.0 and 159.9, but I./FJR 6 blocked the Russian incursions quickly and cleared them out in a counterattack. Losses suffered during this engagement weakened the battalion significantly, however, and on 27 December it was pulled back behind the front and replaced by II./FJR 2.

On 28 December, the battalions of 2 FJD moved into the sector from which the 13th

This Jäger open fires on the enemy with his submachine gun. The Fallschirmjäger proved themselves time and again to be courageous men; after receiving punishing artillery barrages, the Fallschirmjäger let the enemy come close to their positions, so that they could open fire on him from a closer range.

The photo of this Oberjäger on the Eastern Front is particularly interesting. The grade chevron with braid trimming on the collar and the epaulettes are easy to recognize here. In addition, he is wearing the army insignia of a Fallschirmschütze; therefore he is a former member of the Fallschirm Infantry Battalion of the army, which was established as the counterpart to the paratrooper riflemen of the Luftwaffe. As is typical for life on the front, the service standards of personal hygiene cannot always be upheld. For example, soldiers often had to neglect daily shaving in combat areas.

Panzer Division had been relieved. They took advantage of the inactivity of the enemy over the next few days to send out recon patrols. A captured Russian officer revealed under questioning that the enemy planned a renewed offensive. In the beginning of January 1944, air surveillance reported concentrations of enemy tanks and infantry near the left flank of the division. While the enemy's combat troops were fought off on 4 January, the following morning the Russians began their carefully planned major offensive with strong artillery support and rocket launcher fire. Their goal was to encircle Kirowograd.

Surrounded by superior enemy forces, the Fallschirmjäger once again rose to the occasion and transformed every foxhole and command post into a stronghold. Nevertheless, their losses were immense and the resupply of ammunition and rations

This Gefreiter is taking a bite of fresh bread. Even though the butter might have frozen in the Russian winter, the warm, fresh bread was always welcome.

failed to materialize. Battalions in those days were melted down to the size of companies; companies were sporadically cut off from others and had to stand on their own. Losses of up 60–70 per cent weakened the troops' combat power. The enemy, too, suffered heavy losses. The battalions' resistance was so powerful that even though the encirclement succeeded, the city remained firmly in German hands.

In the meantime, the 2 FJD troops marched in to relieve the beleaguered force, so that the Russians had to open the cordon around the city. Kirowograd became a Monte Cassino for the Fallschirmjäger in Russia. In a teletype from 14 January 1944, the General of the Pilots and the chief of Luftflotte 4 (Air Fleet 4) Otto Dessloch wrote:

> To the 2nd Fallschirmjäger Division!
> The 2nd Fallschirmjäger Division, in spite of heavy blood sacrifices, caused the enemy serious losses and destroyed more than 150 tanks in the defensive battle in the area of Kirowograd on 5 January 1944. Standing at the focal point of the enemy attack, the division played a decisive role in preventing large-scale attempts to break through in this combat sector.
>
> To this brave Fallschirmjäger division and their tried and tested commander, Generalleutnant Wilke, I would like to express my thanks and deep recognition for this great deed, and with reverence I commemorate their dead.

The coming weeks proved to be relatively calm, but were marked by heavy recon patrol activity. On 6 February, the division received orders to march to Tscherkassy, to relieve the encircled troops there. Heavy snowstorms delayed the move until 11 February, however. The original plan, to reach the assembly position near Tischkowka by foot, was dismissed, and on the morning of 12 February the relocation began at the train station of Schewtschenkowo. Because not enough trains stood ready, I./FJR 6 could only

While against the massive Russian infantry attacks, machine guns were particularly valuable tools. Often enough the Fallschirmjäger positions were nothing more than a flat rifle pit dug into the frozen ground.

This photograph illustrates the fight for Kirowograd especially well. Without supplies, and often cut off from the other comrades, the Fallschirmjäger held their positions literally down to the last man.

The Fallschirmjäger suffered heavy losses in Kirowograd because the attacking Russians outnumbered them so significantly. The units melted together and smalerl and smaller battlegroups stood their ground alone, cut off from their main formations.

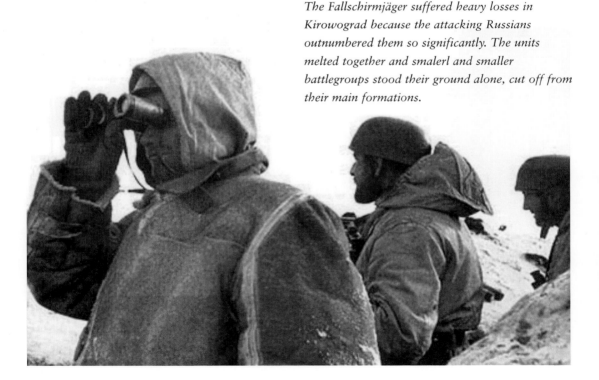

The Fallschirmjäger refused to be satisfied with just fighting off the Russian attacks; they used every opportunity for counterattacks. These Fallschirmjäger are preparing for one such counterattack. The MG42, with its rapid rate of fire, would keep the Russians' heads down until the Fallschirmjäger could infiltrate the enemy positions and fight at close quarters. The phrase 'seeing the whites of the enemy's eyes' took on a whole new meaning, and the attacks were carried out with relentless pressure and determination.

Newspapers were a treasured commodity for frontline soldiers, even if they, after a long road trip from the homeland, were no longer current. This Fallschirmjäger snatched newspapers from a supply train and brought them to his comrades. He is wearing a civilian scarf around his neck for extra warmth, and he has camouflaged his steel helmet with white netting.

begin their train journey on 15 February.

Because the enemy occupied many of the stations on the path towards Tischkowka, the train had to travel via Nikolajew on the Black Sea to Nowo Ukrainka. This detour led to the first battalions of the division arriving on 18 February, too late for the planned deployment because German forces had already blasted through the Russian encirclement. With General Ramcke, who once again took over leadership of the division, the heavily weakened I./FJR 6 received personnel and equipment replacements.

In a snowstorm, the battalions set off to march on foot to Nowo Archangelsk. The Russian winter once again showed its ugliest side, especially for the infantrymen, who had to march through the snow that was at some points as high as their hips. Because visibility was practically nonexistent, each man held onto the belt of

After a major Russian attack is beaten back, the troops can regularly receive supplies once again. Letters and packets from home bring a much-awaited change of pace.

the man in front of him, in order not to become lost. Ernst Lochner, then an Obergefreiter in the 2nd Company, remembers: 'In the late afternoons, we dug holes for ourselves in snow piles and set ourselves up there for the night. Whole groups could stay in snow caves, while two men kept watch to shovel the entrance clear repeatedly. There was no need to keep watch outside; Ivan would never attack in such bad weather.'

The goal was Gniloy Tikitsch, where a battlegroup of the 11th Panzer Division would be relieved. At this time, the individual battalions of the division were so weakened by the losses of the previous battles that the battle groups had to be rebuilt. I./FJR 6 was combined with the remains of FJR 7 and the 2nd Fallschirm Pioneer Battalion; they took the positions between Gniloy Tikitsch and Olchowez.

The thaw that set in at the end of February brought warmer temperatures, but also the seasonal rain and mud that hindered logistics as much as the deep snows of winter. On the night of 3 March 1944, the enemy was able to break through the adjacent front and establish themselves in the Petki sugar factory, as well as on Elevation 208.9. Battlegroups from all units retaliated with a quick counterattack, and managed to retake the sugar factory, and by the evening they had also cleared the elevation.

The greatest problem for 2 FJD, and especially for heavily attacked units like I./FJR 6, was the lack of replacement personnel. Every loss hit the battalion especially hard and the apparently inexhaustible Russian reserves that permitted the enemy to throw more

This well-built position for a MG34 is near Gniloy Tikitsch. The machine-gunner has placed boxes of ammunition next to his weapon in the snow so he can change ammunition belts quickly. To the right of him is a close-combat weapon – the field spade –ready to hand on the parapet.

and more troops into combat presented Finzel with almost unsolvable challenges. On 4 March, the Russians once again attacked with more battalions to the west of the sugar factory. Despite heavy losses due to the Fallschirmjäger's machine-gun fire, they managed to break through FJR 6's position in Olchowez. The 4th Company managed to take the bridgehead in a valiant counterattack. They were also able to fight off a nighttime attack by the Russians, when they tried to break through the line one more time.

Unfortunately it turned out that the enemy's activities in early March had only been the prelude to a larger offensive. On 5 March, the enemy attacked broadly across the front after massive artillery preparations and with strong tank support. Despite FJR 6's fierce defence, the Russians were able to take and hold their location. Because the

Forward-deployed one-man positions were often the forward line of defence against enemy attacks on the Russian Front.

neighboring sectors had also been overrun by the enemy, I./FJR 6 pulled back to Gussakowo.

Oberfeldwebel Rudolf Harbig, holder of the world record in 400m and 800m sprints, a platoon leader of the 2nd Company, was also one of the many wounded. His comrades brought him to a first-aid station on the rear of a self-propelled assault gun, where he succumbed to his massive wounds. Germany not only lost an exceptional athlete in him, but the regiment, above all, lost an excellent soldier.

The rest of FJR 6 were, together with other smaller units, united into Battlegroup 'Fehse'. The battlegroup took position in a kolkhoz near Gussakowo and stood up to massive enemy attacks. Because the ground was frozen, the men could not dig foxholes, and the Fallschirmjäger had to take advantage of natural cover instead. The goal was to cover the move to Talnoje. After successfully defending against Russian attacks, the battlegroup relocated to the train station of Talnoje, where the Russians attacked with renewed fury on 8 March. Supported by the paramedics of the 2nd Fallschirm Medical Battalion, who had put down their Red Cross armbands, they were able to hold off the enemy attacks. Fighting the whole way, Battlegroup 'Fehse' withdrew to the southern shore of the Gorny Tikitsch and went into positions near Kamentschje on the afternoon of 9 March.

In accordance with their orders, the battlegroup relocated to the Nowo Archangelsk area and lined up with 2 FJD again, which had been deployed on the main line of battle west of the River Sinjucha. They were able to hold that position until 14 March; after that the division pulled back into an alternative position near Nowosseliki. But two days later, the enemy broke through that position and seized a strategically important elevation. Because the Russians couldn't be thrown out of that position through counterattacks, the heavily battered division escaped to Kuzaja Balka. Under strong enemy pressure, the main line of battle was pushed back to the Bug River west of Perwomaisk, where the Russians had already built three massive bridgeheads.

At the Bug, the enemy attacked again with undiminished vehemence. The Fallschirmjäger succeeded, however, in countering a breakthrough in the ranks of their neighbours on the left flank, but this success did not improve the situation significantly

After the Stahlhelmhöhe had been cleared of the enemy, recon patrols stayed close to the enemy. Here the remains of a Russian tank serve as cover from the fire of enemy snipers who may be lurking. The Fallschirmjäger are equipped with submachine guns and a Panzerfaust; an army machine-gunner stands ready to deliver support fire with his weapon.

as a whole – the front had to be pushed farther back. By the beginning of April, the division was no more than 500 men strong, yet it fought on. In April they received the order to relocate to the positions around the Dniester. The Fallschirmjäger had a few days' break from the fighting behind their own lines, because the condition of the division was poor beyond all imagination. Two weeks later field reinforcements arrived under the direction of Oberleutnant Backhaus: 640 fresh-faced Fallschirmjäger with no experience. Given the circumstances, no regard could be given to their inexperience, because the division became entangled again in heavy battles with the Russians on the Dniester bight.

Subordinate to the 3rd Panzer Division, the Fallschirmjäger went up against the Russians on 10 May 1944 as part of Operation *Bulwark*. They succeeded in a quick manoeuvre to push forward into the so-called Stahlhelmhöhe (lit. 'steel-helmet heights') and to entrench themselves there. Despite enemy counterattacks, the assault on the Russian bridgehead continued during the following day, and around evening the Russians pulled back to the other side of the Dnester. The Wehrmacht report from 12 May 1944 announced: 'In the destruction of the enemy bridgeheads on lower Dniester that was reported yesterday, the troops under the leadership of the General der Infanterie Buschenhagen, defeated seven enemy infantry divisions as well as parts of an artillery and anti-aircraft division.'

On this day, 2 FJD was released from the frontline by the order of the LII Corps. Their release was due to the losses suffered during the last operation, which were too great to sustain. The units prepared for return transport to Germany. On 20 May 1944, the Fallschirmjäger boarded the wagons and headed home.

CHAPTER FOUR

The Reorganization in Cologne-Wahn, 1944

On 15 January 1944, the reorganization of FJR 6 officially began in Cologne-Wahn. Major Freiherr (Baron) Friedrich August von der Heydte was the commander of the new regiment. From his time in Italy as the chief of staff of 2 FJD, he already knew the regiment well, and he was a dynamic and experienced leader. It is telling that the complete reorganization of the regiment had already been started when the former I./FJR 6 was still on its mission in Russia. The regiment not only released two of its battalions to become the heart of new Fallschirmjäger regiments, but it also suffered such heavy losses in Russia that by the beginning of 1944 all that remained of Major Liebach's proud regiment were a handful of survivors.

The reorganization of FJR 6 took place on the military training ground in Wahn near Cologne. This contemporary picture shows the main entrance to the administrative building.

These barracks were home to officers and men in the Wahn camp. Later, the roof of their lodgings would serve as a control tower in their Fallschirmjäger training.

In December 1943, when Major von der Heydte received the order that he was to take over command of the new regiment in Wahn, he was in a hospital in Munich, still under recovering from a plane crash in Italy. Oberfeldwebel Geiss, a seasoned Fallschirmjäger, was the one to lead the cadre. Under von der Heydte's direction, the body of commissioned and non-commissioned officers was reformed. He remembered well the achievements of FJR 6 in the battle for Rome, so he took the necessary steps to get as many old hands as possible in his new unit. Due to his management, some recovered Fallschirm-

Hauptfeldwebel Karl Hentschel, the 'mother' of the 1st Company, displays the means of transport provided for the company first sergeant – the service bicycle.

jäger received the order to report to Wahn instead of returning to the old 1st Battalion on the Eastern Front.

The heart of Major von der Heydte's force soon consisted for the most part of combat veteran NCOs of FJR 1, 2, 3, 5 and 7, as well as the former Ramcke Brigade. Even the bearers of the Narvik Shield and the Crete cuff title were included. The young volunteers from other areas of the Luftwaffe, and with whom the regiment was overflowing at the time, were only 17 and 18 years old. They were to receive the Fallschirmjäger training in the French jump schools, and then immediately return to Wahn for further training. But there was not time for this. So Major von der Heydte took initiative and let the jump training take place in a simplified form directly in Wahn.

Albert Sturm, at the time a Gefreiter in the 7th Company, remembers: 'In Wahn there was no jump school like there was in Wittstock and Dreux and elsewhere. So the barracks roof took the place of a jump tower, and we jumped over the training field. In Wahn, I never had to pack my own parachute, learning that would have taken too much time. The older Fallschirmjäger did nothing else all day but pack our chutes.'

The training programme was full, and the timeframe was tight. Major von der Heydte employed unconventional training concepts that he himself designed for the

jump and combat training of his regiment. Based on the experiences of the officers and NCOs, the basic elements of an infantryman's trade did not have to be repeated again and all the focus could be given to the young Fallschirmjäger. FJR 6 received training at night and close quarters combat. He even managed to get a squadron of Junkers Ju 52s and a flight of Heinkel He 111s assigned to his command , so the training could be carried out three-dimensionally.

The Fallschirmjäger could only dream of regular work hours. The quick tempo of their training, with frequent combat and jump exercises, meant that their schedules were full until late into the night. The staff soldiers and specialists also put in endless overtime.

In the coming weeks, more old and young Fallschirmjäger arrived to strengthen the regiment. Some of the

Gefreiter Albert Sturm.

This picture shows soldiers of the 3rd Company preparing for jump training. Some of the Fallschirmjäger are not only wearing padded knee protectors, but also the elbow pads that went with them, but were seldom worn.

For the young Fallschirmjäger, completing the practical elements of jump training was a great adventure. Even the best education and training on the ground could not replace an actual jump out of an aircraft.

Oberjäger Schlemmer oversees preparations for jump training. The Fallschirmjäger are about to board the Ju 52 that stands ready to deliver another parachute drop.

This Fallschirmjäger is standing in the correct jump position in the side door of a Ju 52. With a strong leap, he is about to catapult himself out of the door and take up the so-called 'eagle position'.

In a straight body position, this Fallschirmjäger springs out of an aircraft. The 9m-long suspension line is visible in the top left of the picture. It will soon pull open his pack and release the parachute.

With an opened parachute, this Fallschirmjäger floats towards the earth. With rowing movements, he is trying to turn himself into the wind so that he will be able to perform the correct landing roll.

officers and NCOs could claim previous service in the Fallschirmjäger instruction battalion. A new recruit of special heritage was the regimental clergyman, the Jesuit father Otto Stöckle, who was assigned to the regiment at Major von der Heydte's request through military channels by the Jesuit Provincial Superior, Father Rösch. Because the staffing schedule did not allow for a priest for FJR 6, Father Stöckle was brought in as a private.

Werner Eul, a Oberjäger in the regimental staff, remembers how he was affected by the reorganization:

Before the reorganization of the sixth I was with FJR 7 in Russia. My old acquaintance Heinz Gabbey had been requested by Major von der Heydte as a Hauptfeldwebel; he had recommended me to the Major and then I was requested in Cologne-Wahn. When I reported to him, Heinz Gabbey said 'He will be a wonderful instructor!' A few

With signs like this, the individual companies in Wahn marked their territory. On the left of the sign is the military symbol of the 1st Battalion, the head of a bull. The 2nd Battalion used a comet, while the 3rd Battalion used an eagle's claw.

At the Wahn base, Fallschirmjäger liked to take pictures for their loved ones at home. The company sign was a popular place for such souvenir photos.

Oberleutnant Emil Preikschat and Oberfeldwebel Karl Hentschel pose proudly in front of their company sign.

days later, I was supposed to report to the 1st Company of Oberleutnant Preikschat as the new squad leader. As a former minor clerk, I was not so sure that I would make a wonderful instructor.

In the office I met Hauptfeldwebel Karl Hentschel. I announced myself to him by saying: 'Oberjäger Eul by the command of Herr Major von der Heydte transferred to Herr Oberleutnant Preikschat's 1st Company as a clerk.' In this way, I transferred myself into a new assignment in the 1st Company.

Oberjäger, later Feldwebel, Werner Eul.   *Oberjäger, later Feldwebel, Eugen Griesser.*

Eugen Griesser, at the time a Oberjäger in the 5th Company, also remembers this time:

When I came to the new regiment in the middle of February 1944, I first had to report to the Regimental home in Aschersleben, where I received my marching papers to Cologne-Wahn, where the regiment resided for their reorganization.

I had expected to find Hauptmann Finzel and the rest of the 1st Battalion there, instead there really were three completely new battalions. The officers and NCOs were all experienced soldiers, some of them even had high commendations, and all the teams already had experience on the front.

We all knew the commander, Major von der Heydte, from Italy. One of his former staff officers, Hauptmann Mager, was the chief of the 2nd Battalion. I was to report to him, and was assigned to the 5th Company as a squad leader. Those who hadn't jumped before were quickly sent to Dreux to jump training, in the 5th, however, we only had experienced Fallschirmjäger, as much as I can remember. Most of the time we spent training the company in attacks, etc., and close-combat exercises with and without weapons. Because the NCOs brought a lot of fighting experience to the training, the exercises became very realistic.

Another FJR 6 soldier, Obergefreiter Dietrich Scharrer, at the time in the 7th Company, here reflects back on life in Cologne-Wahn in 1944:

On 6 January 1944, I was released from sick leave. I was to report to the replacement training battalion in Gardelegen, because my unit, III./FJR 6 under Major Liebach, stood on the mission at Monte Cesima. I did not know when I was supposed to leave to go there. In January, I finally arrived at my new unit, FJR 6 under Major von der Heydte in Cologne-Wahn.

We were in the barracks in an external camp. It reminded me of my time doing Reich Labor Service; then we had also lived in barracks. I was assigned to the 7th Company; one could barely call us a company, because we were so few. Over time, however, our barracks filled up. My first company chief was Oberleutnant Count von Bethusy-Huc, who later took over the difficult company. An officer followed him, who had been transferred to us from the police, but whose name I can no longer remember. After that came Oberleutnant Endres, who led our company in Normandy. In this formation, the 'new' 6th Regiment was different from the 'old'. In the 'old' 6th, we had all been volunteers directly from different parachute forces. We had served together as recruits and had been together at the jump school in Wittstock. Now we old recruits were thrown together with recruits, who were coming directly from basic training, and soldiers who had been in other areas of the Luftwaffe: loadmasters, radio operators,

Gefreiter, later Oberjäger, Dietrich Scharrer.

A squad of Fallschirmjäger climb into a Ju 52 for a practice jump. Major von der Heydte took charge of two squadrons of Ju 52s for training purposes, so that airborne deployment could be an integral part of combat exercises.

and so on. It seemed like a serious crime to us, but actually it was a good mixture. The good companionship quickly affected us positively. In order to make the regiment ready for deployment, an emphasis was placed on intensive squad training. In addition, through the influence of the regimental commander, Major Friedrich August von der Heydte, the regiment also received good jump training. Our most important experience, however, was improvising! The ground exercises took place between the barracks.

Because we had no time to teach the young Fallschirmjäger to pack their own chutes, we old-timer Fallschirmjäger packed them at night. (An old-timer? I was 19 at the time!) There was no regular schedule according to service regulations because above all we had to fulfil the training exercises. Therefore we never got a long night's rest. I gladly shared my experience and what I had learned at jump school. In this way we were successful, in the six required exams – no one from my squad suffered an injury during jumping. The bombing of civilians in Cologne interrupted our training period, after which we had to recover corpses for a whole day. Mentally, this was a great challenge, because as German soldiers we couldn't even comprehend an attack against civilians. This attack on our homeland was a terrible experience.

As part of the training, the 7th Company undertook a practice march with full gear. After a short time our platoon leader, Leutnant von Socha, gave his MP40 to a

The parachute jumps for Fallschirmjäger recruits first took place over the flat Wahn Heath; later, in the context of combat exercises, they were also made over uneven ground. On the Elsenborn drill ground, FJR 6 troops here carry out a final exercise for to test their readiness for action.

machine-gunner and carried the machine gun. That was impetus for me to do the same. In principle it wasn't difficult, because I was marching directly in front of the machine-gun section. The company soon looked a bit strange: both officers and NCOs schlepped the heavy weapons, and the recruits carried the lighter weapons. The exemplary behavior of Leutnant von Socha illustrated the well-tried Prussian principle: don't ask others to do things that you won't do yourself.

On 20 March, General Student [the commander of the Fallschirmjäger arm] arrived at the troops' drill ground in Wahn, in order to observe FJR 6 and to get a picture of Major von der Heydte's progressive training plans. Major von der Heydte spent a lot of time with the subunits, in order to oversee the training personally. He knew that little time remained to bind his soldiers into a regiment. Therefore, the training proceeded at a

Fallschirmjäger take the opportunity to pose for a photo during training. These two photographs perfectly illustrate uniforms and equipment of FJR 6 at this point.

quick pace.

On 1 April 1944, he declared the regiment ready for action. Without exaggeration, it can be said that FJR 6 was at this point in time the only Fallschirmjäger regiment in the Wehrmacht ready for the complete range of operations. All members of the regiment were trained parachutists.

The full strength of the proud regiment amounted to 4,500 officers and men. Three battalions and regimental staff with the associated supporting companies stood ready for complicated air-landing operations and ground combat.

The battalions consisted of three Jäger (light infantry) companies and one company armed with heavy machine guns and mortars. The light infantry companies valued the development of firepower, so every squad had not one, but two machine-gun sections at their disposal. The light infantry companies were for the most part armed with the Karabiner 98k rifles, but Major von der Heydte managed, in addition to the MP38s and MP40s that were usually issued to the platoon and squad leaders, to get submachine guns for their second-in-commands also, as well as models of the FG42, the weapon that had been specially designed for deployment by parachute troops. Particularly good marksmen received the semi-automatic, self-loading G43.

The 13th Company was conceived as a heavy artillery company, and in addition to medium and heavy mortars, it also brought into the field 10.5cm rocket launchers, the so called Nebelwerfer. The 14th Company was an anti-tank unit with PaK 40 anti-tank guns and three tank-destroyer platoons, each divided into six tank-destroyer troops. They had 8.8cm *Raketenpanzerbüchse* 54 anti-tank rocket launchers, as well as the reliable Panzerfaust [lit. 'armour fist']. Leutnant Degenkolbe's pioneers of the 15th Company received, in addition to the usual explosives, two of the flamethrowers that

On 26 April 1944, the men of the 1st Company congratulated their company chief, Oberleutnant Emil Preikschat, on his birthday. This picture shows the Fallschirmjäger wearing the third model coveralls, that is, the second model pattern with modified camouflage. Even the Fallschirmjäger helmets seem to be covered with the same camouflage pattern, in sand or dark-green.

the enemy feared so much. Everyone knew that the regiment would be deployed to the front as soon as they were needed. Therefore, many of the Fallschirmjäger used their time in the homeland to get married, an an eyewitness remembers:

> A Feldwebel came to us in the business office and filed a request to be married. Before our company chief, Leutnant Emil Preikschat, could grant this, proof of Aryan descent had to be solicited. When the documents were finally present, I called the Feldwebel in and showed him the papers. His grandfather had been identified as a Jew. If this information had landed in the wrong hands, he could have been released from service and sent to a concentration camp. The Feldwebel stood before me, with his Crete cuff title and his chest fully decorated. A real warhorse and an experienced soldier from the front, and cried. I threw the piece of paper in the oven, where it burned up right away. I wrote him a replacement certificate: 'The original not able to be located, grandfather probably Catholic.' Now the Feldwebel could marry and everything was well.

At first the regiment relocated on 2 May from Cologne-Wahn to the Elsenborn troops' drill ground, where combat exercises with live ammunition took place over the next five days, and the regiment demonstrated its combat potential. The challenging training in Wahn had been worth it: FJR 6 was a hard-hitting formation.

On 6 May 1944 General Ramcke, the commander of 2 FJD, visited FJR 6, as he later recollected:

Having congratulated Oberleutnant Peikschat on his birthday, the 1st Company marches to breakfast with precision after the morning roll call.

During the relocation of the regiment to Elsenborn, these Fallschirmjäger pose one more time for a photograph. The second from the left (No. 1) is Hauptfeldwebel Karl Hentschel, while the fifth from the left (No. 4) is Oberjäger Werner Eul.

The regiment stood before me in a square open to one side. Fifteen companies of 200 men each. The companies were divided up further. Uniform: battle uniform. An iron wall in camouflaged field-grey under the round helmets of the Fallschirmjäger troops. In the first rank, the 'old hands', fighters from Holland and Belgium, from Crete and Africa, from Sicily and southern Italy, and from the wide front in Russia. Chests decorated with well-earned medals for bravery, with Wound Badges in silver and gold, and with the badge awared for completing Fallschirmjäger training, showing the diving eagle.

Oberstleutnant von der Heydte had used the time well. Every man of the regiment had carried out his required jumps at dusk and in the dark, and also participated in a gliding dive in a military glider from a height of 3,000m. The weapons training was excellent: Panzerfaust and Panzerschreck, pistols and rifles, submachine guns, heavy and light machine guns, heavy and light mortars, as well as recoilless guns... The regiment was ready for battle.

To protect ore transports from northern Sweden, FJR 6 was intended for deployment to the Aland Islands in the Baltic Sea. This movement did not take place, however. In spite of all facts being kept top secret, the wildest rumours circulated about the future deployments: Sweden, Russia and Italy were all options.

Oberst Friedrich August Freiherr von der Heydte, commander of FJR 6

Hauptmann Rolf Mager, commander of the II./FJR 6, bearer of the Knight's Cross, of the German Cross in Gold, and the golden Luftwaffe Close-Combat Clasp.

Hauptmann Emil Preikschat, commander of the I./FJR 6.

Hauptmann Horst Trebes, Commander of the III./FJR 6, bearer of the Knight's Cross.

Oberfeldwebel Graf, Oberfeuerwerker (chief gunner) of the 1st Battalion.

Oberjäger Templemann, 1st Battalion.

Feldwebel, later Oberfeldwebel, Werner Eul, 1st Battalion

Oberfeldwebel Hans Morthorst, Bekleidungsverwalter (uniform administrator), 1st Battalion.

Feldwebel Dattko, uniform administrator, 1st Company.

Feldwebel Gruellich, WuG Troop, 1st Battalion.

Feldwebel Kammerer, Küchenverwalter (cooking administrator), 1st Battalion.

Oberjäger Löw, 1st Battalion.

Oberjäger Mikus, 1st Battalion.

CHAPTER FIVE

Deployment in Normandy, 1944

In order to strengthen the defence against the anticipated Allied invasion of Northwest Europe, FJR 6 relocated in mid May 1944 from Elsenborn via Maubeuge, Amiens, Rouen and Caen to the narrows of the French Cotentin peninsula. Tactically, they were the assigned reserves for the LXXIV Corps; the regiment adopted a switch position between

In FJR 6, the NCOs formed the backbone of the companies. This photo shows two Oberfeldwebel, a Feldwebel and an Oberjäger studying a map in preparation for an exercise. The two Oberfeldwebel are experienced fighters – the armbands worn on the left sleeve of the pilot's blouse indicates their service in Crete and in North Africa. Each company considered itself lucky to have such battle-tested soldiers in its ranks.

Mont Castre and Carentan. The regimental staff was in Gonfreville, north of Périers, the 1st Battalion under the command of now-Hauptmann Emil Preikschat in the area from St Jores and Monte Castre, the 2nd Battalion under Hauptmann Rolf Mager near Lessay, and the 3rd Battalion under Hauptmann Trebes between Carentan and Périers.

In their planning, the corps assumed that the Fallschirmjäger were the best candidates for anticipating the modus operandi of the Allied air-landing operations, and therefore the best able to go up against them. The regiment was assigned to the 91st Airborne Division, under II Fallschirm Corps.

In expectation of the enemy attack, Major von der Heydte kept the Fallschirmjäger busy. In addition to the usual patrols and nighttime aircraft scouting assignments, he ordered smaller exercises. According to General Eugen Meindl's battle instructions from 11 May 1944, a third of the troops always had to be in position day and night in the possible landing zones.

Amongst other things, the goal was for the Fallschirmjäger to become accustomed to the terrain of Normandy, and to improve how they used natural and man-made positions. Major von der Heydte put in place effective defensive arrangements. Aircraft observation posts were created, with anti-aircraft guns arranged in a 360-degree pattern and covering every attack altitude. Furthermore, whole fields were

Whenever possible on operations, the Fallschirmjäger set themselves up in houses. Here Feldwebel Kurt Wiemer of the WuG Troop stands in the doorway of outbuildings on a farm in Normandy.

planted with 'Rommel's asparagus', long wooden poles designed as air-landing obstacles, in order to prevent military gliders from landing.

Under the command of Generalfeldmarschall Erwin Rommel, who pushed the building of coastal fortifications with great urgency, whole stretches of land were flooded, turned into death traps for parachutists. On the coast, the rule of thumb was to allot one division for every 10km of defensive line. FJR 6, however, was assigned an area 20km wide and 15km deep, and therefore had no systematically arranged bunker positions. Once more, this shows the army leadership's almost limitless trust in the

The 9th Company lie in position near Meautis. The Fallschirmjäger's positions are disguised and made rainproof with tarpaulins, bushes and plywood sheets.

combat power of the Fallschirmjäger, because this key position secured the entrance over land to Cherbourg. An Allied landing on the Cotentin peninsula could build into a wave that rolled into the heart of France.

What concerned the Major even more was uneven tactical line presided over by diverse commanders. Rommel, who visited the regiment in their positions shortly after his arrival, proposed that the invasion be defeated directly on the coast, practically at the water's edge, while Generalfeldmarschall von Rundstedt wanted to let the enemy set foot on the coast, in order to close in on him with armoured counterattacks, and drive him back to the ocean.

The regiment's neighbouring units were as diverse as the tactical opinions about how to handle the invasion. Battle-tested troops with experience on the Eastern Front were located next to reserve units with outdated material and captured weapons, and eastern battalions consisting of volunteers and former Russian prisoners of war. The

Fallschirmjäger realized that they had only themselves to rely upon in the upcoming battles. The higher powers of the army recognized the heterogeneous nature of the defensive forces in Normandy, and demanded every base commander give his written word of honour that no matter how desperate things became, he would hold his position and not desert it. Without suffering any consequences, Major von der Heydte, however, refused

In the last days of May 1944, General Eugen Meindl, commander of the 2nd Fallschirmjäger Corps, visits FJR 6 in their positions at Mont Castre. Major von der Heydte leads the General through the positions and voices his concerns about the size of the assembly area and the problems with logistics.

Positioned in a field fortified with so-called 'Rommel-asparagus' to prevent the landing of parachute and gliderborne troops, this Fallschirmjäger also has a machine gun on an anti-aircraft tripod. Very likely, the nearby command post is equipped with a field phone so the alarm can be sounded quickly.

to sign this on the grounds that it was dishonourable.

At this time, the regiment had access to 70 motor vehicles. This fleet of around 50 different brands and makes, so repairs and part replacement became a logistical nightmare. In a brief period of time, many of the vehicles failed and had to be retired because of mechanical problems and damage. Even though the regiment was well equipped for infantry deployment, they were seriously hindered by the lack of motorized mobility. The promised anti-tank guns also never materialized; at the beginning of June, Major von der Heydte wrote to General Student saying that they were 'completely prepared for any air-landing invasions, but only partially prepared for ground combat because of insufficient anti-tank weapons and a lack of vehicle equipment.'

In the first days of June, indications of an enemy invasion spread. Encoded radio transmissions from the French resistance were intercepted, and the informants to the Luftwaffe did not miss the increase in enemy air transport formations in southern England. Telephone connections were regularly cut, and often the German units' communications with one another relied on the activities of the resistance and the ability of signalers to repair the wires. It could only be days before the invasion happened; the enemy waited on the weather and the tide.

Eugen Griesser remembers this time well:

Communications were an essential part of the German defence system in Normandy. These signallers are laying cables for field phones, but they also have to repair those lines cut by the French resistance fighters.

In the days before the invasion a tense mood reigned. Everyone knew that the invasion had to come; we just did not know when and where exactly. The resistance continued to make trouble, cutting electrical wires, shooting up individual vehicles, and so on. On 2 or 3 June, a farmer who was friendly to the Germans gave us two rabbits that he had slaughtered. The day after, we went to pay him a visit and offer our collective tobacco rations in thanks. We found him lying in his clean living room with a crushed-in skull; his wife and children had disappeared. Someone, probably his murderers, had drawn the sign for the resistance in coal on the wall.

Given such events, the Fallschirmjäger were especially vigilant.

When the Alsatian drivers of the regimental supply train all deserted, one thing became clear: soon it would start! On 5 June, Allied bombers attacked tactically important points such as bridges, roads and railway stations. The 3rd Battalion carried out a map exercises for its officers and platoon leaders; they focused on the destruction of an enemy airborne operation in the battalion's staging area.

The highest powers of the army planned a war game/map exercise in Rennes for the morning of 6 June 1944; it would be led by the Chief of Staff of the Wehrmacht, General Walter Warlimont. All division commanders with their staff were required to

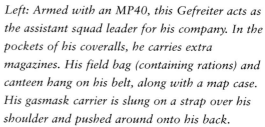

Left: Armed with an MP40, this Gefreiter acts as the assistant squad leader for his company. In the pockets of his coveralls, he carries extra magazines. His field bag (containing rations) and canteen hang on his belt, along with a map case. His gasmask carrier is slung on a strap over his shoulder and pushed around onto his back.

Below right: In his free time, this Oberjäger visits the fortifications of the Siegfried Line, known by the Germans as the undefeatable Westwall. He is wearing the second model of camouflaged coveralls, which were modified with additional pockets for signal cartridges. His rank is displayed via the wings sewn onto his sleeves. Because the Fallschirmjäger had to be prepared for attacks by the French resistance at all times, this soldier has two hand grenades ready on his belt as well as a pistol behind the left hip. As the squad leader, he is carrying field glasses around his neck, an indispensable piece of equipment for scouting and combat.

Below left: A Feldwebel of the 2nd Battalion views the ground in front of his position near Lessay.

participate, along with the commanders of units of troops that were subordinate to the army and the respective corps. This order also affected Major von der Heydte. Because he planned to drive to Rennes with General Erich Marcks, the commander of the LXXIV Corps, he decided not to depart on the evening of 6 June, in order to use the protection of the dark to make it to Rennes, but instead to spend the night with his regiment because of the critical overall situation. During the daytime the Allied planes darkened the skies; therefore the departure with General Marcks was planned for 0500hrs on 6 June.

During the night of 5/6 June, the communications officer of FJR 6, Oberleutnant

Dietrich, received word from Luftwaffe command that the Allied air transport units stationed in England were showing signs of heavy activity. Dietrich reported to Major von der Heydte. Contrary to the relaxed approach of his superiors, von der Heydte ordered his regiment to prepare to march and for battle. Ground observers had already been assigned to track the Allies' movements in the night sky and report anything suspicious. While the battalions prepared, Oberleutnant Dietrich had the assignment to inform the neighboring army units. The radio connection, however, refused to function; they could not figure out why. Acting more out of desperation than anything else, Dietrich tried to establish a connection via the French public telephone network, and surprisingly it worked. Apparently the resistance had scruples against harming property of the French state. Major von der Heydte finished a late dinner and shaved, 'in order to appear respectable going into a possible battle', he explained later in his memoirs.

Shortly after midnight, the first reports from the ground observers arrived: enemy paratroopers were landing between the coast and Carentan. Shortly thereafter, they received the news from the 3rd Battalion that the enemy paratroopers had landed north of Carentan. It turned out that the men of FJR 6 were the first to identify enemy soldiers having landed in Normandy; in this case, it was the pathfinders of the 101st US Airborne Division, who had landed between St-Come-du-Mont, Baupte and Carentan, in order to direct with light signals the paratroopers who followed. Exactly seven

Observing possible enemy movement, this Fallschirmjäger has field-modified his jump smock by adding a rather large pocket to the left sleeve.

minutes after midnight, a ground observer noticed approaching enemy transport planes and reported them to the regimental command post.

The Allied plan involved the following strategy. In the morning hours of 6 June, US and British combat troops – supported by Polish, Canadian and other Allied contingents –were set to land at five different points on the coast between Quineville and Ouistreham and form bridgeheads. As quickly as possible, they were supposed to expand and consolidate these individual bridgeheads by landing heavy armour. An airborne attack by British paratroopers on the bridges over the River Orne and the Caen Canal would support the landings by sea, as would an attempt by American paratroopers to take the town of Carentan. In this latter sector, the Allies had divided the beaches into two areas, with Carentan as the decisive point between them: the beach northeast of Carentan was called 'Omaha', while the beach directly north of Carentan was 'Utah'. As long as this town was in Germany hands, these two sections could not be consolidated, and there was a real danger that German forces could isolate and annihilate the American troops deployed on 'Utah' Beach.

The leaders of the Allied troops decided that landing soldiers by sea only would be too costly in lives and materials. Yet they believed the German coastal defences to be stronger than they actually were. The powerful paratrooper units and airborne infantry that were deployed behind the backs of the defenders were supposed to pull German forces away from the coast and lock them in the interior, in order to weaken the resistance on the beaches and simplify the landings there.

The western flank of the landing zone became the area of operations of the US 82nd Airborne Division and the US 101st Airborne Division, two particularly powerful

Especially in the bocage of Normandy, these well-camouflaged machine-gun nests were highly dangerous for the Allies. The Fallschirmjäger expertly used the terrain and the firepower of the dreaded MG42 to their advantage.

divisions of paratroopers and airborne infantry. They were assigned to form a bridgehead between St-Marie-du-Mont, St-Germain-de-Varreville, west of Picauville at Meredet and northwest of Carentan. They planned to blow up the bridges over the Douve and occupy the causeway over the Meredet, in order to make the advance towards Cherbourg possible. Similarly, the western outlets of the dam near the 'Utah' Beach section had to be taken, so that the advance from the landing zone into the interior could take place without losing any time.

Prior to the invasion, recon aircraft had already supplied the Allied planners with photographs of the area of operations. They had recognized the artificially constructed flooding at the juncture of the Meredet and the Douve, but they had overlooked the swamps to the north, which had been created to defend against airborne operations, and reached out the railroad Carentan–Cherbourg embankment. This oversight was due to the dense vegetation growth in and around the water west of St-Mère-Eglise that made, for example, La Fière appear to be fields and pastures. What actually awaited the American paratroopers there was a 600m-wide flood.

Rudolf Thiel, an Obergefreiter in the regimental combat platoon, remembers what happened on the night of 5/6 June:

Arthur Völker, my bunker mate, had indigestion. He believed that this always happened to him when something was in the wind. I, too, could not hide my inner unease. After the relative quiet of the past weeks, I was worried about the massive bombings of the interior. Something was coming our way!

The rations had been miserable again that day: lots of pearl barley and a little fish, a lot of marmalade and a little sausage. We hoped it would stay quiet that night and that there would be no false alarms. Arthur and I were assigned duty on the high lookout post, an airy, windy task. A strong breeze blew in from the sea; now and again the moon shone through the clouds. It was not cold, just nippy; there on the high perch one got really knocked about.

At 2400hrs I had to relieve Arthur; until then I tried to catch a few winks of sleep. It didn't work, sleep wouldn't come. My unease grew stronger from hour to hour. I tried to read by the light of my Hindenburg light, but I could not concentrate. What the devil was being set in motion out there? The night was so calm, there was no noise of motors. Only the wind blew through the poplars. I had to relieve Arthur soon, and because I couldn't sleep anyway, I decided to relieve him earlier than scheduled. I dressed, belted up, checked my submachine gun and magazine, and crawled out of the bunker. The fresh air made me shudder slightly and I listened carefully to the night. It was strange; this much quiet wasn't normal. I had the feeling as if something treacherous was lying in wait for us. I went to the observation perch and called up: 'Arthur, come down. I can't sleep and will relieve you now!'

Arthur climbed down the ladder and said: 'Shitty wind, the damned cold, nothing particular to report' and disappeared into the darkness. I climbed up to the perch and looked at my watch. Ten minutes to midnight. I hung my field glasses around my neck, loaded and secured my submachine gun, and made myself comfortable. After a few minutes I heard the familiar but distant noise of airplane motors. 'Donnerwetter', I thought, 'that's not just a few. Hopefully they're not going to unload on us.' I looked at my watch again and held the binoculars up. It was 0007hrs when I looked to the northwest and saw all kinds of red flares and glaring white light signals. That could only mean one thing to any experienced soldier: The enemy is attacking!!!

My mind told me: this is the invasion. After the initial moment of shock, like a crazy man, I turned the crank on the field telephone that connected the observation post with the regimental command post.

Right away I was connected with the service's clerk who sat next to the telephone. 'Obergefreiter Thiel reporting, combat platoon, red and white light signals sighted direction northwest, loud airplane noise, the enemy is attacking!' The phone at the command post was not hung up right away, so I heard how Oberleutnant Peiser gave the clerk the order to get the Major right away. Then I heard the quick steps of the Major and fragments of his speech: this afternoon – French – damn it – no alarm. The Major: 'Combat platoon, report!' I said: 'Obergefreiter Thiel reporting, combat platoon. A large amount of light signals in the direction of the coast and Cherbourg. The enemy is attacking. This is the invasion, Herr Major, should I sound the alarm?' I looked at my watch: 0011hrs. The Major: 'Sound the alarm. Send Oberfeldwebel Geiss to report to me immediately!' He hung up.

I, too, hung up, and yelled as loud as I could: 'Alarm! Alarm!' And again and again: 'Invasion, invasion!' While doing so, I shot out two full magazines of submachine gun ammunition. I climbed down from the perch and Oberfeldwebel Geiss and other comrades were approaching me, looking sleepy and distraught. Everyone thought that it was just an air alarm, because an airplane motor inferno reigned above us. Oberfeldwebel Geiss sprinted to the command post, we took to our positions and our foxholes and waited for the unknown monster: invasion!

Because of the reports of his ground observers, Major von der Heydte ordered his regiment to march, in order to confront the enemy. The scattered state of his battalions was not exactly conducive, however, to such a massive relocation.

After midnight the Fallschirmjäger received reports of the first battles against American paratroopers south of Carentan. The 3rd Battalion encountered the enemy first between St-Georges-de-Bohon and Rougeville, where three companies of American paratroopers landed. The 13th Company of FJR 6 absorbed the enemy fire and achieved good results against the Americans, who were disoriented by the nighttime landing in an unknown area. Obergefreiter Günter Prignitz in the 13th Company:

St-Georges-de-Bohon lay about 14km behind the coast. I belonged to the company troop of the 13th Company and lay with a total of 16 men divided into four tents,

Obergefreiter Günter Prignitz was the company bugler of the 13th Company. We can see the bugle secured to his belt, a sign of his connection to the traditions of Jäger troops. This photograph was taken the evening before the D-Day invasion.

directly next to the churchyard. We had placed a regular observer with a battery commander's telescope in the church tower. A half an hour after midnight on 6 June, I heard our ground observer calling: 'Alarm – parachutes – military gliders!' while firing off his weapon.

The first thing I heard when I left my tent was an American soldier, who had landed in a giant tree, saying 'Oh, oh, broken leg!' His parachute still hung in the treetop, and he was on the ground. I disarmed him and spoke calmingly to him. His wounds weren't bleeding. He was probably the first American prisoner of war of the battle of Normandy.

A second parachute lay laterally across one of our tents, the paratrooper who belonged to it, however, was not to be found. A Feldwebel ran around to the back of the tent and yelled: 'Halt! Password!' Only at daybreak when we found him dead did we understand why the American hadn't reacted.

Units of the 101st Airborne Division jumped between 0100 and 0200hrs, but their landings were heavily dispersed. They were unable to band together, and FJR 6 attacked immediately. The 3rd Battalion reported that Oberfeldwebel Peltz was bringing in the first prisoners of war. They were locked up in the church of St–George-de-Bohon for later questioning. Günter Prignitz remembers that 'Numerous battles with American soldiers took place around our tents and soon we had 30 to 40 prisoners locked up in the church.' Alfons Mertens, at the time a Fahnenjunker-Feldwebel (officer candidate sergeant) in the regimental signal communication platoon, noted the confusion of the night:

The communications situation the night of 6 June was anything but clear. We couldn't get any connection to the neighbouring units or senior positions. Partisans and sabotage groups had cut the wires, so we had to send out messengers and maintenance men to establish contact with the other units. One of my messengers, a young boy who had just turned eighteen, returned to me in the morning, distraught. I had sent him to the headquarters of the 91st Airborne Division; he had found the headquarters deserted and destroyed. He had found the commander of the division,

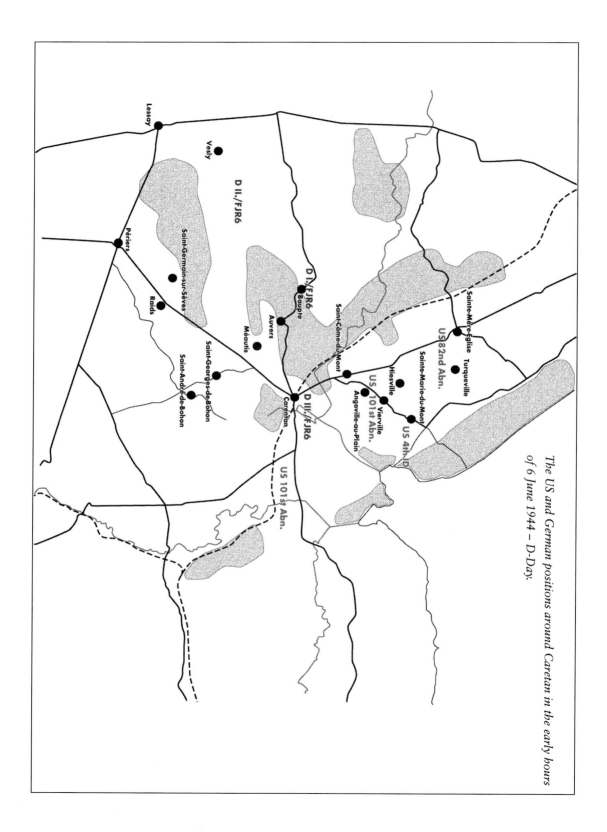

The US and German positions around Carentan in the early hours of 6 June 1944 – D-Day.

General Falley, lying shot dead on the side of the road. At that point, at the latest, it became clear that we only had ourselves to rely upon in the next few days.

At 0400hrs the American paratroopers landed in the area of Raids and once again, after an exchange of heavy fire, the invaders were defeated. In fact, the Germans managed to take prisoner a major, a captain, a lieutenant and 73 other ranks. The remains of the enemy landing force pulled back to the southwest. Eugen Griesser notes the first contact between the Fallschirmjäger and the Americans:

The American paratroopers were mostly young boys around 20, big and strong guys. They wore combat uniforms with sewn-on pockets in which they carried around half a colonial wares stores: rations in cans, chewing gum, chocolate, reserve ammunition, pictures of naked girls and even explosives. It was no wonder that some of them just exploded under fire from the rifles. Each of them had a large combat knife tied with a bootlace to their lower leg. Many others had a second dagger on their belt, a jackknife in their pants' pocket, and a pocket knife in their jacket pocket. The American pocket knives were very useful, because not only did they contain a knife blade, but often also a saw, bottle opener, an awl and a small screwdriver. Unfortunately I lost my American pocket knife later.

The Americans were equipped with small metal frogs for their nighttime attack. They were a child's toy that clicked when you pressed on it. The idea was that they would communicate through this clicking and be able to recognize each other. At night, sounds carried especially far, and therefore this idea that the Americans had, to communicate in the dark with these children's toys, wasn't very intelligent. If they really had ribbited like a frog, no one in the swamps would have noticed it, but the sound of these metallic clickers was so clearly unnatural, that one would have had to be deaf not to notice it.

Oberfeldwebel Peltz took some officers prisoner from their scouting groups early in the morning. They were crowded around a map, shining their dim flashlights on it. They were so concerned with reading the map that they didn't even notice that they had been encircled. They also hadn't set guards; these guys were that sure of their victory.

At 0600hrs on the morning of 6 June, Major von der Heydte arrived in Carentan to interrogate the captured Americans. The pathfinders of the 101st Airborne Division were particularly striking; they had shaved off their hair except for a thin stripe in the middle, and they had painted their faces with red and white. 'Now they're sending us their Indians', Hauptmann Trebes said as he led Major von der Heydte to the prisoners.

Except for the usual information, including their name, rank, unit and age, the Major received no other information from the Americans. However, the deployment of elite divisions such as the 'Screaming Eagles' was enough evidence that this mission was no localized attack, but that it had to be part of a larger-scale operation. This information was directly passed on to LXXXIV Corps, except for the neighboring 709th Infantry Division, with whom they could not communicate.

FJR 6 was the first German unit to fight against the Allied invasion. The men of the 3rd Battalion near St-George-de-Bohon encountered the pathfinders of the American paratrooper units in foxholes like this one. This Jäger has camouflaged his position well and built a fire crest for his Karabiner 98k rifle. Next to him, on the left, lies a hand grenade within easy reach. He also has field glasses, to monitor the battlefield, and his steel helmet is fitted with foliage camouflage.

The enemy engaged the command post in St-Georges-de-Bohon with mortar fire. It only had limited effect, however, and Oberleutnant Prive took action against them with an assault detachment from Rougeville; he drove the enemy back towards St Georges de Bohon. Caught in this pincer attack, and surprised by this textbook manoeuvre, the Americans had no adequate response. Prive's platoon took more than 60 prisoners in this action. Later on, some of the American units' stragglers came voluntarily with hands lifted to the Fallschirmjäger's positions. At this point the situation became clear: those Americans who had landed near the 3rd Battalion west of Carentan were probably dropped in the wrong place; those paratroopers who were captured south of Carentan were probably part of a diversionary manoeuvre or a reinforced recon operation. The enemy paratroopers' main attack could be found in the direction of the coast or farther west by St-Mère-Eglise.

From the north, the Fallschirmjäger heard the noise of more fighting. Coastal Defence Battery W5 lay in that direction and farther up the coast towards Cherbourg was the Marcouf Battery. There was supposed to be an anti-aircraft unit in St-Mère-Eglise, therefore it was possible that these positions had already taken combat fire, similarly for the army unit at St-Come-du-Mont. So Major von der Heydte decided to travel towards the sounds of battle in a sidecar motorcycle to investigate. In his memoirs, he describes the situation:

> On a narrow street, enclosed by bushes, I came to the place called Sainte-Marie-du-Mont, which, according to the map, was the last built-up area before the coast. In the middle of the village there was an old church with a pretty, and very tall, tower. After we had gotten a hold of the key to the tower, I climbed it and had a unique gorgeous picture in front of me that I will never forget. The ocean lay before me, deep blue and practically motionless. On the horizon numerous battleships lined up into an almost closed chain. Between the ships and the shore there was a brisk back-and-forth traffic of craft that were transferring the American soldiers to the shore. The Americans only met resistance from a single German bunker that – from my point of view it was to the right of the ships – was shooting at the landing soldiers. The Americans tried to take cover from the fire, in as much as it was aimed at them, with artificial fog [smoke]. I only needed a few minutes to get a clear impression of what was going on here. The location Sainte-Marie-du-Mont was not occupied by German troops; according to the signs in his office, the local commander appeared to have left in a hurry. I, too, had no reason to stay any longer in this place, upon which the American soldiers were marching in an exposed order. The location lay about 5 kilometres from the coast, and the Americans had covered about half of the distance. I hurried to return to the regiment on my motorcycle; I met the tip of my regiment on a large street towards Cherbourg in a village called Saint-Come-du-Mont. There I gave my first combat orders.

Major von der Heydte ascertained with disappointment that the army unit stationed in St-Marie-du-Mont had cleared out, down to the last man, and were unable to be found. Only the W5 strongpoint, supported by the Marcouf coastal battery, offered ironclad counterfire on the coast. Nevertheless, the Americans succeeded in landing on 'Utah' Beach relatively unharmed; they even managed to unload their first tanks. These actions showed that in this portion of Normandy only FJR 6 was in a position to offer serious resistance against the enemy. The regiment's lack of motorization proved to be a major handicap in this hour, because in order to put 'Utah' sector under massive pressure, it would have required the combat power of the whole regiment. Both American elite divisions had landed scattered in the area for which the neighbouring 709th Infantry

Division and 91st Airborne Division were responsible. There were still able to take the strategically important point St-Mère-Eglise and establish it as a firing basis without too much opposition from German antiaircraft units. At this point, though, Major von der Heydte could not have known that because the radio connection to the neighboring units was inconsistent at best and there was no communication whatsoever for the purpose of coordination.

Near St-Come-du-Mont, Major von der Heydte encountered the 4th and 8th Batteries of 191st Artillery Regiment, the 3rd Battalion of the 1058th Grenadier Regiment, and the 3rd Battery of 243rd Anti-aircraft Regiment; without hesitation, he took these units under his command. Both units had been defeated in battle by enemy troops, and had left from their positions. The ammunition situation was also inadequate; the infantrymen as well as the artillery had to be supplied from the reserves of FJR 6. Over the radio, Major von der Heydte was promised the forces of the 635th Eastern Battalion as soon as possible, but their exact time of arrival remained uncertain, and it was hard to estimate what kind of combat power the battalion had.

I./FJR 6 met with Major von der Heydte in St-Come-du-Mont early in the afternoon. From Hauptmann Preikschat, the commander of the battalion, he learned that the 2nd Battalion under Hauptmann Mager was following and should arrive soon in the village; enemy air attacks had separated the two battalions. On the way to St-Come-du-Mont, the battalion had exchanged fire with smaller, dispersed groups of American paratroopers. Steadily covering themselves against the enemy both on the ground and from the air was exhausting for the Fallschirmjäger. Without hesitating long, Major von der Heydte set the 1st Battalion marching towards St-Marie-du-Mont in order to build a defensive wall against the Allied troops marching inland from the coast. As much as possible, it was important to hold the village: 'If the enemy pressure became too much, the battalion was ordered to fall back towards the eastern edge of Sainte-Come-du-Mont, while maintaining a delaying fight with the enemy', von der Heydte remembered. The infantry battalion took a supporting position by St-Come-du-Mont; due to the status of their personnel and their equipment, they were no longer in a position to lead an attack. The batteries of the 191st Artillery Regiment were annexed by the 13th Company of FJR 6, in order to deliver counterfire against enemy heavy weapons.

The 2nd Battalion received the order to perform recon on both sides of the large National Road towards Cherbourg, in order to ascertain if the village of St-Mère-Eglise, which was elevated, was still free from enemy troops. In doing so, the battalion's right flank was supposed to stay in contact with the 1st Battalion as much as possible. Near Turqueville, the battalion had to swing in towards the coast and, together with the 1st Battalion, perform a pincer action to constrict and destroy the landing forces at 'Utah'. In order to provide a reserve and to secure the key position of Carentan, the 3rd Battalion remained for now near St-Come-du-Mont.

The 1st Battalion moved against St-Marie-du-Mont in a hurried tempo. Hauptmann Preikschat was aware that his battalion for the time being only had themselves to rely upon against opponents of unknown strength. Nevertheless, his principal order was to prevent the Americans from building a bridgehead on the coast and, if possible, from uniting with the airborne troops and the neighboring landing zones. Shortly after moving through St-Come-du-Mont, Hauptmann Preikschat let his men go into open formation: the 1st and 2nd Companies were on the right of the main road, the 3rd on the left. As they crossed the height of Angloville-au-Plaine, the battalion was surprised by the sudden landing of American airborne troops in military gliders. Unplanned, the 1st Battalion had arrived at the centre of an Allied airborne operation; they seized initiative, however, and – following the motto 'offence is the best defence' – the Fallschirmjäger set upon the Americans and fought their way through their ranks. Eugen Scherer, Leutnant at the time, and leader of the 4th Company, describes the situation:

> Our battalion's attack progressed well at first and we rushed immediately into the paratroopers of the 101st Airborne as they landed from military gliders. A gory battle developed on the disorderly grounds. Man against man and group against group. It wasn't possible for the battalion to have any unified leadership, as new enemy units, which we had to fight, kept landing in the middle of the battalion's actions. We took hundreds of prisoners from the 501st and 506th Airborne Regiments and sent them to our rear, unarmed, with only one or two men to accompany them, because we assumed, as the regimental commander had promised us, that German soldiers would be following up behind us.
>
> Unfortunately, we lost time because of this battle and could no longer reach St-Marie-du-Mont by nightfall. Also, even though battle noise could be heard from this direction, we could no longer establish communications with II./FJR 6 near St-Mère-Eglise, who were under fire.

Unhappy with their results so far, the battalion formed an all-around defence in an open field for the night. As darkness came, the 1st Battalion then lost the support of the 4th Battery of the 191st Artillery Regiment: a fire ambush of American naval artillery on the battery position led to the loss of 27 men, and caused the battery officers to issue an order to abandon the position.

The 1st Battalion also came under heavy fire from naval artillery. In the course of the night, more enemy gliders touched down in the middle of the men of the 1st Battalion, these aircraft carrying supplies for the American paratroopers. From prisoners, Hauptmann Preikschat learned that other, powerful airborne forces in military gliders had landed in the area of St-Marie-du-Mont. Almost at the same time, a recon troop brought news back that St-Marie-du-Mont was occupied by enemy tanks. The men deployed there, the 3rd Company of the 1058th Grenadier Regiment, were defeated and in scattered formation had to pull back to St-Come-du-Mont.

Given these facts, Hauptmann Preikschat decided on the morning of 7 June to pull the battalion back to St-Come-du-Mont, as recommended, and to prepare themselves to defend there. During their rapid crossing of the area around Vierville, the battalion ran into an American ambush that broke up and to some extent scattered the unit. The Fallschirmjäger companies engaged in firefight in order to fight clear a path for their own forces. Because the American tanks from St-Marie-du-Mont also joined in the attack, and further American reinforcements closed the ring around the 1st Battalion, casualties increased dramatically until finally Hauptmann Preikschat gave the order to 'Save yourselves if you can!' The 4th Company under Leutnant Scherer, supported by Leutnant Krüger's anti-tank weapons, tried to hold back the US tanks.

In small groups, the Fallschirmjäger tried to break out of the encircled area below the castle of Vierville and to withdraw towards the locks of La Barquette. The flooded areas, which had been created to hinder the Allied airborne landings, thwarted them in this plan, as the enemy now used the swamps to their advantage. South of Angloville-au-Plain, as they waded through the reedy marsh, the Fallschirmjäger were attacked anew by strong American units. The Germans suffered heavy casualties – during the night, more American airborne soldiers had landed in this area via parachute and 150 military gliders, and they now occupied the area.

The Fallschirmjäger tried, at the edge of the swamp or while standing in mud up to their chests, to fight through the ring of Americans to the southwest. The result was further close combat with the American paratroopers, which cost the remains of the 1st Battalion bitter losses. Only a few hundred metres away from their own positions, the Fallschirmjäger were gunned down by Americans lying in ambush near La Barquette. The men of the 1st Battalion made some gruesome observations, as Jäger Manfred Vogt of the 4th Company remembers:

> In the chaos, I had lost my weapon, and I lay with an older Obergefreiter under a hedge for cover. At the edge of the swamp we observed how a few Americans gave one of our wounded a good once-over. With fists and the butts of their weapons they beat the poor guy and kicked him with their boots. When he could no longer move, one of the Americans put his foot on the guy's head and pushed him into the water until he drowned. So those were the 'Sing-Sing' methods of the American paratroopers.

During the night, the staff doctor, Dr Roos, the leading medical practitioner of the regiment, tried to break through in a Kübelwagen to the 1st Battalion under the protection of the Red Cross, in order to offer medical relief. He did not make it – Roos fell into an American ambush and was shot. Some Fallschirmjäger found him dead in his Kübelwagen near the church of St-Marie-du-Mont.

Oberleutnant Wilhelm Billion, leader of the 1st Company, called to his men: 'Either we get out of here or we get captured. But that is not an option for us!' A few minutes later, he fell from a bullet to the head.

Some members of the 3rd Company withdrew towards the direction of their own troops, and occupied a small street and the houses around it. An American tank unit tried to proceed down the street and to break through the Fallschirmjäger positions, but was prevented by the concentrated fire of the Panzerfausts. A US Stuart tank was stopped in the middle of the crossing and went up in flames. The commander, standing in the turret hatch, did not manage to escape the tank, and he burned to death at his post. He unwittingly gave the crossing its name: 'Dead Man's Corner'.

Obergefreiter Karl-Heinz Mayer, at the time in the 3rd Company, was wounded in the action by an American sniper:

This picture, taken after his deployment to reforming FJR 6 in Cologne-Wahn at the beginning of 1944, shows Jäger Mayer. He is wearing the standard uniform of the Fallschirmjäger: pilot's blouse, jump trousers, combat boots and a field cap made from the blue-gray Luftwaffe cloth.

The Americans had posted sharp-shooters in the trees. Even when one of them was hit, he did not fall down, because these boys had belted themselves in. I was a machine-gunner. A sharpshooter hit me in the face, in the left cheek. The bullet dug its way through my collarbone into my right breast. He probably wanted a clean shot to the head, but the smallest movement on my part probably saved my life. I crawled into the gutter by a house on the corner. I don't know how long I lay there, but at some point American soldiers stood in front of me. They yelled at me to stand up. One of them kicked me a few times in the side because he wanted to get at my gravity knife. I just wanted some water, but they didn't understand me. One of them threw me some chocolate, then he realized how badly wounded I was and gave me something to drink. The war was over for me.

On the evening of 7 June, Hauptmann Preikschat's men, most of them wounded and unable to fight, accepted the offer of surrender from Colonel Johnson of the 506th Parachute Infantry Regiment. The battalion had lost over half its men since the retreat towards Vierville. Only 25 men under the leadership of Leutnant Stenzel

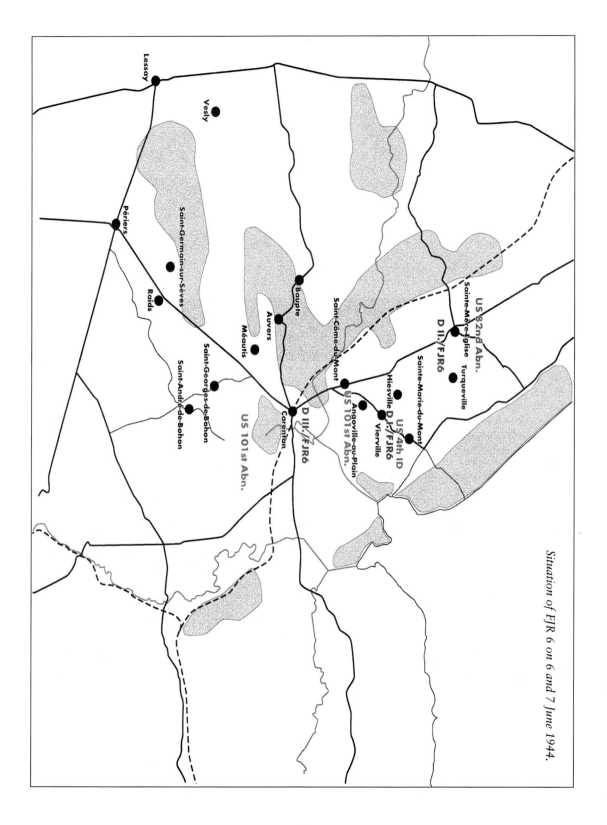

Lessay

Vesly

Périers

Saint-Germain-sur-Sèves

Raids

Baupte

Méautis

Auvers

Saint-Côme-du-Mont

Sainte-Mère-Église

US 82nd Abn.

D II./FJR6

Turqueville

Saint-Georges-de-Bohon

Saint-André-de-Bohon

Sainte-Marie-du-Mont

Hiesville

D I./FJR6

US 4th ID

Carentan

D III./FJR6

Angoville-au-Plain

Vierville

US 101st Abn.

US 101st Abn.

Situation of FJR 6 on 6 and 7 June 1944.

managed to escape from the enemy and fight their way back to their own troop. On the evening of 10 June, the only thing they had to report to Major von der Heydte was the destruction of the brave 1st Battalion.

Their comrades expected execution at the time. According to the order of the American general Maxwell Taylor, during the first days of the invasion no German prisoners were be taken, so the American paratroopers prepared to execute the survivors of the 1st Battalion. Only the selfless interference of an American captain, who had been taken prisoner by the German Fallschirmjäger the night before and had been well treated by them, saved Hauptmann Preikschat's men from death.

While the 1st Battalion moved against the enemy, Major von der Heydte had established radio connection with the neighboring German forces. From the 709th Infantry Division, he learned that they were preparing an offensive in Montebourg on the morning of 7 June. Therefore, the 2nd Battalion under Hauptmann Mager departed right away; they received the order to go around St- Mère-Eglise via Tourqueville and move against the 'Utah' landing zone and, in an extension of the 1st Battalion's position by St-Marie-du-Mont, seal off the beach section. With the US paratroopers cut off from

Normandy's terrain, which is covered thick hedgerows, made both the Allied advance and the German, defence difficult; luckily for the Fallschirmjäger, it also happened to be unsuitable for tanks. Here, in the shade of a hedge, a group of Fallschirmjäger takes cover from fighter-bombers, the most terrible of German enemies in Normandy.

their amphibious reinforcements, it would be possible to take the American airborne troops in a pincer move.

In the meantime, the 3rd Battalion was supposed to put pressure on and destroy the remains of the American paratroopers who had landed during the night. Scouts from FJR 6 reported that enemy groups had entrenched themselves in the villages of Graignes and Tribehou. Because these units could threaten the regiment's rear, the 3rd Battalion advanced against them; only the 9th Company was directly assigned to secure Carentan. The occupation of Tribehou occurred without great difficulties, but a sudden radio report to the regimental command post stopped the operation: American recon troops had been spotted near Carentan and the 3rd Battalion received the order to return as soon as possible to the city. While the battalion was marching back, the 9th Company reported that the Americans for now had pulled back in the face of the greater numbers of the German troops. At 2100hrs the battalion took position, and the city was secured.

The early phase of 2nd Battalion's operation was proving difficult. Because of heavy Allied air attacks, progress was slower than planned and they were forced to spread out widely. The open area south of St-Mère-Eglise facilitated quick progress, but Hauptmann Mager's runners were unable to establish contact with the 1st Battalion. To top it all off, troops from the 505th Parachute Infantry Regiment had dug themselves in here and directed heavy field artillery fire at the 2nd Battalion. The Fallschirmjäger managed to advance to Turqueville and fall into position here, when they came under shelling from both directions: from St-Mère-Eglise came mortar fire, while from the ocean they were battered by huge naval artillery shells the size of boulders. Nevertheless, Hauptmann Mager tried to complete his assignment, and Eugen Griesser received new orders:

> Our battalion was supposed to offer flanking protection to the 1st Battalion, who advanced on St-Marie-du-Mont, against the American paratroopers, whom we suspected were northwest of us. Suddenly, we were under heavy fire from St-Mère-Eglise. Hauptmann Mager had no radio connection with the anti-aircraft division that was supposed to be in this location, so he put together two recon troops. 'You do this!' he said to me.
>
> We left everything that rattled and clanged with the platoon HQ and went stalking. Our approach lasted longer than suspected, because we were partially moving across open ground, which we had to do quite carefully, and because we had to go around some forward-deployed American posts. Coming from the location [St-Mère-Eglise], we already heard the firing sounds of American mortars. The fact that no combat noise could be heard in the area meant that the anti-aircraft units had either been destroyed, or that they had cleared out of their positions. But we had no idea how strong the enemy in St-Mère-Eglise was. Best-case scenario: only a heavy company with their howitzers; worst-case scenario: hundreds of Americans and more.
>
> We managed to push forward into the heart of the objective and one thing quickly

became clear: St-Mère-Eglise was occupied by at least one battalion. Until then we hadn't seen any vehicles, but our chief would be unable to ignore a battalion with mortars on our flank.

Suddenly, from a window two metres to the left of me, a submachine gun started firing, and from the other side of the square machine guns clattered. But they were not aiming at us; the fire was directed at a second recon troop somewhere to our right. We stood in the blind spot of the shooters in the window, and had not yet been discovered. Gerd Kerl and I pulled out our hand grenades and tossed them into the window. The firing from the window stopped right away. I shot off a few bursts of gunfire from my submachine gun, to be sure, and looked into the room; apparently we had blasted a radio station. Now one of the machine guns from the church tower was shooting at us, so it became time to return to the battalion. We ran along the alley, as fast as our feet could carry us, and I believe we could have broken any world record in this moment. An American emerged from behind a house corner, planted himself in our path, lifted his rifle and yelled something at us in English. We just ran over him, we couldn't have stopped anyway, we were running that fast.

Once clear we just threw ourselves behind a hedge, in order to catch our breath; then we slipped back to the battalion. After we had made our report, we just had enough time to pick up our things from the company troop and drink a sip of cold coffee, then our first attack on St-Mère-Eglise began.

Dietrich Scharrer, by then an Oberjäger in the 7th Company, also led a recon troop:

Around midday on 6 June, I received the assignment from our platoon leader, Leutnant von Socha, the lead a recon troop and gather information about the enemy. We advanced from cover to cover, bush to bush, in the specified direction, intending to use our machine gun for fire support. At that point, we hadn't seen anything of the soldiers on the other side.

In this way we entered into a disastrous situation. Even before we got our machine gun into position, Obergefreiter Walter Klute was pushing through a hedge and was halfway through when we heard a short burst of gunfire. Because Klute took a round directly in the chest, he was dead right away, our first casualty. We had established contact with the enemy; our assignment was fulfilled with this, and we pulled back. When we reported the strength of the enemy and his position to the company, Leutnant von Socha gave me a proper dressing down for having lost someone in our first deployment.

Some of the 2nd Battalion were successful in breaking into the Americans' positions. The US units, however, were connected to one other via small, portable radios, so they could easily request fire support from mortars. The Americans soon brought down mortar fire on the 2nd Battalion positions, and the men of FJR 6 had to pull back to Turqueville.

In the course of the night, Hauptmann Mager received tactical information from his recon units, and formed a very clear picture of the numerical superiority of the enemy troops: The flanks and rear of the 2nd Battalion were threatened by American units, and in order to prevent his battalion becoming encircled and destroyed, Mager decided to withdraw to St-Come-du-Mont.

That night, 30 American military gliders landed directly in front of 2nd Battalion's positions, bring supplies and reinforcements for the troops in St-Mère-Eglise. In the open field of the landing site, the Americans were easy targets for the Fallschirmjäger, who quickly overpowered them. The Germans took supplies from the American supply boxes: fruit juice, chocolate, cigarettes, cans of meat and everything that a hungry soldier could want.

Dietrich Scharrer remembers his experience of the engagement:

On 7 June, my group and I were supposed to join a scouting troop of the 5th Company. We found the 5th Company quickly; they lay well camouflaged in a bush behind an earthwork. I told my soldiers to be quiet and take position between the groups of the 5th Company. Then I understood what we had planned here. In front of us lay a wide field, on which American military gliders were landing. When the first sailor touched down, fire from our gun barrels greeted him. It was a mean surprise for the Americans to have so much heavy fire rain down on them during the landing. Many of them paid with their lives, they must have suffered great losses. Afterwards we searched the field to haul scattered Americans from their hideouts. My group returned back to the 7th company.

On the morning of 7 June, the Fallschirmjäger broke away from the enemy and occupied a defensive position in front of St-Come-du-Mont. This move soon proved to have been the right decision, because scouts reported strong enemy units approaching from the direction of the 'Utah' section, and from St-Mère-Eglise towards St-Come-du-Mont. If they had stayed any longer in Turqueville, it would have cost FJR 6 a second battalion.

Meanwhile Major von der Heydte had secured the area from St-Come-du-Mont to Carentan with two companies from the 3rd Battalion and brought III./1058th Grenadier Regiment into deployment near Basse Addeville to guarantee the safe return of the II./FJR 6. An energetic advance by American tank units, however, broke through the grenadiers' defensive positions. The 9th Company of FJR 6 stabilized the army unit's front, and once again the Fallschirmjäger destroyed some enemy tanks with close-combat tactics.

The Americans now attacked the Fallschirmjäger positions around St-Come-du-Mont from the north and east. In a delaying battle, FJR 6 still managed to fight off the enemy assaults, but the danger of being encircled remained. A division of American light tanks penetrated into the positions of the 3rd Battalion during the fighting. Obergefreiter Fischer managed to bring one of the vehicles to a halt with a Panzerfaust directly in front of the battalion's command post. Because the American ground troops had reported the position of the Fallschirmjäger to the naval artillery, FJR 6 troops by St-Come-du-Mont also received heavy fire from the sea. One element of uncertainty was the resilience of the subordinate army battalion, whose Georgian companies were given a particularly tough hammering by the Allied air attacks. At first in smaller groups, later in larger ones, the Georgians trickled away from their positions and turned themselves over to the enemy. 'After three days, no more Georgians could be found', Major von der Heydte remembers in his memoirs.

From a covered position, a squad leader gives orders to his men. The Oberjäger is wearing the typical battle uniform of the Fallschirmjäger, and he carries only the most essential equipment: a field bag and canteen. The Fallschirmjäger avoided carrying all unnecessary personal equipment during battle.

In the meantime, enemy tank forces marched on Pont l'Abbé, a village northwest of Carentan. Further elements III./FJR 6 were deployed to clean up the breaks in the line, but it turned out that a row of smaller towns and homesteads had been occupied by the Allies, and winning them back would only lead to splintering the forces of the 3rd Battalion. Major von der Heydte therefore announced the return to Carentan. But he soon learned that his own troops, probably the company of 191st Pioneer Battalion who had been stationed in Carentan until then, had blown up the northern bridge over the Douve. Now FJR 6 found itself in a pinch, with Americans in front of them and on their flanks, and cut off by the flooded areas behind them. Major von der Heydte did the only correct thing: instead of waiting until the Americans rolled up and destroyed the 2nd Battalion with their numerical strength, he ordered a retreat into the area south of the Douve.

In the morning, a heavy barrage of American field and naval artillery beat down on the ranks of the 2nd Battalion. The enemy increasingly used phosphorous grenades, which caused intense burns for their victims. With smoke grenades the Americans then lay out a thick obsuring curtain, under the cover of which their combat troops could sneak in and settle themselves in hedges and trees. Dietrich Scharrer remembers:

> With three submachine-gunners and Gefreiter Herbert Peitsch, who had a rifle grenade launcher, I was supposed to cover the withdrawal of the 7th Company. We spread ourselves wide across the position and waited until the order came to retreat. Then we slid slowly under cover into the trenches along the street.
>
> Suddenly we were under small weapons fire from the left! I couldn't make out the origin of the fire and therefore could not figure out the enemy's positions. Gefreiter Peitsch ran across the street, sat down with his legs apart and began to bombard the tree line in front of him with rifle grenades. He was so calm while doing so, as if nothing could happen to him. But the way he sat there made him a perfect target for sharpshooters in the trees. On this day, for the first time, Gefreiter Peitsch showed stubbornness and cold-bloodedness on the front. He hit a sniper in the tree with a rifle grenade. The sniper fell out of his hiding spot and ended up hanging from a tree branch. Peitsch turned to me and said 'Oberjäger, look at that – I feel sorry for him!' Peitsch mastered situations like this with his rifle grenade weapon. On his own, he shot up two Sherman tanks and died in the process. Posthumously he received the Ritterkreuz [Knight's Cross] for this action.

At the same time, the Americans succeeded in breaking through the defences of III./1058th Grenadier Regiment, and forced the remains of the battalion to flee. In mindless flight, the battalion was pushed back towards the west.

The 13th Company's position also came under heavy fire, as well as the regimental combat platoon deployed to protect them, the bicycle platoon, and the messenger section. The powerful shells of the naval artillery caused great losses among the Fallschirmjäger and destroyed some of the heavy weapons that were so necessary to providing fire support. At 0545hrs the Americans stopped the barrage but did not immediately follow up with their ground troops, so that the available elements of FJR 6 had chance to regroup along the St-Come-du-Mont–Carentan road and place the remaining mortars into a secure reverse-slope position. Soon, however, the American infantry showed up and stormed the new defensive line, and were only pushed back in bitter close combat. Nevertheless the enemy succeeded in entrenching themselves on the western edge of St-Come-du-Mont and bringing up further tanks into position. Because the Americans were now unhindered by German defences on the coasts, they could land reinforcements of men and armour; this build-up led Major von der Heydte to the conclusion that the position on the road towards Carentan could also not be held for long. The swamp between St-Come-du-Mont and Carentan represented a formidable hindrance for the Allies, as FJR 6 could quickly take a new defensive position on the northern edge of Carentan.

II./FJR 6, meanwhile, pulled back passed Housville through the flooded fields and over a railway bridge towards Carentan. During this process, the battalion lost its heavy weapons, because these could not be transported across the swamp. Through radio contact with the 3rd Battalion, Major von der Heydte announced the arrival of the 2nd Battalion in Carentan area. The support weapons of III./FJR 6 were set up to cover the withdrawal route. While the few mortars, submachine guns, anti-tank guns and 2cm anti-aircraft cannons could not match the firepower of the Allied artillery, Oberleutnant Pöppel's company nevertheless managed to shut down an advanced command post with well-aimed mortar fire. The 3rd Battalion, however, also found itself under fire. The Fallschirmjäger regretted the beautiful sunny day, because the wonderful weather brought further infantry attacks, in addition to the harassing fire of the American big guns.

The 2nd Battalion needed longer than planned for the march through the flooded area. Wading and sometimes swimming, the Fallschirmjäger had to cross the swamp to then proceed along the railroad embankment. From their position on top of Elevation 30, they observed further landings of transport gliders near St-Mère-Eglise. Bomber fleets thundered above their heads, destined to unload their deadly cargo over the Vire bridges.

The bicycle platoon, under the leadership of Leutnant von Cube, still managed to establish and maintain communications with the retreating 2nd Battalion.

Those from FJR 6 who were following Major von der Heydte through the swamp towards Carentan had as difficult a situation as the 2nd Battalion – further pieces of gear and equipment sank into the water. A handful of Fallschirmjäger who attempted to save the machine guns at least, drowned for their efforts. Sanitäts-Fahnenjunker-Unteroffizier (Medical NCO Officer Candidate) Hehle, an excellent swimmer, managed to save the lives of some of his comrades in the swamp. When von der Heydte's combat squad finally reached dry ground, the Major found the 3rd Battalion already in position. His small troop was temporarily incorporated into an extension of the defensive line.

Shortly after 1000hrs, the pickets of the 3rd Battalion reported that the tip of II./FJR 6 could be seen approaching through the path in the marsh area. The Americans also noticed the movement of the withdrawing Fallschirmjäger; they attacked the German troops, who were moving forward slowly and with difficulty because of the terrain. Now the heavy weapons of the 3rd Battalion opened a devastating fire on the Americans, thus giving their comrades the chance to climb up the railway embankment and cross over the Douve on the railway tracks. The 8th Company of the 191st Artillery Regiment even managed, by firing six tank shells, to destroy the church tower of St-Come-du-Mont, in which the Americans had set up an observation post. The US troops were apparently too surprised by the fire assault to cover the railway bridge with their own mortars or machine guns; therefore the 2nd Battalion succeeded in reaching the safe side of the Douve. Leutnant Degenkolbe, the leader of the Pioneer Platoon, stood ready to transport the men across the water with inflatable boats, but luckily this dangerous undertaking was not necessary.

Engineers cross a river with an inflatable assault boat.

By throwing up a curtain of fire, the 3rd Battery of the 243rd Anti-aircraft Regiment prevented low-flying enemy air attacks for the duration of the crossing of the railway bridge. A skilful feint prevented the American infantry from going after the 2nd Battalion in earnest. By running along the hedges and firing from changing positions, the men of the bicycle platoon and the regimental combat platoon gave the enemy the impression that the defensive position was occupied by strong forces.

By the Ferme Pommenauque, the recently arrived 2nd Battalion took up its position right away, and defended the area against a strong American recon unit that wanted to work its way forward in the direction of the bridge to Carentan. The 6th Company under Leutnant Brunnklaus went after the enemy unit and destroyed it.

Immediately after his arrival, Major von der Heydte let Hauptmann Trebes inform him about the situation. The area west of Carentan was completely flooded around the Douve and therefore safe from enemy attacks; east of the city the ground was swampy and unfit for tanks. The supply situation of the regiment was particularly worrisome, given the significant material losses they had suffered, especially in terms of vehicles and heavy weapons. FJR 6 also had to provide supplies for the units placed under them. Many of the ammunition and rations reserves were lost with the vehicles; furthermore, the fighting had led to a disproportionate use of ammunition. At the regiment's special request, one of the ammunition storehouses, 'Melon', was assigned to them by the 91st Airborne Division. The Waffen und Geräte Trupp (WuG; Weapons and Equipment) that

Here Leutnant Degenkolbe's men keep the enemy heads down with well-aimed hand grenades. In the foreground, their comrades secure the flanks with their submachine guns. The Fallschirmjäger wore little equipment during operations: only weapons and ammunition were carried, with perhaps an additional field bag and canteen.

showed up there found a well-marked and well-prepared storehouse that was, however, completely empty. The replacement storehouse 'Mulberry', which lay 50km from Carentan, was in the process of being relocated, so no ammunition could be received from there. One thing was clear as day to FJR 6: Carentan was the linchpin of the right wing of the Allied invasion army, because as long as the city was in German hands, the Allies could not unite their 'Utah' and 'Omaha' landing zones, nor push forward into the flank of the German defence.

Major von der Heydte had some of his troops go into position along the flooded areas by the Douve, west of the homesteads, over the northern and eastern edge of the city. At the same time some of the Georgian army volunteers who had recently arrived from 635th Eastern Battalion were deployed to strengthen a rear position in the south of the city. Parts of the 2nd Battalion relocated at night to the eastern edge of Carentan because the forward-deployed observers reported American troops approaching the city from 'Omaha'.

The Americans' first goal, to take Carentan by midday on 6 June, had already failed, but it was expected that the Allies would commit everything to get the city under their control as soon as possible. Indeed, two hard-hitting and large task forces stood ready to storm Carentan, along with the 101st Airborne Division and the 1st Infantry division. Eugen Griesser remembers the early phases of the engagement:

> Our group lay on the northern edge of Carentan in the first floor of a house. From there we looked onto the National Street, which gave us a clear view into the city, and all around there was a broad field of fire. To the left and right of the street, American soldiers were working their way forward; it was definitely a whole platoon sent to scout ahead. When our machine gun opened fire, they scattered and went under cover. A short time later, enemy fighter-bombers appeared and fired on the houses along the street. The Americans tried one more time to bring their recon troop into the city, but quickly discovered that their fighter plane attack had not cleared us out of our position. It didn't last long until their artillery open up to shoot the way clear for them. Everything that you can imagine came at us: mortars, fire, even naval artillery from the sea. It went on and off like that for days.

Carentan became the Cassino of the Normandy invasion front. Like the old 'sixers' had done in Kirovograd, the men of this FJR 6 transformed every building into a fortress. They lured the Americans into traps, manoeuvred around them and cut them off from their own lines. As soon as a US combat unit believed they had secured one section, the

During the heavy Allied shelling from the sea, the Allies also used phosphorus shells. These caused serious burns, and such injuries were beyond the limited capabilities of the aid stations.

Fallschirmjäger appeared from an unexpected direction and engaged them in crossfire. In a countermove, the enemy artillery, in tandem with the fighter-bombers operating during the day, turned the city into a landscape of ruins.

A group of engineers was assigned the task of blowing up the Taute bridge, which led to Carentan train station. Gefreiter August Gönnermann and his comrades took their positions along the bridge and began to wire the explosives. The importance of their task soon became clear, as a strong American force tried to take the bridge, which they believed to be unwatched, in a quick attack. The Fallschirmjäger allowed them to advance to within close range, then opened fire on them and threw the Americans back.

The commanding subordinate officer tried to set off the explosives with an electrical fuse, but because of a technical failure, this was unsuccessful. Despite the enemy fire,therefore, Gefreiter Gönnermann jumped out of his foxhole on the side of the street and set off all the explosions manually. Just in time, and with a huge leap, he managed to get himself to safety as the charges exploded behind him. Only after a full five minutes could the Fallschirmjäger recognize that the destruction of the bridge had been successful; so thick was the smoke. The cloud of dust that formed from the explosion proved that the task had been completed; the bridge was completely destroyed.

On the afternoon of 9 June, the battalion doctor of 439th Eastern Battalion reported to the regimental command post of FJR 6. He explained the situation of a battlegroup formed from the remains of his battalion, II./ 914th Grenadier Regiment and a mixed anti-aircraft unit – they had set themselves up in defensive positions at the mouth of the Vire around a railway bridge. On the same day, Major von der Heydte received the order to take the battlegroup located at the Vire under his command. Recon troops of II./FJR 6 established contact between the battlegroup and the

This photo shows August Gönnermann on 4 September 1944. Notice the wide, comfortable combat trousers. Many veterans preferred to wear their uniforms one or two sizes too big, because freedom of movement and comfort were more important to them than a dashing appearance.

main Carentan defence. However, they also soon ran into the enemy, because the Americans had crossed the Vire with their tanks in the combat team's area and were pushing forward towards Carentan. Major von der Heydte reorganized the battlegroup (it had now been driven back to Carentan) and deployed them as the Battlegroup 'Becker' on the right flank of III./FJR 6 near St-Andre-de-Bohon.

On the morning of 10 June, the enemy attacked from the east and the southeast, supported by a whole tank battalion. FJR 6's outer defences slowly pulled back towards the main line of fighting, and prevented the Americans from pursuing them decisively. Once again artillery and fighter-bomber attacks rained down on the Fallschirmjäger's defensive line before the ground troops stormed the area. In the north of Carentan, the enemy infantry had attempted an early-morning crossing of the canal in inflatable boats, but they were destroyed in the crossfire.

The Fallschirmjäger were harassed by constant artillery barrages and air attacks, and the Americans finally managed to break through the German lines in the area of 635th Eastern Battalion. In response, 8th Company, FJR 6 (8./FJR 6) led a quick counterattack that managed to push back the enemy successfully, so the German troops could once again take their former positions.

Around 1500hrs, the enemy artillery barrage stopped suddenly. An American Jeep under the protection of a white flag arrived at the street bridge of St-Come-du-Mont toward Carentan. Two German prisoners of war, accompanied by some American soldiers, delivered a message from the commander of the 101st Airborne Division, General Maxwell Taylor: a message written in German in which General Taylor demanded the Fallschirmjäger's capitulation with the advice, 'Bravery has been well served.' If they resisted they would face further bombardments.

The letter was given to the commander in the foremost position, Hauptmann Mager of II./FJR 6. He established radio contact with Major von der Heydte right away in order to save time, because the answer was already clear. Mager wrote a reply on the missive in English: 'Would you surrender in the same situation?', and sent the messengers back to General Taylor. At the same time, under orders from Major von der Heydte, 4./191st Artillery Regiment fired off a demonstrative bombardment on the southern edge of St-Come-du-Mont with their last high-explosive shells.

During these negotiations, the weapons were silent only for a short period. In a hurry, both sides secured their wounded and fallen, moving them away from the frontlines. One of the American captives from the first days was a doctor, a captain named Dr Thomas Urban Johnson, who helped the German military doctors to treat the wounded. The bandages and medicines taken from the prisoners turned out to be helpful supplements to their own materials, because the reserves of painkillers and bandages were quickly dwindling.

The pause in fighting was brought to an abrupt end when the American paratroopers carried out a heavy attack near Ferme Pommenauque, north of Carentan. The Americans once again received additional support from their artillery and fighter-bombers. The 10th and 11th Companies of FJR 6 were in the hot seat of bitter defensive fighting and managed to hold the position, but with heavy losses. Recon troops brought new, worrisome news. During the night of 10/11 June, the enemy had gone around the right flank of the regiment near St Fromont and had taken up positions there, about 15km southeast of Carentan, with tank units. Strong Allied forces, which had managed to cross the Meredet, were also positioned by Amfreville, 16km northwest of the city. Furthermore, sabotage units were spotted attacking supply vehicles and messengers. On the afternoon of 10 June, Major von der Heydte issued the following regimental command:

1. Enemy: ...

2. Battlegroup 'von der Heydte' defends Carentan as they have previously and prevents the forward advance of the enemy towards the south or west over the swamps that surround North Carentan.

3. Main Line of Resistance: Le Port 1,500m north Tribehou–salient by Rougeville – western edge St-George-de-Bohon–western edge of the Tauteniederung [Taute Lowland]– Taute Canal on the eastern edge of Carentan–the southernmost bridge on Carentan street – St-Come-du-Mont – Pommenauque – southern edge swamp to Le Moulinet.

4. The following will be deployed:

On the main line of resistance
II./914 from Le Port to salient by Rougeville,
635th Eastern Battalion on the right up to the southern edge of Carentan
II./FJR 6 up top the northwestern edge of Carentan,
III./FJR 6 northern edge of Carentan up to and including Pommenauque
III./1058 from the western edge of Pommenauqe up to Le Moulinet
borders between
II./914 and 635th Eastern Battalion northern edge of Culot–Canal les Gonfres
635th East-Battalion and II.FJR 6 southwestern edge of Carentan–Taute Canal
II. and III./FJR 6 L'Hopital (to III./FJR 6)–Peneme
III.FJR 6 and III./1058 southern exit of Carentan–southern edge of Pommen-auque–western edge of Liesville

At my disposal and to receive various oral commands:
439th Eastern Battalion in the area north of Cantepie
Regimental Combat Platoon (FJR 6) in the area of le Moulinet
Regimental Bicycle Platoon (FJR 6) by Cantepie

Regimental Pioneer Platoon (FJR 6) in the area Meautis and Carrefour of Chemine
1st Platoon 2./1049 in the area around Sainteny
3./243rd Panzer-Jäger Division (Anti-tank Division) between Auvers and Baupte

5. With this the following are relieved:
III./ FJR 6 – the 635th Eastern Battalion and vice versa
II./FJR 6 – Parts of the 635th Eastern Battalion between Dassine le Flot and L'Hopital
15./FJR 6 – the security of III./1058 by Meautis

6. Heavy infantry weapons
The parts of the 4th, 8th, 12th and 13th Companies of FJR 6 that are still capable of combat will be gathered into the Nahde Company and immediately assigned to the regiment. They will go into position so that they can function as the central point of the II. and III./FJR 6. Nahde Company has their own permission to fire on any targets that they deem worthwhile. They will be fighting against the targets that will not be targeted by the artillery. They will use all their weapons during the day, and at night all weapons except the 1st Infantry cannon barrage fire.

7. Artillery
4./191st Artillery Regiment, 8./191st Artillery Regiment and 13./914th Artillery Regiment will be gathered together under commander II./191st Artillery Regiment as Artillery Group 'Rock'.

Assignment: To go into position so that Artillery Group 'Rock', with all their guns, can be in front of II. and III./ FJR 6, and have an effect with all their components in front of the main line of resistance. Artillery Group 'Rock' has permission to fire on all targets within the context of the present ammunition supplies.

Point of main effort: Artillery barrage, concentration of fire on all main critical points, at destroyed railroad and street bridges eastwards and north of Carentan and at the harbor of Carentan, fighting known enemy heavy weapons.

8. Areas of fire barrage: ...

9. Conduct of combat: Because it is to be expected that the enemy will pound the main line of resistance with artillery and bombs according to their plan, the main line of resistance will be thinly occupied with infantry (seamless observation, strong security for all positions, through which it would be possible for the enemy to infiltrate). Behind the main line of resistance, troops should have prepared and be occupying blocking positions.

Namely: The 635th Eastern Battalion on both sides of the road crossing 2,750m southwest Carentan church. Assignment: prevent the enemy from infiltrating along the Carentan–Périers road.

III./FJR 6 with front toward the northwest in the line street crossing 500m northwest Carentan–Elevation 30 southwest Carentan. Assignment: prevent infiltration into the city from the northwestern direction.

Regimental Bicycle Platoon (FJR 6), 439th Eastern Battalion and Regimental Combat Platoon (FJR 6) with front towards the east in the line southern edge Cantepie–Le Moulinet. Assignment: prevent the enemy from infiltrating into the artillery positions.

From the collective battalions, the assault reserves are to withdraw and prepare to destroy any infiltrating enemies who appear along the blocking positions or perpendicular to them. These assault reserves are to stick together in about platoon strength, are to be equipped with sufficient close-combat supplies, and are to maintain a state of heightened readiness.

10. Ammunition supply: ...

11. Ground reinforcements and demolitions: ...

12. Light signals: like 'AVI'

13. Passwords and recognition signals were not made known to the regiment. As of 6 November 1944 0500hrs, in the area of the Battlegroup 'Saustall' [Pig Stall]. Until then the old passwords.

14. Message connections: ...

15. Regimental Combat Post: western exit of Cantepie

Around 1745hrs, two strong US companies were able, with artillery support, to infiltrate the German defensive lines along the railroad bridge; elements were able to push forward to Carentan train station. Hauptmann Mager dispatched the 6th Company under Leutnant Brunnklaus to restore the situation, in cooperation with the 8th Company. In a pincer movement, they managed to annihilate the Americans. Around the same time, a patrol of the 5th Company captured three American medical orderlies, who apparently had lost contact with their unit. Major von der Heydte sent the men back to their own units with a message written in English. The message stated that due to their high losses, the Americans could surely use their medical practitioners, and that Major von der Heydte hoped that the American commander would one day know how to return the favour.

Once again, the 635th Eastern Battalion proved the weak link, with serious breaches of its line in many sectors. (At one point, two Eastern battalions took up positions near Carentan, but then quickly defected to the enemy.) Major von der Heydte regrouped his troops and from then on only FJR 6 fought in the important areas – the army units took over securing the flanks. In this way, the front could be held on 10 June against increasingly strong enemy attacks.

But despite the German bravery, the lack of ammunition and other essential provisions was soon readily apparent. The bridges and streets to the German rear were destroyed or impassable, so that barely any provisions could make it through to the fighting troops. While the Americans could land all necessary materials through their 'Utah' landing zone, Allied air supremacy prevented effective German resupply. Only one anti-aircraft division, which appeared in Carentan by accident, not by plan, gave itself to the regiment's command and proved to be a valuable help.

Eugen Griesser remembers the serious deficit in supplies:

On the evening of 10 June, I only had a little ammunition left for my submachine gun: two full magazines on my belt in a bag and one in the weapon. Because we barely received any ammunition resupplies, I had little more than my 08 [pistol], the bayonet, the spade and a few hand grenades. The war could not be won with this meagre arsenal, however, and some of my comrades had it even worse off.

The Luftwaffe put in a rare appearance over Carentan on the night of 11/12 June. Transport Ju 52 planes threw down 13 tonnes of supplies over the edge of the city, including urgently needed ammunition for rifles and machine guns. Major von der Heydte implored the command of the 1st Fallschirm Army in Nancy for more air supply, but no promises could be made and the drops never materialized.

In a nighttime operation from 10 to 11 July , the Americans attacked the road bridge at St-Come-du-Mont, but did not move forward from their positions in front of III./FJR 6. In actions such as these, and in contrast to the German situation, the Americans displayed their material wealth. Where the soldiers of the 101st Airborne Division could go no further, they simply pulled back and demanded plentiful air and heavy artillery support. For hours, the men of FJR 6 were subject to punishing bombardments that reduced their positions to rubble and ashes, burying whole troops and platoons.

The Fallschirmjäger did not yield, not even when the ammunition situation worsened. Rifle ammunition had to be collected in order to refill the belts of the machine gun. Every position was held literally down to the last cartridge; only once that was fired would the Fallschirmjäger pull back.

After a three-hour firefight the enemy eventually succeeded in entrenching themselves in the Ferme Pommenauque and infiltrating Carentan from the northwest.

Again the Americans pushed forward to the train station and occupied part of the building there. In order to close the hole in the defence between the remains of III./FJR 6 and the 13th Company of the regiment, the 6th Company, moving on their own initiative, threw themselves against the enemy at Pommenauque.

Leutnant Brunnklaus and his men managed to fight through to the road bridge and establish a connection with the remains of the 3rd Battalion located there. Once again, events came down to bitter close-quarters combat between German and American paratroopers. Leutnant Brunnklaus fell in the dense struggle, hit in the back by a pistol bullet.

Meanwhile the combat reserves of the 2nd Battalion took on the task of recapturing the train station. Cut off from their own forces, the Americans couldn't hold the building and were slaughtered to a man. Dietrich Scharrer celebrated his 20th birthday on this day:

After a firefight with American paratroopers, Gefreiter Herbert Peitsch takes a cigarette break.

11 June was a particularly hot day. We lay in our positions, the sun burned down on us, and our canteens were empty. I collected all the flasks and during a break in the firing, I ran to find water. After I had filled the canteens with water, I discovered two glass bottles behind an open door. I suspected that spirited cider was in them and took them back for my comrades and me. We figured out that the bottles were too old and that the good cider had turned into vinegar. So for my birthday we toasted with a mixture of water, vinegar, and sugar.

Around 1500hrs, Major von der Heydte arrived at positions along the Hiesville–Carentan rail line, in order to get an overview of the enemy position. While the 6th Company deployed to the right Carentan–St-Come-du-Mont road had won ground in their operations, the 3rd Battalion fighting to the left of the road remained under heavy fire from enemy mortars. Furthermore, parts of the 439th Eastern Battalion and the III./1058th Grenadier Regiment, which had been sent as reinforcements, had been apparently scared off and had advanced no further. At first individual men, then soon whole groups, fell back because they had run out of ammunition. Across improvised bridges, the Americans could land on two positions along the southern shore; they could now speedily reinforce their ranks. Even tanks were brought into play in large numbers.

In the face of the overwhelming superiority of enemy numbers and weapons, and in response to the completely inadequate provisions situation, especially with regard to ammunition, Major von der Heydte decided to pull his troops back from the northern and western edges of Carentan and then reform on the southwestern perimeter of the city. Holding onto the present positions would have led to the annihilation of his men.

At 1705hrs Major von der Heydte reported to the 91st Airborne Division: 'All leaders of Jäger companies have fallen or been wounded. Hardest fighting on the city limits of Carentan. The last of the ammunition has been fired; at 1800hrs we will vacate Carentan and fall back to Elevation 30–Pommenauque. This line can only be held if ammunition and provisions arrive.' The tactical leader of the 91st Airborne Division confirmed receipt of the radio message, but did not answer it.

The Fallschirmjäger had to disengage from the enemy in leaps and bounds, so as to disguise their manoeuvre. Eugen Griesser remembers the situation:

> In Carentan train station, my unit held the baggage storage rooms. During a break in the firing, the commander [von der Heydte], Hauptmann Mager, Hauptmann Hermann, and another Oberjäger came over to us. 'What's the status with you?' the Major asked. 'We can still give the Amis hell', I said. 'But when the ammunition's gone, it will be difficult.' The commander knew how serious the situation was, because the other sections had the same to report. 'Hang in there as long as possible', he said. Then he unfolded a map and showed us the prepared positions in the rear. 'Before the [support] fire is completely stopped, pull your men back to here', he said to Hauptmann Mager and Hauptmann Hermann. As he left, he patted me encouragingly on the shoulder and moved on, ducking.

The battle for Carentan was largely determined by American material superiority. Fighter-bombers swooped on individual targets, and machine-gun nests were wiped out by concentrated heavy artillery fire, before the US infantry advanced. In this manner, and supported by strong tank units, the Americans able to entrench themselves on the eastern edge of Carentan and push farther forward. The city literally had to be taken by the Americans house by house.

Now the Fallschirmjäger had to pay the price for the way that German tank reserves had been stationed deep in the French hinterland. The 17th SS-Panzer Division 'Götz von Berlichingen' was moving towards them from Bordeaux, but it could only move forward under the protection of darkness – during the day, the Allied planes turned the march into a suicide mission. The men of FJR 6 still had only themselves to rely on.

Parts of the 5th Company under the leadership of the beloved Hauptmann Otto Hermann were still trying to push back the enemy through powerful counterattacks. In this way, the Fallschirmjäger came to a open piece of ground, and they suspected that the opposite side was occupied by the enemy. Some young daredevils wanted to cross the field first, but Hauptmann Hermann held them back. According to an eyewitness:

> The Hauptmann called to them: 'I am in command here, therefore I will go first!' He rose from under cover and went forward in a crouch. He had barely covered 50 metres when the Americans open fired on him from all sides. Heavily wounded he fell to the ground. Suddenly the young boys lost the desire to attack. An old Gefreiter pushed the medic forward. 'You're the Sani [medic], now it's your turn!' But the medic stubbornly refused to leave his position.
>
> The Gefreiter pulled out his pistol, shot down the medic, and called: 'Is there another coward who wants to leave the Hauptmann out there to rot?' We then gave covering fire while he and a few other volunteers recovered the Hauptmann.

The Fallschirmjäger took the heavily wounded man to the next aid station. Shortly thereafter, the Hauptmann succumbed to his wounds.

The situation became ever more desperate for the individual battlegroups, because soon the ammunition for the automatic weapons became scarce, and the enemy kept adding reinforcements to the battle. Furthermore, one depot did not have the necessary ammunition on hand, while the personnel of another explained to the men of the WuG Troop that they were not responsible for Carentan. So while the Fallschirmjäger were going against American tanks with empty weapons, a depot administrator refused them the ammunition that could have helped them keep control of Carentan.

On the way to the regimental command post, Major von der Heydte met the chief of staff of the 17th SS-Panzer Division 'Götz von Berlichingen', who had driven ahead of his troops in order to investigate the situation. When Major von der Heydte reported to him, in accordance with protocol, that he had just given the order to evacuate the city, the SS man flew into a rage, because his division had been redeployed specifically with the assignment of securing Carentan and leading a decisive counter-attack in the region. He thrust aside Major von der Heydte's objections and produced the orders for the subordination of FJR 6 to the 17th SS-Panzer Division, and thus removed the Major from his command.

Directly after arriving in Carentan, Major von der Heydte informs Brigadeführer Ostendorf of the 17th SS-Panzergrenadier Division of the situation. Despite the immediate danger of losing the city to the Americans, Ostendorf hesitated to lead his troops into battle right away.

The eventual arrival of a fresh division gave the Fallschirmjäger hope that Carentan could still be held. Their disappointment was that much greater when not a single SS man took up a position within the city itself.

On the evening of 11 June, while his Fallschirmjäger were clearing out the last positions in Carentan, Major von der Heydte reported to the division's command post, and Brigadeführer Werner Ostendorf. He accused von der Heydte of cowardice, but he was eventually forced to take back his untenable accusations when the commanding general of LXXIV Corps, General von Choltitz, joined the conversation (like a 'Deus ex machina', according to von der Heydte's memoirs) to express his admiration of the Major for the resistance he had maintained for six days in Carentan. General von Choltitz coined the phrase the 'Lions of Carentan'. Nonetheless, the Fallschirmjäger felt that the Waffen-SS had left them in a lurch. Had the SS reinforced the city, Carentan would not have been vacated on 11 June. Their main benefit of the 17th SS-Panzer Division for the paras was they could supply some ammunition and rations. Gerd Schwetling, an Obergefreiter in the 6th Company at the time, had low opinions of these particular troops:

> The 17th SS was one of the new divisions that has been put together in the spring and basically had no combat experience. Maybe that's what caused their snobbery. They hadn't had any interactions with Fallschirmjäger yet. Looking back on it, it doesn't surprise me that a high-ranking SS officer, who had run across my path in the half-darkness, had jumped to attention and saluted me quickly. He probably thought that he had run into a superior officer.

The new line of defence southwest of Carentan was much shorter than the old line, and therefore it could be occupied by Fallschirmjäger in denser positions. But after six days of ceaseless deployment against a more powerful enemy, the men of FJR 6 were burnt out and completely exhausted. As a precautionary measure, Major von der Heydte pulled them away from the frontline so they could catch their breath; he left the rest of the army infantry in their positions overnight.

The Wehrmacht report from 11 June 1944 stated: 'Under the leadership of Major von der Heydte, 6th Fallschirmjäger Regiment distinguished themselves in heavy battles in the enemy beachhead, and in the destruction of the enemy paratroopers and air landing troops landing in the area.' Yet despite the clear appreciation of the performance of FJR 6 since the first day of the Allied landings, there were further attacks on Major von der Heydte. These attacks only stopped after General Kurt Student and General Eugen Meindl, independently of each other, declared that they would have acted in the exact same way in such a hopeless situation. Outvoted by three generals, the 17th SS-Panzer Division (now only referred to as the 'Kiss My Arse Division' by the Fallschirmjäger), supported by II./FJR 6, fell in on 12 June to storm Carentan. FJR 6, now subordinate to the division, took over securing the right flank, with the assignment

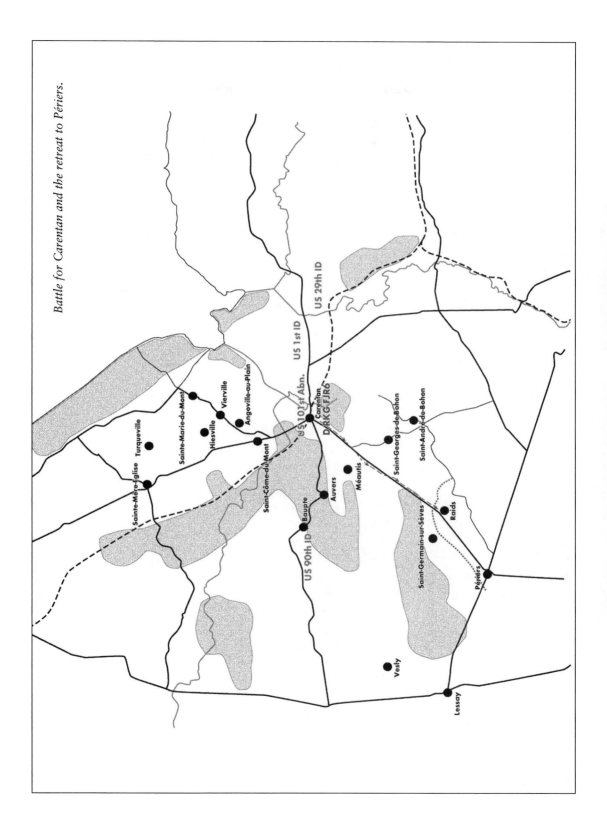

Battle for Carentan and the retreat to Périers.

to occupy and hold Carentan train station while the SS division undertook a counterattack from Carentan towards the coast.

At first, the Americans seemed impressed by the tank units of the Waffen-SS, and they pulled back, but it turned out they only partially retreated to escape the hail of bombs and rocket fire from the air support they had quickly called in. Surprised by the intensity of the Allied air attacks and the firepower of the enemy artillery, the Waffen-SS forces quickly came to a standstill and were caught in the enemy's fire. The SS approached the battle with a 'murderous idealism' (as Oberleutnant Martin Pöppel later

described in his memoirs), but without prior battlefield reconnaissance and sufficient artillery support, spirit alone was not enough to win the city back from the Americans.

The men of FJR 6, meanwhile, managed to occupy the train station according to their orders, and prepare themselves to defend it; the fighting of the past few days had given them enough knowledge of the area and the fighter-bomber attacks were nothing new to them. Some Fallschirmjäger couldn't conceal a certain Schadenfreude at the fact that the Waffen-SS, with all their pomposity, had failed miserably in Carentan.

Hurrying in with the regimental combat platoon, Major von der Heydte ordered all his officers to round up all scattered and fleeing SS grenadiers and incorporate them into the Fallschirmjäger – some of the grenadiers could only be convinced at gunpoint. Major von der Heydte inspired the bunch of men who had been thrown together; transfer papers to the Luftwaffe were filled out for the SS men, and he accepted volunteers into the Fallschirmjäger troop. The nearest messenger carried the documents to the corps command post, from where they were sent on to the Reichsluftfahrtministerium (Reich Air Ministry). Thus FJR 6 had received

The battle for Carentan developed into a French equivalent of the Cassino battle for the Fallschirmjäger. The constant bombings by the Allied air forces left large portions of the city in ruins, like the train station here. Here one Fallschirmjäger and two SS men rush through a shot-up building. The Fallschirmjäger is armed with a Panzerfaust, because the Americans had penetrated the city with tanks.

reinforcements. While the losses suffered in the battle of Carentan were not made up in the least, Major von der Heydte preferred even this small number of new men as replacements, as opposed to the actual big fat zero that had received as official replacements.

While the 17th SS-Panzer Division, heavily wounded, pulled back to their original jump-off position, FJR 6 pulled back and were reunited in their positions having suffered minimal losses. One regimental company continued to hold off against the Americans. One of the most important roads into Carentan was kept free by firing machine guns along it from covered positions. The American paratroopers of the 101st Airborne Division, trying to advance, were forced to stay in place by the concentrated fire. When the US soldiers, despite a German bombardment and their own heavy losses, finally managed to push forward, the Fallschirmjäger evaded them and fell back into other prepared positions, from which they continued their resistance with the remaining mortars. The company finally withdrew on the evening of 12 June to the regiment's new positions, as now three American divisions with strong tank support attacked the city from three different directions and occupied it.

Brigadeführer Ostendorf now accused Major von der Heydte of not having held his position. But in the face of his own defeat, he was unable to counter Major von der

The scene at one of FJR 6's first-aid stations near Périers. Here the Fallschirmjäger and the SS grenadiers deliver wounded to the doctors, and then return to battle.

Heydte's cool response that FJR 6 simply covered the retreat of 17th SS-Panzer Division and followed their general reduction of the front.

The news now arrived that an attack by the 100th Panzer-Ersatz Division (Tank Replacement Division) about 10km west of Carentan had not improved the German situation in the region. Accompanied by some officers, the commander was said to have left his troops during the battle, as though fleeing. The situation was tumultuous because some of the troops had surrendered to the enemy, while others dug in their heels and tried to hold out. Major von der Heydte sent his 3rd Battalion out to stabilize the situation, because if the Americans were to advance successfully in that sector, it would be possible to cut off and surround FJR 6 and the 17th SS-Panzer Division. Because Major von der Heydte recognized the general helplessness of the Waffen-SS, he moved the regiment to pre-prepared positions in the rear, southwest of Carentan. The terrain there was not well suited to tanks, and therefore the next four weeks were mostly determined by infantry actions. Nevertheless, the enemy artillery was still a great danger and the non-stop Allied fighter-bomber attacks were giving the Fallschirmjäger a tough fight. In the land battles, however, the men of FJR 6 were particularly tough opponents for the Americans. It took the Allies 24 days to wrest 18km of land from them between

After the operations in Carentan, FJR 6 pulled back at first to the line at Elevation 30–Pommenauque. This Jäger belongs to one of the tank-killer units and carries a Raketenpanzerbüchse 54, a lightweight anti-tank weapon called the Ofenrohr (stove pipe) by its users. As opposed to th120e Panzerfaust, which was constructed as a single-use weapon, the Ofenrohr could be used multiple times, and with significant results. This man is wearing a steel helmet painted with camouflage specks and covered in wire mesh in order to attach more camouflaging natural material.

FJR 6 lost most of their heavy weapons in the first days of the D-Day invasion. This Panzerabwehrkanone 40 anti-tank gun is one of the last remaining anti-tank weapons of the 3rd Battalion. It performed an important service in the fight against enemy tanks. To the left of the picture, a tank-killer team stands ready to give cover should the gun team have to change positions.

The Fallschirmjäger often used captured weapons in the defence of Normandy. This troop is using a US Browning machine-gun on a tripod mount. When the captured ammunition was used up, the men would resort to their own weapons. Normandy's landscape was not only covered in hedgerows; it also included wide areas of open, coverless terrain. In relation to trench digging, Major von der Heydte's maxim 'sweat saves blood' takes on a deeper meaning.

Carentan and Périers, the outer points of the new defensive line, where FJR 6 took up their positions between Raffoville and the River Sèves.

At this time, the remains of the 1st Battalion, the so-called 'Emil Unit', relocated via Paris and Weissewarte to the air base at Güstrow in Mecklenburg to form a new 1st Battalion. On 17 June Werner Haase, an Obergefreiter in the 14th Company, found time to write a letter to his family:

> My dears,
> You have probably waited for a few lines from me for a while. Today's the first time it has been possible for me to write to you. I'm sure you know from the radio or newspaper how it's going here with us. This is the first letter that I can say comes directly from the battlefield. Until now I have always gotten away unscarred, and I hope that I continue to do so. Everything's going okay. I was deployed to the point that was, at first, the weakest point. You'll have heard on the radio, how there was a battle for one city that had to be given up after a few days. Our regiment has shrunken down to only a few because of this city. If you find an old newspaper, you'll be able to read more about it. I'll only give away the name of our commander: Major von der Heydte...
> To a soon and healthy reunion! Greetings,
> Werner

The reunion never happened. On 20 June 1944, only three weeks after his 21st birthday, Werne Haase fell victim to an enemy sharpshooter. Because his foxhole could be seen by the opponents, his comrades only managed to get to him after darkness fell; they brought him to the main first aid station where it was discovered that one small, clean shot

This is the only known photograph of Werner Haase in uniform.

From his foxhole, this soldier engages the enemy in fire with his rifle. Even though no official emblem was supposed to be worn on the steel helmet, the Luftwaffe eagle is particularly visible on this photograph.

In the hedgerow-filled Normandy landscape, camouflage was essential for any position; it offered protection and concealment from the ever-present Allied fighter-bombers, and allowed the defenders to keep their position concealed from enemy infantry for as long as possible. This Jäger has disguised his position well with bushes. A large-meshed camouflage net serves as a cover to his steel helmet. This net has a shroud on the front that can be pulled over the face in order to further disguise the contours of the head. Natural camouflage materials like twigs and leaves can also be woven into the net.

that gone through his left armpit. The bullet had gone straight into his heart.

At the beginning of July, the remains of 17th SS-Panzer Division were relieved by the 2nd SS-Panzer Division 'Das Reich'. This division had a lot of experience in the field at this point, and worked well with the Fallschirmjäger.

FJR 6 also received replacements at this time, although the 830 new men could not completely make up for the losses they suffered. In addition, many of the new arrivals needed uniforms and weapons in order to be ready for battle. Major von der Heydte wrote in his memoirs: 'About a third of them didn't even have a steel helmet, over half had ripped footgear, their training and their morale were even worse than it had been with the original regiment.' Obergefreiter Franz Hüttich had a similar impression:

This group makes up an anti-tank unit. Note the common appearance of the Fallschirmjäger's camouflaged coveralls and steel helmets. Only the man in the middle is wearing a steel helmet designed for other army and other Luftwaffe ground units. The Fallschirmjäger also are not carrying the special cartridge belt for Fallschirm troops; instead they have attached leather ammunition pouches for the Karabiner 98k rifle onto their belts. It was unusual for Fallschirmjäger to be carrying bags for their gasmasks on their chests; the gasmask canister itself was attached to the carrying strap, and not the gasmask bag designed for Fallschirmjäger.

Among the replacements were many young boys around 17 or 18 years old, that had absolutely no combat experience and had basically been brought into the military directly from the school benches. They were no well-trained Fallschirmjäger, whom one could send into battle without concern. There was no evidence in their behaviour of training or jump school. We had to teach the boys everything, and because we were constantly deployed into combat, they had to learn very quickly if they weren't going to fall in battle. Others came from the practice of Heldenklau ['hero-stealing', the process of recruiting soldiers from other divisions] in the offices and air bases, redeploying them to a new troop. These were men from ground personnel that hadn't held a weapon in years; they had voluntarily signed up for the Fallschirmjäger troop after hearing the persuasive talks of the recruiters. Some had been threatened with deployment to the Waffen-SS, because the ranks of the fighting troops urgently needed to be filled up.

Searching the sky for enemy aircraft, this Fallschirmjäger is sporting the latest fashion in FJR 6: a scarf made from a rather large piece of a camouflaged American parachute. This adaptation not only shows that he has victoriously fought the American airborne soldiers, but it also protects his neck from the chafing of the woollen collar of his pilot's blouse. The peak of his field cap can be seen sticking out of the chest pocket on his jump smock.

The regiment only just managed to equip, clothe and arm the new arrivals. Major von der Heydte reorganized the companies of FJR 6, so that battle-experienced Fallschirmjäger would be standing shoulder to shoulder with the young boys. Nevertheless the companies were not more than 30–40 men. The Americans were getting bogged down attacking the defensive positions between Périers and St-Germain-sur-Sèves, which were echeloned in depth. The newly formed 16th Company, which had been created out of the bicycle platoon and the regimental combat platoon, had counterattacked and cleared up a breakthrough in the main line of resistance by the American infantry on 4 July. Obergefreiter Thiel and his group managed to take 15 prisoners during this action. He received an Iron Cross 1st Class for his efforts.

Having completely captured the Contentin peninsula, the Americans now channelled more and more reinforcements into the Carentan sector. The American paratroopers of the 82nd and 101st Airborne Divisions, after suffering heavy losses in the battle against FJR 6, had been relieved from the frontline. Now the Fallschirmjäger faced a new and no less tough enemy, the US 90th Infantry Division.

Now and then the regiment received visits from propaganda company reporters and photographers, and they had to adopt heroic poses.

This anti-tank team proceeds down a sunken road, typical of Normandy. In order to be less visible from the air, the Fallschirmjäger prefer to move in the shadows of the hedges.

The 16th Company – formed from the regimental combat platoon –stands ready for the commander to assign them with special tasks. Here the Fallschirmjäger prepare for a recon patrol. The machine-gun team members carry belted ammunition around their necks, ready for loading. Other men would carry further machine-gun ammunition, in addition to their own combat gear.

This Fallschirmjäger is watching the terrain in front of his foxhole. The wire netting on his jump helmet also holds a piece of camouflage material in place, most likely cut from an American parachute.

The Americans planed to advance from Périers towards Coutances, while the city St Lô would be taken from the north, in order to then drive towards St Malo and form a cordon reaching to the ocean. But FJR 6 stood in the way of this plan, because they still held the key blocking positions. St-Germain-sur-Sèves was secured to the north by the River Sèves, and to the other sides by flooded areas. Because the village lay on a small hill, the Americans called it 'Sèves Island'. In the preliminary stages of what was called Operation Cobra, the US 90th Infantry Division received the assignment to take this location. For this task, they were given all available artillery weapons and command of the mortar divisions of the neighbouring units, and were also promised strong air support.

At 0600hrs on 22 July, bombardment began on the positions of 11./FJR 6, which was defending the area north of St-Germain-sur-Sèves. Two battalions of the 358th Infantry Regiment, 90th Division, advanced on the road over the river, supported by combat engineers and tanks. The Americans managed to push back the forward-deployed members of the 11th Company, and build a bridgehead at the crossing. In the open swamp terrain, the enemy had little cover, so that due to the defensive fire from 6th Fallschirmjäger Regiment's companies to the left and right, their losses soon amounted to 200 men.

Major von der Heydte realized that the American advanced had to be stopped.

The pioneers under the command of Leutnant Degenkolbe were not spared the exertions of combat. Quite the opposite, in fact. Because of their special knowledge of explosives, the pioneers would often have to tackle the threat of Allied tanks. The Fallschirmjäger in the middle here is carrying a flamethrower, one of the weapons that the Allies particularly feared. The Pioneer Platoon had access to two flamethrowers during the battle in Normandy.

The flamethrowers were a valuable and effective weapon in the fight against the Americans, who were supported by strong tank elements. Repeatedly, the pioneers were called upon to perform special combat assignments with their flamethrowers.

Because of the high losses in the past weeks, the only part of the regiment that was available for this responsibility was the 16th Company under the leadership of Oberfeldwebel Alexander Uhlig. Because they were designated for special deployments, they stood at the ready near to the regimental command post. Uhlig himself remembers:

Operation *Sèves Island* began for me on the morning of 22 July, with a conversation that the regimental commander had called me in for. He shared with me that in the previous night or early morning hours, the enemy had broken through our main line of resistance in III./FJR 6's sector. They needed to be pushed back immediately. There was no answer at the time to my question about the strength of the enemy. The commander hoped, however, that we were dealing with just one combat patrol that I could push

Oberfeldwebel Alexander Uhlig, bearer of the Ritterkreuz (Knight's Cross).

130

The WuG Troop is taking over an American Jeep and trailer captured during the fighting. The vehicle is going to be checked, evaluated and taken into service within the hour.

back with 16./FJR 6 strength 5:27. I received complete freedom of action, the right to subordinate soldiers from other companies, and the assignment to push back the Americans over the Sèves, so that the former main line of resistance could be restored. Whenever possible, I was supposed to bring two or three captives along so that we could learn about the details of the regiment, their units and their strength. I returned to the company, and let them know about the deployment assignment. We marched off on foot towards the area of our mission. We only carried light weapons with us (rifles, pistols, submachine guns, hand grenades and rifle grenades), and thus we were well equipped for the close combat we were expecting. Because of enemy's ground-attack aircraft, which had control of the air space, we made slow progress.

Around 1300hrs, the company was bombarded with mortars in a sunken road northeast of Remeurge. Three men and one Oberjäger were injured. Two men brought them back to the nearest first aid station. I had the unit spread out to go into full cover, and scouted the terrain in front of us with Gefreiter Ahlbrecht (the company messenger).

The terrain north of the Sèves–St Germain road was occupied by the enemy in a breadth of about 800m. To the east of Closet I encountered a blocking position of 9./FJR 6. Between the two positions our whole main line of resistance was in

American hands. Unfortunately we weren't just dealing with a single combat patrol, but with a whole unit of more than 300 men. With my few people, a frontal attack against this enemy ... did not seem promising. Therefore I decided to attack the enemy's flank in the wing where his numbers were spread the thinnest, i.e. his right flank near Sèves. The company crouched and crawled behind hedges and earthwork towards Sèves, along the whole length of the American breach without being noticed. When we got there, I took some of 6./FJR 6 and began the flank attack around 1800hrs; it surprised the enemy, who certainly must have been counting on a different direction of attack. Within the next three hours, the enemy was pushed back around 350m in close combat, and so they lost about half of their ground. During this battle we lost none of 16./FJR 6. The medic could easily deal with light scratches immediately, and lightly wounded men voluntarily stayed in battle. After returning the two litter bearers, the company had at this time a strength of 4:24. On the American side several soldiers had fallen. We had been unable to take prisoners at this time. When darkness fell, the fighting ceased.

Afterwards we heard the enemy digging entrenchments. He was probably preparing a defence for the next morning against a German attack from the same direction as earlier. That gave me the idea of surprising him again; so instead of

Even the much-feared 'Green Devils' could not stay in the frontline forever. Here men of FJR 6 are using their well-earned time of rest behind the lines to maintain uniforms and equipment, clean themselves up and enjoy food from the field kitchen.

attacking the position he was currently reinforcing, we would attack his newly formed flank. For that I would need good reinforcements. First I spoke with a tank commander from an SS-Panzer regiment, that had been sent to Sèves to support us. He promised to support my attack with three tanks from his unit the following morning. I also went to the commander of II./FJR 6, Hauptmann Mager, but he could promise me no support. Afterwards I searched out the command post of III./FJR 6 and spoke with Hauptmann Trebes. He gave me command of a group with the strength of 1:15, which was equipped with two heavy machine guns; this group had been placed under his command as a reserve. Because these men had little experience on the front, I didn't want to send them into an attack on the next morning, but I still could use them. Because the Sèves lowlands absolutely had to be blocked according to my plan, and heavy machine guns with a firing speed of 1,300 rounds per minute would be excellent for this task, I sent the group northeast of the Sèves to take up position on a sunken road. From this position, they could see the whole Sèves lowland and had a completely free field of fire. Thus it was possible to block any retreating enemies or enemies trying to move behind us. My assignment to the group was: to build up and camouflage the machine gun position in the remaining hours of the night. They did not have permission to fire during my morning attack ... they were free to fire only on retreating or advancing enemies.

On 23 July at 0730hrs, it was absolutely still. Low-lying cloud cover had appeared that prevented enemy ground-attack planes from engaging. Three Panzers waited on the street towards St Germain at the Sèves town exit. The 16th Company stood ready to march from their old position across from the Americans. An Oberjäger assigned a group of six men to every tank. The attack was supposed to start at exactly 0800hrs by firing all weapons from the road running northwest. After that the Panzers were supposed to drive forward, with the groups assigned to them following. Surprisingly, the tank commanders rejected this plan. For this kind of attack, the complicated terrain left them too open to enemy tank-killing units. I changed the plan and ordered the three groups to attack in front of the Panzers. Shortly before 0800hrs the tanks advanced, the men of the 16./FJR 6 jumped out of their positions to the tanks.

The firefight began and suddenly, almost to the exact minute, the American artillery unleashed a heavy barrage on the area behind us. The fire gradually shifted back to our initial position and came closer and closer to us. We were forced to attack, so to speak. During the pandemonium, our opponents disappeared into their foxholes. Because of this we could storm forward and so escape the artillery fire. Unfortunately the Panzer on the left failed early in the operation because of mechanical failure; the Panzer on the right had become immobilized under a collapsing roof in a farm in Closet. Nevertheless we made progress. Certainly the enemy had not realized how inferior our numbers were, because the first US soldiers surrendered themselves; others tried to withdraw through the Sèves lowlands. At this moment, the concealed machine guns opened their fire and thus cut off their

Here we see men of the 16th Company, amongst them their company commander, Oberfeldwebel Alexander Uhlig. Uhlig is shown wearing his pilot's blouse with the shirt collar comfortably folded over the wool collar of the tunic to avoid chafing the skin on his neck. As an old hand, the Narvik Shield and Crete cuff title can be seen on his left sleeve. As he had also served as an observer, he also wears the Observer Badge along with his other decorations.

return path. In a sunken road on the southeastern edge of the Sèves lowlands, we drove the opponents together and began to take prisoners.

The captives had to put down their weapons and were marched to the regimental command post in groups of 20–25, with one of my men to lead each group. Once I only had a few men left it became clear to me that we must have taken more than 200 prisoners. Around 1100hrs the battle was successfully concluded. I occupied the recently re-taken main line of resistance with the heavy machine-gun group assigned to me and with some men from other units who had been scattered. Afterwards I returned to the regimental command post with the remains of 16./FJR 6. Here I reported my successfully completed assignment to the commander. He commended me. In the large hall of the farmhouse, 11 American officers were collected. They were being handed tea when the commander introduced me to them as the leader of the whole offensive operation. The last successful battle of a unit of the German 7th Army in Normandy was over. As a result of it, we had brought in not only the two to three prisoners that the commander had requested, but exactly 234. On the morning of 24 July, I learned confidentially from Heinz Gabbey, the Hauptfeldwebel of the

TheSE Fallschirmjäger, most likely men of the 16th Company, are getting ready to engage the US 90th Infantry Division near Séves Island.

regimental staff, that the commander had submitted my name for a Knight's Cross of the Iron Cross. I received it on 29 October 1944.

Around 1430hrs the forward-deployed outposts of FJR 6 reported enemy activities in the Sèves lowlands. The Fallschirmjäger opened fire on three Americans, but realized shortly afterwards that they were dealing with army chaplains, who had slipped into the combat zone unarmed and unnoticed. A Protestant pastor, a Catholic priest and a preacher from the Salvation Army were searching for wounded survivors among the corpses strewn throughout the river meadow, which was open to constant fire from both heavy machine guns. Disregarding the fact that what was occurring was an act of humanity, American fighter-bombers attacked in a low-level flight, covering the field with fire. When the airplanes turned away, some American medics arrived to help the army chaplains and Major von der Heydte ordered that his Fallschirmjäger should help them recover their wounded; he offered the Americans a three-hour ceasefire. In return, the Americans sent over wounded Fallschirmjäger from the 11th Company, who had been taken into captivity the day before during the advance of the 358th Infantry Regiment. During the ceasefire both sides recovered their wounded and fallen without danger.

Major von der Heydte issued the following report to 2 FJD on 23 July 1944 at 2345hrs:

This is the sunken road that Oberfeldwebel Uhlig's battlegroup used as a starting line for their action against the 90th Division. Two MG42 machine guns are used to protect the flanks and lay crossfire on the open ground ahead.

The enemy – US 90th Division – attacked the middle and left wing of the regiment yesterday with the whole 358th Infantry Regiment, supported by the 344th Artillery Regiment and probably also the Artillery Corps. The attack was fought back. Oberfeldwebel Uhlig led the operation to repair this breach. With a combat team of only 30 men and support of one Panzer, they predominantly destroyed an American battalion (I./ 358). 234 unwounded prisoners were taken, including the battalion commander and 11 officers. According to the captured papers available to the regiment, the 358th Regiment, that stood ready south of Gonfreville before the attack, was supposed to break through the German main line of resistance east of Sèves and then swing east and take the area around St Germain.

On 25 July, FJR 6 observed from their positions as 2,000 Allied planes blanket bombed the area towards St Lô. FJR 14, the Panzer-Lehr Division and some other neighbouring units felt the effects of this attack. At this time, the enemy formed up west of St Lô with strong tank forces. They were able to break through and destroy the German defensive positions and, with a quick advance, take St Lô.

FJR 6 received the order to relocate to St-Sauveur-Lendelin and build up a defensive line there along the railway line Combernon–Belval–Ouville, because an attack by the 3rd US Armored Division had broken through in the Périers–St Lô sector and was now approaching the Périers–Coutances road. The 2nd SS-Panzer Division 'Das Reich' offered ten tanks for this operation. The goal was to make it possible for the German forces escaping from the north to withdraw. Despite heavy attacks by American armoured units, FJR 6 managed to hold the position on the railway at the north edge of St-Sauveur-Lendelin and to build up a point of main effort on the Périers–Coutances road. The already weakened regiment suffered fresh losses, 150 men.

On the next day, the commander of the 2nd SS-Panzer Division sought out the command post of FJR 6 and oriented Major von der Heydte to the situation east of his own positions, where his units had been surrounded again by Americans and where he faced the threat of being completely encircled. He wanted to try to withdraw his beleaguered division with the Fallschirmjäger covering his retreat, and then retreat themselves. He closed his report to Major von der Heydte with the words, 'I am an old tank man. This breakthrough is decisive, the war in France is lost.'

Major von der Heydte could not meet the SS officer's wish right away. This was due to the fact that the reinforced 16./FJR 6 was in the area of Sèves at the time, in order to feign continuing occupation of this region by German troops. In addition, the danger of fighter-bomber attacks was still great for a day march. Major von der Heydte drove ahead, however, to investigate the new positions near Coutances. In the grey dawn, FJR

The Fallschirmjäger had little in terms of tank-killing weapons to use against the American tank forces. Nevertheless every position was bitterly defended, even when the paras were faced by a technologically superior opponent.

'Elastic defence' was the tactic of choice against the overwhelming numerical Allied superiority in Normandy. After their successful counterattack, these Fallschirmjäger are occupying their positions again and get ready for the next attack.

6 began reconnaissance patrols, because they were unsure of the enemy status and positions needed further information. As expected, the results were sobering. Admittedly, the Americans were moving from Périers slowly, but American tanks from St Lô had advanced to the south and threatened to attack along the road toward Coutances. FJR 6 had barely swung to the east to face the Americans when the regiment received enemy contact and engaged in a skirmish. During this clash, the 11th Company was surrounded by American troops and completely destroyed.

Major von der Heydte gave the order for the 16th Company under Oberfeldwebel Uhlig to hold the Sèves position one more day, and then to regroup with the regiment in Coutances. Because of their inferior numbers, the 16th Company could not resist the broad breakthrough by the 90th US Infantry Division and swerved in a delaying action towards Périers. The Fallschirmjäger succeeded in drawing off some of the 90th Division and slowing down their general advance. For a total of three days, Oberfeldwebel Uhlig and his troop waged a small war against the Americans and tied up enemy forces in this manner, forces that otherwise would have been deployed to go after the relocating main German units. Finally, near St Michel, south of Périers, the ring around the rest of the 16th Company became ever tighter until escape from this encirclement was impossible. The 16th Company pressed the enemy hard for days. On 30 July, Oberfeldwebel Uhlig

The average age of FJR 6 men in Normandy was 17 years. Despite their youthful appearance, these young men have just fought the bloody battle for Carentan. This group of the 10th Company is led by Gefreiter Georg Schober.

and the rest of his men were taken prisoner.

In the encircled area around St Lô, serious disagreements arose between the Waffen-SS and the Fallschirmjäger. While the SS reported that a battalion commander of FJR 6 had suffered a nervous breakdown in combat, and that the Fallschirmjäger were no longer holding their positions, Major von der Heydte's men countered, with irony, that the Waffen-SS would hold their positions until the last Fallschirmjäger. Moral sank further when the commander of the SS division died of wounds and his second-in-command took over.

Under the protection of darkness, FJR 6 broke away from the enemy and moved several kilometres, according to orders. (Under such strong pressure from his opponents, von der Heydte barely noticed his promotion to Oberstleutnant.) On the following day the regiment received the order to break through to Percy via St-Martin-de-Centilly with the rest of the 2nd SS-Panzer Division, but it was not until dawn the next day that the German forces were able to depart. The Fallschirmjäger initially rode on the Panzers during the operation. At first, fog supported their operation and offered

This older Fallschirmjäger has covered his combat helmet with finely woven camouflage netting – it is possible that he has used the cover of an American steel helmet. A braided cord disappears into the left pocket of his coveralls, probably attached to a pistol.

During the breakout from the encircled area around Coutances, the Allied fighter-bombers remained the Fallschirmjäger's greatest concern. The worried face of this young machine-gunner shows more than words can say.

cover against air attacks, but by 0800hrs the fog had dispersed and fierce fighter-bomber attacks began.

Near La Corbière the leading tank came under enemy attack and the Fallschirmjäger had to dismount and regroup in trenches to the right and left of the road. They also determined that III./FJR 6, who had been in the back of the column, had gone missing along with its whole carrying tank. The SS had probably become lost. Because the SS commander on location refused to follow the advice of von der Heydte, the Fallschirmjäger Oberstleutnant decided to seize the initiative. A recon troop reported that enemy ahead was too strong. At the same time, the part of the column believed to be missing had returned and reported that a path over St-Denys-le-Gast was free from enemies.

Part of II./FJR 6 managed to disengage from the enemy quickly and mount the tanks, while the rest of the battalion under the direction of Oberstleutnant von der Heydte tried to fight their way through on foot.

The Fallschirmjäger who had found the way out near St-Denys-le-Gast were able to use the gap in the Allied cordon to get through without enemy contact. However, the Fallschirmjäger mounted on the fleeing SS vehicles came under a large-scale air attack south of St Denys. They suffered bitter losses. Hauptmann Trebes, commander of the 3rd Battalion, was amongst the fallen – during the air attack he sought cover under a tank that was then targeted by the American fighter-bombers. The survivors still managed to meet up with their comrades who were travelling on foot; having travelled via St Denys in a march of 60km, they met up at La Mancelliere, southwest of Percy. Here they discovered that some of the 2nd Battalion under Hauptmann Mager were still missing, but contact was re-established one day later. Oberstleutnant von der Heydte recalled later how the defensive position near Percy was only a cordon of single outposts, without any strength to resist a major assault.

Because American tanks were on the Hambye–Villedieu road, and because FJR 6 had no tank-destroying weapons left, Oberstleutnant von der Heydte decided to march more than 50km to avoid Villedieu towards St-Martin-de-Bouillant. The 353rd Grenadier Division could be found there, and the Oberstleutnant would put his troops under their command. When American tanks moved into St-Martin-de-Bouillant that afternoon, FJR 6 was divided into two battlegroups, one group that had roughly the strength of a company. The other group headed through to Alencon, according to orders.

Many of the men of FJR 6 have powerful memories of this chaotic period. Hermann Wübbold, at the time an Obergefreiter in the WuG Troop reports:

On the evening of 25 July, our boss, von der Heydte, called Wern to him. [Waffenoberinspektor (Chief Weapons Inspector) Heinrich Wern, leader of the WuG Troop.] He also called me to him, stating that four ears hear better than two. He explained that the enemy would march forward without any more resistance and that our troops could no longer offer effective counter-fire due to our heavy losses. He gave the order for us to move during the night towards Villedieu via Gavray. On 27 July, we were supposed to blow up the large ammunition storage dump left behind at our deserted position in St-Michel-la-Pierée, near St-Sauveur-Lendelin. During

the morning, we – Waffenoberinspektor Wern, Oberfeldwebel Günter Friebe and I – set out towards Coutances. We made it there despite the air attacks. We rode farther on the National Highway towards St Lô. Meanwhile it had grown cloudy so the fighter planes could no longer attack.

Günter Friebe was from Großgiesmannsdorf in Upper Silesia. Three weeks before this fateful trip he had said to me: 'Listen to me, and pay attention to what I have to say. I'm not going to come back from this war. I will fall here. My wife Maria recently gave me a daughter. Her name is Katharina. I just got this message the day before yesterday. You have to promise me, that

Obergefreiter Hermann Wübbold.

you will inform her about my fate.' In the weeks that followed he repeated this plea to me over and over; the last time he did so, on the evening of 26 July, one day before his death, he said it so urgently. Until this day I've been unable to forget that. Before the last trip, Wern said to me: 'Sit in the back. I'll drive, otherwise you'll fall asleep.' I hadn't slept for two days and nights. Without thinking much about it I put on my steel helmet, for the first time. Günter Friebe sat in front of me in the passenger seat. I bent forward and tried to sleep. After seven kilometers we left the street and headed north. Suddenly I looked ahead and cried out 'Turn around! There are Sherman tanks and American soldiers ahead!'

Wern turned the car around and headed to the right. In the curve, a shell struck directly above Günter Friebe. The car ran towards the right into a roadside ditch next to an apartment building. After a short period of unconsciousness, I came to, and was quickly aware of my situation. Friebe was no longer there. On the seat in front of me there was only unrecognizable flesh and blood to be seen. Wern had lost his right arm and been hit heavily by shell splinters. My hands, face and legs were bleeding. The wounds were not serious; I at least was able to leave the car and crawl into a pipe under the street.

It was around 1400hrs when claustrophobia forced me to leave the pipe, cross to the other side of the street and run into a sunken road. After going around 50 metres, I spotted a Sherman tank about 30 metres off, headed straight for me. Through the bushes, I hadn't been able to see it early enough. GIs marched behind it. On the right side there was an entrance to a field; I fled there and let myself collapse. After a while I crawled towards a rampart that was overgrown with shrubbery. I was still wearing my steel helmet. It looked very similar to the American ones; the American soldiers probably thought that I was one of them. At the forward edge of the frontline, the Americans weren't taking any German prisoners. They exterminated them instead. If they had recognized me, my life would have ended right there.

This is the helmet that saved Herman Wübbold's life in his encounter with the American tank. It is easy to recognize the spot where the shell splinter broke through and ripped open the helmet's outer shell, sticking in the foam rubber padding underneath.

The worst part of it was the thirst. I finally fell asleep from exhaustion and when I woke up it was almost dark. First I took off my steel helmet and noticed that shrapnel had pierced it. The splinter was still sticking in the inner padding.

Led by nothing more than a feeling, I headed towards my comrades. To do so I had to cross the American lines. I met up with the last rearguard of our troops along some railroad tracks. I was allowed to ride on a Kübelwagen for part of the way. When day began to break, American fighter-bombers unceasingly directed heavy attacks at the fleeing masses of soldiers and vehicles in the sunken roads. They did not spare the many medical vehicles carrying wounded soldiers. Even a single soldier was enough to warrant the fighter-bombers' target. Around 0600hrs, I reached my comrades from the WuG Troop. They had spent the night celebrating and drinking. When they saw me, they instantly sobered up. From the last discussions with the commander, I knew that the Americans would expand their encirclement. My urgent advice was to relocate to the south as quickly as possible; they followed my advice and so we were spared being taken prisoner by just a few hours.

On 29 July, at 0200hrs the regiment received the order to attach themselves to the SS-Panzer regiment and head along the route Ouville–La Penetière–Maupertuis–Percy. Albert Sturm remembers the move:

At some point the Americans had broken through the front on a broad scale and we were – we heard with surprise – to be loaded onto trucks and transported to this open gap in the front. When we arrived there, the 1st Platoon of the 7th Company, at the time ten men strong, received the order to push forward into open territory and seek out contact with the enemy. The other platoons received similar orders and the rest sequestered themselves around various street intersections. Our recon troop set out. Everyone who has been on the front knows the feeling of pushing forward into the unknown when you aren't exactly sure where the enemy is located. We set up security in all directions, jumped from hedge to hedge, slipped through sunken roads and occasionally took short cigarette breaks. At least two hours passed and we still hadn't seen anything of the enemy. An uncanny calm settled around us; because we had been consistently under fire for eight weeks, the silence gave us a bit of the creeps. Nonetheless, our attentiveness waned a bit in the afternoon sun. We became careless and ran into a trap set by the Americans!

While we were climbing over a hedge, we made the mistake of not sending out only one man to scout ahead until the next hedge; instead, we all climbed after each other in a single file. The first few were already over when I saw our three comrades standing with hands lifted and their belts unstrapped. American soldiers had surrounded them in a half-circle and were pointing their fire-ready weapons at them. I threw myself back behind the hedge; my comrades sprinted off right away. We dashed to a hedge that ran parallel and went into position. I reported to them what I had seen, and we made plans to get the three out. But how? After a brief deliberation we circled around the hedged area and hoped to intercept the American troops. But we didn't have any luck. The

143

Americans had slipped off; perhaps they believed that we were getting reinforcements. We searched as long as we could. Then we received the order that we were to go back to our meeting point at the street intersection; we arrived around 1700hrs. A whole army camp had been deployed; for the first time in a while I saw German tanks again, and not just Panzer IVs, but many, many tanks. As I had heard, these were the combat elements of the 2nd SS-Panzer Division 'Das Reich.' The rest of our regiment was gathered, plus men from Organization Todt (OT; a Nazi engineering and works organization) and many who had been scattered from all types of combat divisions. Surprised by the large collection of men, we asked our way through to the 7th Company; our platoon leader reported to the company commander, Feldwebel Otto Netzel, who was happy that our reappearance increased the size of the company to about 30 men again. At that time that was quite an accomplishment to have a company with the strength of a platoon. We were informed about the situation. The Americans were trying to close us in. The only question was if we would be able, with the other troops that had joined us, to break through a gap in the encirclement or if we would have to fight our way out. Now and again I saw our commander drive by in a Kübelwagen alongside some high-ranking official from the SS.

I was pleased that two comrades whom I had known since basic training, Klaus

During their withdrawal from Normandy, the paratroopers had to be careful. The Allies had absolute superiority in the air, so movement along roads was best done in the shadows cast by buildings, hedgerows and trees.

Klapprat and Günther Koch, had found each other. They had their canteens full of cider; we all partook heartily and then lay down to sleep against a hedge. Our rest did not last long, because the 7th Company received the order to mount tanks. We learned the following: the tanks would drive as the advanced guard, while FJR 6, the SS and the other foot troops would follow along both sides of the road in single file. Dispatch riders as well as the commanders of the various units would maintain communications between the Panzers and the infantry.

It was already dark when the tanks drove off. About ten Panzers drove close together along the road; they could not deviate from the road because to the right and left there were hedgerows. The 7th Company sat on the first three tanks, Klaus and I on the third, the command tank. Klaus, Günther and I had always tried to stay close together, but on this evening, Günther sat on the first tank. It is a strange feeling to ride through the night on a jolting metal monster. Now and again a dispatch rider would come up to our command tank and gave the commander a report, whereupon we would slow down or ride faster. The distance between the marching troop and us could not be too great, because if we really were to break through, then the troop would need our tank support. The whole night passed like this.

Near La Penetière in the morning, strong American forces attacked the battlegroup, and an intense battle ensued in which the Fallschirmjäger maintained the upper hand, but were separated from most of the SS-Panzer units and continued the march west alone. Albert Sturm continues:

Around 0330hrs the tank commander said to us, after having received a report, 'Boys, it looks like we've made it, we've just come out of the encircled area!' Many of us had been dozing and we were jolted awake by this news. We were thrilled just once to have escaped. Ten minutes later we drove by a lonely farmhouse; the maids who had just got up to milk the cows waved happily at us, and day began to break. The morning fog lay over the fields; the low mooing of the cows being milked reached us. The street curved away ahead of us. As soon as the first Panzer disappeared around the curve and the second one followed it, the peaceful daybreak was over. The American anti-tank weapon gave a short, dry roar. We saw that the tank standing in the curve had been hit and that the force of the explosion had sent the comrades who had been riding on the tank flying away. We jumped down from the tank right away. Klaus and I ran forward to see what had happened to the first tank, the one that Günther had been sitting on. The comrades on the second Panzer were more or less unharmed, expect for a few bruises.

Meanwhile, all hell broke loose; cracking and popping could be heard from every corner and the air was rife with iron. Under cover of a hedge, Klaus and I crawled around the street bend and what we saw when we lifted our heads out of cover was anything but encouraging. The first tank was burning up, and around it lay a few

A machine-gun team runs along an embankment to better cover. This photo shows a three-man machine-gun team with the machine-gunner (carrying the MG42) accompanied by two ammunition carriers. The man to the left of the picture is wearing an army steel helmet, while his two comrades are outfitted in para helmets.

lifeless Fallschirmjäger. We tried to make out if Günther was among them, but we couldn't recognize him and so we hoped that he had got away. Klaus and I lay exactly between the opposing positions and the anti-tank artillery; armour-piercing rifle grenades and curtains of fire from machine guns on both sides swept over us. It was time to pull back and under cover of the hedge we managed to do this fairly easily.

When we reported to our tank, our commander Oberstleutnant von der Heydte was also there giving orders from his Kübelwagen. We, the 7th Company, were supposed to take over the left flank to the left of the road. Springing from hedge to hedge, we were to find the enemy line and remain in front of it until our combat forces closed up the lines.

So we left our tank and snuck along the side of the hedge. The farther we moved from the road, the cleaner the air became. Then we received the order to turn back in and the 7th Company was again darting forward from hedge to hedge. We communicated without many words; two comrades always moved forward over each hedge, running across to next one, peering over it, levelling their weapons, and then giving us a sign. When we saw that to our left and right the same manoeuvre had been carried out, we darted forward and occupied the next hedge. After we had six such manoeuvres behind us, we came under intense infantry fire.

We lay behind our concealing hedge and awaited further orders. Now our other comrades arrived, who had been on the move on foot all night, and filled out our line. Meanwhile, it was starting to get light and the Americans began to shoot at us with mortars. We looked up to the heavens – it was still a bit too hazy, but soon it wouldn't be long before it was light enough for the fighter-bombers, our worst enemies, to appear in the skies. Around 0630hrs we received the order to set out. Klaus and I exchanged meaningful looks. Until then we had still hoped that Günther would somehow turn up again. We had spoken to every available comrade about it, but he was not to be found. From that morning, Günther Koch was counted as missing in action.

We still had a half an hour until we had to leave; so we lit cigarettes, drank the rest of the cider from our canteens, strapped our equipment together and stuck hand grenades into our belts where we could easily grab them. So we sat around waiting for the zero hour. Klaus didn't have long to wait, because a mortar landed directly next to him. It must have hit him hard; he jumped up, screaming like an animal and ran towards the back. I ran right after him, but before I could reach him, two medics grabbed him and laid him on a stretcher. When I breathlessly reached the stretcher, Klaus was already unconscious. The medics told me that he had received multiple splinters in the chest, and they marched off towards the first aid station with Klaus

Crouching alongside a building wall, these Fallschirmjäger are taking cover while Allied aircraft pass overhead. The men are part of a tank-killer team. Their Raketenpanzerbüchse, also dubbed Ofenrohr ('stove pipe'), is a good weapon against the numerous Allied tanks.

In a short sprint, this machine-gunner crosses an exposed street corner. The gunner is carrying his MG42 on his shoulders and has an ammunition belt hanging around his neck, while both his comrades carry ammunition boxes.

on the litter. By the time I reached my position again, I was pretty drained. It's not a nice feeling to lose two good comrades within two hours and then have to start an attack. A machine-gunner, who was lying to the left of me, called out to me: 'Don't get worried, Albert, we'll do it!' His expression under his combat helmet was reckless as he looked over at me.

And then it was time. We jumped up and stormed the enemy. From the street we heard the humming of tank motors; everything was exploding on all sides. We roared and rushed forward. The Americans didn't engage in close combat, instead they just retreated while firing madly. To the left of me the machine-gunner dashed forward, shooting from the hip with his MG42, chasing after the Americans with spurts of fire. In this way we moved through one hedge after another, and then abruptly the attack lost momentum. The machine-gunner next to me suffered a mental breakdown in the middle of his all-out attack. His assistant grabbed the machine gun and jumped into cover. We all threw ourselves to the ground and also search for cover. In front of us stood – presented as though for an exercise – a Sherman tank, firing with all its guns. With our small arms we could do nothing against it; we were nailed to the spot by the tanks. Crawling or running we got to safety behind a hedge and called for a tank-killer unit. The boys still schlepped their Ofenrohr ['stove pipe', the nickname for the Panzerschreck anti-tank weapon] around with them, but they unfortunately had no ammunition left for it. At any rate, we were still able to take out a few of the Shermans with the Panzerfaust, but in the long run, that didn't help us. There was no way through.

We stayed down under cover and learned that the whole attempt to break through had failed. On the street, our tanks had ground to a halt and were fighting for mere survival. Meanwhile the fighter-bombers joined in the attack, so that there really was no more chance of accomplishing anything. Then the order came to disengage from the enemy. The 7th Company was supposed to cover the withdrawal. Ha, what 7th Company? How many of us were left? But an order is an order. A few of us tried to hold off the enemy for our retreating comrades. We had been given the good advice to hold east of Coutances after we had ourselves pulled back. There was a chance that there would be a pipe there through which we could get out. We were lucky that the Americans made no serious attempts to go after us...

On the street, however, the fight raged with increasing intensity; the Americans wanted to break through with their tanks, but a Panther tank held out bravely. Even though there were constant attacks, eventually the street became calm. Now there was an uncanny stillness. We received a signal from the 7th Company. We made our way across the field through the bushes. After a short time we came across the farm that had stood there so peacefully in the grey of morning. Now it was shot up and burned out. We hurried on because all of a sudden American soldiers were swarming all over the place. Although there was on a few of us, we split up completely – it was every man for himself. Today I could no longer tell you where I crept around and how long it was until I had a solid street under my feet again. It was easier to march on the roads than to fight my way through the exposed open land that felt like a death trap. After I marched along for a while, completely alone, I heard the sounds of tanks behind me. I jumped over the nearest hedge into the ditch on the side of the road and looked apprehensively towards the direction where I heard the rattling of chains. How happy I was to see the national identification cross on the iron monster!

Immediately, I came out from my cover, stood at the edge of the street and waved towards the Panzer coming quickly towards me. The turret hatch opened, the tank throttled back its speed and a commander dressed in black gave me a sign to jump up. I set off at a trot and jumped up onto the vehicle from behind, whereupon the Panzer set off at full speed again. The commander did not ask me that much; he just let me know that I had to take care of myself. In response to my question where we were headed, he said dryly, 'We'll find a gap, and we'll break through.' Then he secured the hatch tightly and a hellish ride began. The Panzer had additional armour around the turret made out of metal plating, and behind it I made myself as comfortable as I could and watched the skies. At high speed the tank made quite a lot of noise, but I still could hear significant sounds of combat up ahead. At first I wanted to jump down from this monster, but somehow I had the feeling that everything would be all right with the tank under me and the steel plating around me.

Then we were right in the thick of it, driving towards a mid-sized village with quite a large church. The Americans were sending fire across the main street with their artillery. It was a hilly terrain and I watched the American infantry storming down the hill. None of this bothered my tank; it thundered through the small city and shoved aside everything that stood in its way. Mounted units came rushing out of the surrounding farm buildings, carriage drivers beating wildly at the carthorses. Loaded trucks were trying with all their power to break through, infantrymen of all types were running around, with American shells falling between them everywhere. If I were to ask myself today, how long the chaos lasted, I would no longer be able to say, but at some point we had moved through it. I stayed on the tank until we arrived at a rear position late in the afternoon. The Panzer was sent to the front again, and I said my goodbyes to my tank comrades who had brought us through so well.

The regiment proceeded to St-Denys-le-Gast via Roncey, and learned there that American tank units were moving on every major road; the tanks had to be avoided. The Fallschirmjäger literally fought their way through the rural terrain, often using gaps in the American marching columns to cross roads unnoticed. Sometimes the Fallschirmjäger were creeping through ditches alongside roads on which American tanks were rolling directly next to them. They were able to cross the River Sienne at two points, using damaged bridges. Eugen Griesser:

Every battalion assigned a few platoons to secure the flanks and a rearguard for the retreat out of the encircled area. The commander had ordered that the assembly area for soldiers with minor wounds near Alençon also be used as a gathering point for soldiers who had lost contact with the regiment. There he also wanted to leave information about the location of the regimental command post, so that everyone would be able to find his company again.

Events played out as they had to. Our platoon ran aground in a sunken road against a company of American Sherman tanks with accompanying infantry in half-tracks. We managed to take out the first two tanks with limpet mines and explosives before the column could respond, and before the half-tracks had enough time to fan out and displace their infantry. (The sunken roads and narrow streets in Normandy were not well suited for these kinds of moves.) The Americans had to manoeuvre quite a lot to get their destroyed tanks out of the way. One of us, unfortunately I can no longer remember who, threw a hand grenade into the foremost half-track and we took advantage of the confusion to work our way into the bushes and split up. Because there were at least two companies of American tank engineers on the street, a firefight in this situation would have been pure idiocy. Strangely, the Americans did not pursue us; perhaps they thought our numbers were greater than they were.

We marched through the night and the next morning we came upon the baggage train of some army unit. A military police motorcycle and sidecar stood at the gate of a farmyard: a policeman guarded the motorcycle while two others checked the baggage train. Military policemen liked to act self-important, and these three were particularly harsh. The Feldwebel demanded our papers and our marching orders. 'What do you mean you're headed to the assembly area for minor casualties? You all look perfectly healthy!' 'Where's your unit?' and so on. The policeman refused to understand that we had been separated from our unit and therefore had no written marching orders, although we were already on our way back to our regiment. He began to ramble on about desertion, so a couple of us offered to polish his face for him. Then he wished us a good day and waved us through. During the return trip out of the cordon our biggest threat was the fighter-bombers, so we were always happy to have foul weather and fog, because only then could we march safe from such aircraft.

After a few narrow escapes, we decided to avoid regular tactical groups and to march alone, so that we formed small, separate targets. During the next flyover by the fighter-bombers, we waved our hands and even our helmets – the fighter-bombers rushed down on us but waved with their wings, because they believed we were Allied soldiers. As long as we moved separately, this tactic worked very well, but as soon as we were marching with other troops, we had to jump into the ditches in the road when the aircraft passed by.

In Tincebray we ran into the battalion. Hauptmann Mager was happy to have us there again, because the Normandy battle had annihilated the regiment and we had been reported missing. He sent us to the commander right away. He greeted us joyfully, but took us down a notch right away because of what had happened with the military police. They had reported our interaction with them to their superior right away and he had informed the whole regiment. It's strange how well the bureaucracy functioned while all around us whole divisions were being annihilated.

On 10 August, FJR 6 received the order to relocate to the 1st Fallschirm Army in Nancy. Due to high losses of men, the regiment was relieved from frontline duty. Since the beginning of the invasion, FJR 6 had been in action; almost all of its men were sick or wounded at this point. When the order arrived, Oberstleutnant von der Heydte's command was only 40 men strong; little is known to this day about the fate of the other men. Only eight weeks earlier, the regiment had been 4,600 men. 'At least I no longer had to worry about securing transportation', Oberstleutnant von der Heydte remarked, not without sarcasm.

On 14 August, FJR 6 decamped from Tincebray. On the way to Paris, the staff work

The constant battles and physically stressful high-speed marches in Normandy pushed the Fallschirmjäger to their physical limits. The attacks from low-flying fighter-bombers were especially dangerous; they became increasingly frequent, and forced the men into the meagre cover of ditches alongside the roads, but they still took many victims.

that had been laid in place earlier paid off. More and more wounded Fallschirmjäger found their way to their regiment, because Oberstleutnant von der Heydte actually managed to keep the assembly area in Alençon constantly informed about the location FJR 6; the men were literally running after their regiment. Von der Heydte incorporated new men into his unit again, members of other units who crossed paths with our regiment. By the time they arrived in Dreux, 1,007 men were reported as ready for service. From Paris, the regiment relocated to Nancy by motor march.

On the way to Nancy, the Fallschirmjäger learned, in an unnamed town, about the joys of rear-area service. Oberstleutnant von der Heydte described the situation as following:

We arrived in a small town and passed by an inn with the sign 'German Officers' Home'; loud, jarring music was coming from the inn. We weren't really in the mood for loud music; we were just hungry and thirsty. I ordered that we stop in front of the 'German Officers' Home' and went in. I found a few drunk officers from the rear area, who were with some not-so-sober French prostitutes. That got on my last nerve. The German officers, who at first didn't recognize my rank (I always kept my rank insignia in my trousers pocket), wanted to refuse me entrance to their 'officers' mess.' It didn't do them any good. I called a few of my soldiers into the pub and ordered them to arrest the officers present, to strip them of their shoulder straps and to determine what court-martial would be applied to them. I'll never forget the dumbstruck faces of these 'gentlemen' when they saw my rank, which I had pinned on in the meantime, and when they heard that we were Fallschirmjäger.

In Nancy, FJR 6 received the order to relocate to Güstrow, where the reorganization of the regiment would take place. For the Fallschirmjäger this meant, above all, that they could have a rest period and could recover for the future battles that would inevitably come.

While the regiment began to settle down in Güstrow, there were still some scattered soldiers in France. A platoon of the 11th Company under the leadership of Oberjäger Heinrich Fugmann, which had been detached to secure the baggage trains, arrived late

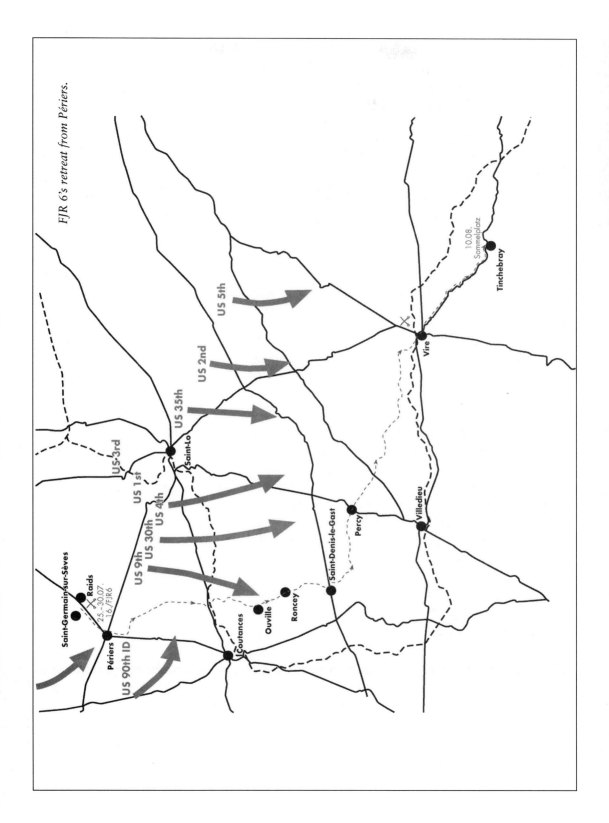

FJR 6's retreat from Périers.

in Paris. Fugmann recounts:

With 25 to 30 men, travelling mostly on foot and hitching rides, we arrived near Paris. On a country road we were stopped by a technical officer, who was travelling in a Kübelwagen; he asked us how the situation on the front was. He took us to a soldier's home, where we got something to eat and had the opportunity to bathe after months of being deployed. From a clothing warehouse that was about to be blown up, he got us new uniforms and, most importantly, fresh underwear, because ours was completely dirty and lice-ridden. On the following day we got lucky one more time. A communication unit, which was primarily made up of female personnel, was supposed to be transported to Nancy with omnibuses and we were allowed to ride along. The communications officer who was responsible for the transport explained that he was happy to share the buses with Fallschirmjäger, because he had to drive through some areas where partisans were operating. Several times on the trip, we were forced to abandon the buses because of low-level air attacks, and these caused several more losses. Some of the women sought cover in the nearby raod ditches and canal pipes, and after the attacks they crawled out of hiding shaking and screaming, completely wet and covered in mud from head to toe. It was a hellish trip and we were truly delighted to reach Nancy. From there we travelled with the train to Güstrow, where more fighter-bombers attacked us during the trip. Some comrades reached our destination, but no longer alive.

Like many of his comrades, Oberjäger vom Fliegerhorst is setting out from Güstrow on his first leave since the beginning of 1944. He has eight days to visit his family, sleep in a real bed again and eat as much home cooking as he can.

The reorganization took place in an air base that was in the process of being built; the 'Emil Unit' also undertook the rebuilding of the 1st Battalion there. Most of the buildings had not yet been finished, so the Fallschirmjäger and the new arrivals had to be quartered for the most part in tents. The reorganization was a positive experience for the veterans; with only a few exceptions, all men and NCOs received eight days of leave.

The whole reorganization had more of a cosmetic feel, because despite intensive efforts, the Luftwaffe was not able to offer enough replacements for the regiment's losses suffered in the Normandy campaign. In addition to the young 17-year-old recruits, volunteers for FJR 6 were found from amongst office and ground personnel, and from pilot school. Franz Hüttich commented on the quality of the new recruits:

> To get the required replacements, a lot of Heldenklau took place. Young boys were attracted with great promises: short, quick deployment, better provisions, higher pay. Flying personnel, older members of the Luftwaffe, who didn't have any planes, and who could be spared in the logistics offices and admin offices, came to us. But we all knew that it wouldn't amount to anything.

Oberstleutnant von der Heydte later described the situation like so:

> The unit hadn't meshed yet. The young replacements constituted 75 per cent of the regiment and they were barely trained or not at all. (Hundreds of members of the regiment had never held a weapon in their hands until they fired the first shot in earnest of their life in their first battle!) The officer corps for the most part was not in a position where they could fill the positions needed for officers.

Nevertheless, the young volunteers fitted in quite quickly, taking the old hands as their role models. At first there were some problems with the new officers, because most of

During the reorganization of the regiment in Güstrow, the experienced NCOs proved invaluable, because there was very little time in which to turn ground personnel, staff soldiers and young volunteers into tough Fallschirmjäger.

them were former pilots and had difficulties adjusting to their new roles. The switch from being a hero in the skies to a Fallschirmjäger officer was so difficult for some that Oberstleutnant von der Heydte had to operate according to the following principle: whoever couldn't obey was kicked out. Also, the promotions in the former core group were not enough to meet the needs for officers and NCOs, and many of the new recruits,

The new arrivals spent a lot of time on the shooting range, and on the training grounds learning infantry tactics. Camouflage techniques and covert movement were also repeated features of the instruction.

despite their rank, did not have the necessary combat experience to lead groups and platoons in battle.

Oberstleutnant von der Heydte was supposed to build up a powerful unit in only six weeks, an objective that, in view of the facts, was set to fail from the beginning. Nonetheless, the trainers set to their task with enthusiasm, using tried and trusted methods. Providing the men with uniforms also proved difficult; for the most part they were unable to furnish them with gear especially designed for Fallschirmjäger and instead had to use regular army kit. Albert Sturm noted that 'Many of the boys were 17 years old, not even really grown up. Therefore they had received an extra ration of milk during jump school. The doctors also ordered that they receive additional milk in order

Oberstleutnant von der Heydte had only two weeks in which to replenish FJR 6 with replacements, and to rebuild the unit. During the reorganization process, he placed great emphasis on making sure that young, inexperienced Fallschirmjäger served alongside the old hands, who could teach them the tricks and knacks for survival in combat.

A Fallschirmjäger platoon is lined up for a marching exercise. The paratroopers are wearing full combat gear.

Marching exercises, in combination with all-terrain training and bivouacs, accustomed the Fallschirmjäger to long marches on foot, as well as to life outdoors.

Before the march, the instructors in charge check the platoon. The baggage on their backs consists of a rucksack with a buckled-on tarpaulin and a hanging canteen. For many of the Fallschirmjäger, there were no more canvas gasmask bags available, so instead they carried the standard-issue metal gasmask container.

to make them stronger while they were with us. No one had any idea, however, how we were supposed to keep that up during deployment.'

Based on the experiences of the Normandy campaign, von der Heydte restructured the regiment. Along with the planned three battalions, he put together an additional fourth battalion. For this battalion he took personnel from the first three battalions, and also brought in additional heavy artillery; thus the regiment's ability to fight off tanks was notably strengthened. Hauptmann von Dobbeler took over command of the 4th Battalion. The newly reformed 1st Battalion was led by Hauptmann Peiser, the reliable Hauptmann Mager retained command of the 2nd Battalion and Oberleutnant Ulmer took over the 3rd Battalion.

Because the time for training was short, formalities like drills were dropped. The programme consisted of combat exercises day and night. If anyone complained about the harsh pace, the old hands just told him, 'Sweat saves blood!' Oberstleutnant von der Heydte spent a lot of time with the training units and for the most part carried out the tactical training of the officers himself. Some in the ranks of experienced personnel were put through sniper training during this time – until then FJR 6 had not had their own sniper troops.

Siegfried Dietrich was an Oberleutnant and communications officer in the regimental staff at the time:

As a communications officer I had to deal with the acquisition of radios, telephones and other necessary equipment. In addition I was responsible for establishing new Funktrupps [radio sections]. Because we had received reinforcements exclusively from units that possessed no ground combat experience, I made sure that one or two 'old fighters' were in each troop. This activity did not occupy all my time. So I gladly took my commander up on his offer to accompany him on trips to the individual battalions and companies.

Major von der Heydte set up a tough schedule for the training of replacements and their incorporation into the ranks of his veteran Fallschirmjäger. This Jäger shows how the foliage loops on the fabric camouflage helmet cover were used to attach natural camouflage material to the helmet.

CHAPTER SIX

Deployment in Holland, 1944

Once more, events on the front threw plans in disarray. Training in the tranquil town of Güstrow was in full swing when FJR 6 received the order to march on 3 September, as Siegfried Dietrich remembers:

> On 3 September, it was a Sunday and we were sitting with a glass of red wine after dinner in the officers' mess when around 2100hrs we received a phone call with the order to march. The first transport train was supposed to stand ready at 2400hrs. This deployment came as a shock to all of us, because the training of the replacement soldiers with no ground combat training had barely just begun, and furthermore we didn't have enough weapons to go into battle. The individual battalions and companies were informed immediately by phone and then dispatch riders followed up and confirmed this with written orders. Because of his general staff training, the Baron wrote precise and careful written orders. Incidentally, during combat operations he carefully dictated all written reports, even if it was midnight or if he had just come back from an attack that he had personally led. Oberjäger Otto wrote them down and he was a very capable secretary.

After the regiment was mobilized, the troop was re-outfitted as quickly as possible, so that the departure time could be kept down to the minute. At 0500hrs on 4 September, the last transport train left Güstrow. The Restkommando (unit assigned to stay behind and sort out relocation and transportation matters) of FJR 6, under Leutnant Mund, stayed behind and then, on 12 September, relocated to temporary barracks in Stendal.

At the train station in Aachen, the Fallschirmjäger had to change trains, and they took the opportunity to stretch their legs. On the neighbouring platform, members of the Allgemeine-SS (General SS) guarded a train with cars whose door openings were blocked with reinforced steel mesh. Numerous hands stretched out from the inside of the train. It quickly became clear that this was a transport of concentration camp prisoners: men, women and children.

The SS men tried to keep the Fallschirmjäger back, but the paras energetically pushed their way through. From the prisoners' bony limbs it was easy to see how underfed they were. Even though the Fallschirmjäger's rations were scarce, the men of FJR 6 opened their bread bags and stuffed rations into the train cars. The SS men approached the Fallschirmjäger and threatened to open fire on them, but they soon found themselves surrounded by more men than they were, so recognizing the hopelessness of the situation, they let the Fallschirmjäger have their way. Shortly afterwards, the troop transport was about to continue on its way to Holland and the men of FJR 6 had to hurry to catch their train.

At the last minute, the regiment received unexpected additions to their artillery. On a storage track, they spotted a Luftwaffe anti-aircraft division that was travelling to Denmark. For their assignment, their batteries were equipped with multiple cannon mounted together. Oberstleutnant von der Heydte saw the usefulness of these weapons for his own regiment and summarily issued his order to the anti-aircraft division. It caused a long discussion with the man in charge of the train station until finally the train cars could be rearranged and tacked onto FJR 6's train. The newly formed 17th Company now had access to more than 12 individual 20mm cannon as well as quad 20mm cannon systems. Now FJR 6 had access to notable firepower as defence against air attacks.

On 8 September, in the early morning hours, the regiment arrived in Tilburg, Holland, and received a written command from a messenger of the LXXXVII Corps. They were to go straight to Moll in the area of Buckenberg. Before marching, however, they had to arm the battalions; fortunately all the promised weapons stood at hand and they could be distributed to the companies quickly. There were only a few small things left to do; for example, they had to draw up shooting charts for the 8.2cm mortar. Luckily among the hand-held weapons there were several boxes of the newest Sturmgewehr 44 (an assault rifle). These were entrusted to the old hands, who accepted the brand new automatic rifles with great enthusiasm.

At this point, FJR 6 was subordinate to the 85th Infantry Division. At the division's headquarters in Turnhout, Oberstleutnant von der Heydte received exact orders from General Chill. Due to the unknown status of the enemy position near Beeringen, FJR 6 was to advance immediately to the threatened Albert Canal Bridge and secure that area, destroying the bridge in the process. The enemy had not, as expected, attacked Antwerp directly, but instead had moved to the east and south of the city. Clear countermeasures had to be taken immediately.

Because the regiment lacked the necessary transport, and because the Allied air forces were carrying out intensive attacks, only a single recon unit, with the strength of a platoon and under the leadership of Oberleutnant Ulmer, could be sent to scout out and destroy the bridge.

The 1st and the 3rd Battalions, meanwhile, were deployed to the Albert Canal, in order to attack the bridgehead near Beeringen. Meanwhile, the 2nd Battalion departed for Gheel, where strong enemy armoured units had crossed the Albert Canal and were building another bridgehead. The order came down from General Student that the positions on the canal were to be held down to the last cartridge. But even this encouragement could not bring about a successful outcome. The engineer company of the SS-Leibstandarte 'Adolf Hitler' (SS Bodyguard Regiment 'Adolf Hitler, the division that grew out of Hitler's personal bodyguard) had been deployed to destroy the bridge of Beeringen; they pulled out of the area of operations without a fight, leaving the task to the Fallschirmjäger. Because the British had larger numbers, the recon troop's attack failed. Oberleutnant Ulmer was wounded and captured during the attack.

Supported by numerous tanks, the British troops of the XXX Corps, including the Guards Armoured Division, pushed forward from Beeringen towards the military training area in Beverloo. A difficult battle ensued, in which FJR 6 managed to hold its positions for some days, but eventually, in the face of the ever-increasing strength of the opponent, had to yield. The available anti-tank weapons and ammunition dwindled quickly, until in a short time the Fallschirmjäger only had hand-held weapons to use in their fight against enemy tanks. The Fallschirmjäger were unable to sway the outcome of this imbalanced fight, in which FJR 6 only had their bravery and intelligence to pit against the British war machines. Nevertheless, they succeeded in taking out 50 enemy tanks with only close-combat weapons. The addition of I./FJR 2 under Hauptmann Finzel could only bring temporary relief. As pressure from the enemy grew, the positions finally had to be deserted. At the same time, the flanks of the other German units gave way and rapid enemy advances threatened to cut off both battalions. On 11 September, the Fall-schirmjäger took new positions between Hechtel and Leopoldsburg.

II./FJR 6 aimed to hold off and delay the enemy in Gheel, but the British were able to expand their bridgehead through massive armoured attacks. Hauptmann Mager's men managed temporarily to hem them in, pushing the British back to the northern bank of the canal and preventing further advances. Without their own tank support and because they lacked artillery, however, the Fallschirmjäger were unable to beat back the British advance guard. In laborious street battles, the British wrested

These two boys are typical of the replacements that were sent to FJR 6 from mid 1944. After a short period of military training, they young men quickly had to prove themselves in battle.

house after house from the Germans.

The 5th Company formed the spear tip of the battalion and received the assignment to take the eastern edge of Gheel in an attack. Ever since the death of Hauptmann Herrmann in Normandy, Fahnenjunker (Officer Candidate) Heinz Köhne had been leading the company. To the east of Gheel lay only flat terrain, and so the company had to advance slowly towards the area, by crawling. They crossed the last few hundred metres in a sprint, and took up position in the building. In good form, Fahnenjunker Köhne rushed his men forward, but halted abruptly when he almost stumbled into an enemy machine-gun nest that had been well camouflaged. Instinctively, he took the machine-gun crew prisoner; he also noticed further foxholes to his right. Quickly they overran and disarmed the Englishmen before continuing on with the attack.

The English proved to be tough opponents; they received the Fallschirmjäger with heavy small-arms fire and mortars. The men of the 5th Company had to wrest every metre of ground from the enemy in close combat. They used bayonets, sharpened shovels, hand axes and sometimes just their naked fists to throw Tommies out of their positions. The reinforcements that they so urgently needed did not appear, and the 5th Company stood alone.

Around evening they reached their objective. The Fallschirmjäger occupied several houses and created overlapping fields of fire with their machine guns. With the

Men of 5./FJR 6 assemble along a Belgian roadside after the battle of Gheel. Although victorious, the Fallschirmjäger are exhausted.

During the 2nd Battalion's divisionary attack on Gheel, the 5th Company go into action one more time. This combat patrol has destroyed a British Sherman tank and is using its wreckage for cover before moving on. The Fallschirmjäger only carry what is necessary for completing their mission: weapons and ammunition.

reinforced company troop, Fahnenjunker Köhne fortified a farmhouse and established the company's command post. During this time his men observed enemy infantry going into position under the protection of a tank, but the infantry did not make a move to attack.

At night a combat patrol reached the farmhouse and established communications with the other elements of the 2nd Battalion. Hauptmann Mager requested a report on the situation from the company leader. When Fahnenjunker Köhne arrived at the battalion's command post, Hauptmann Mager asked excitedly where Köhne and his company had been for the whole day. 'Herr Hauptmann, everywhere where it was crashing and burning, and where it is still burning, that's where we were!' Hauptmann Mager hugged Fahnenjunker Köhne happily, because the 5th Company had been counted as missing since the beginning of the attack. All the companies of the battalion had reached their goal for the day; so far the operation counted as successful.

The deployment of the 2nd Battalion won much-needed time, during which further reinforcements could be brought to the combat zone in order to secure the relatively thin line of defence. Köhne achieved quite a daring feat in Gheel, literally taking action between shots of Schnaps as this act was later called in the frontline newspaper *Der Fallschirmjäger*. In a half-destroyed house on the corner of the Stationsstraat and Nieuwstraat, he discovered the remains of a sign, on which the word 'Bar' could be made out. Driven by a sudden thirst, Köhne investigated the bar more closely, and found the owner in the darkest corner of the cellar. While grenade blasts shook the walls of the bar, Heinz Köhne signalled to the barkeeper his wish for a strong drink. With hesitation, the owner left his protected hideout and poured the Fallschirmjäger a Schnaps at the bar. Fahnenjunker Köhne had barely emptied the glass when he heard from outside the distinctive rattling of tank chains. He made it clear to the barkeeper to pour him one more glass as he prepared his Panzerfaust. He drank up, jumped to the window and landed a shot in the turret ring gear of an enemy Sherman tank. After completing this act, he turned back to the barkeeper and got a third schnapps. The man watched him wide-eyed in amazement; Heinz Köhne emptied his glass one more time, pulled a few coins from his trousers pocket, put them on the bar and left. Oberstleutnant von der Heydte later referred to this deed as the 'Shooting from the bar position'. Fahnenjunker Köhne took down a total of five enemy tanks in the fighting around Gheel and was awarded a Knight's Cross for his deeds.

In addition to the heavy artillery, the tanks gave the British a strong tactical advantage. The Shermans were also used in Gheel to fight against Fallschirmjäger positions with indirect fire. The 7th Company suffered from constant enemy fire, but, admittedly the losses were few. A nighttime assault troop of men from the 1st Platoon under the command of Leutnant Hans Gänzle was sent out to solve this armoured problem. Anton Richter, Oberjäger in the 7th Company, describes the deployment of the assault troop:

It was only a few valiant men. Their weapons were submachine guns, hand grenades and the Panzerfausts that were so feared by the enemy; it was little in comparison to the weaponry that they could turn on us, if we were detected too early. But what did their superiority in manpower and materials count for against the combative bravery, the daredevil nature – paired with cool deliberation – that the young Fallschirmjäger brought with them? They had, in fact, in every man-to-man battle proved themselves to be the stronger than their opponents.

The night, shadowy and opaque, lay like a dark curtain between friend and foe. Heavy drops of rain had been falling for hours. There was not a single dry scrap of clothing on their bodies. And yet this was the perfect weather for this kind of undertaking. Without being noticed, they crossed the canal in an inflatable boat, man by man. Behind this canal lay the Tommies. The front was quiet. It was a deceptive quiet, because at any instant all hell could break loose, if this handful of brave men were to be seen. Any unplanned step, any hasty movement could betray them. Slowly they progressed. Footfalls became loud, unfamiliar whispered sounds could be made out; the presence of a glimmer of light that was instantly extinguished led them to the probable shelter of the Tommies. They continued on. The jackpot had to be here somewhere – the Shermans. Three men from the assault troop worked their way forward, slowly; it would only work if they went impossibly slowly, while the rest secured all sides. Their nerves were on high alert. Two hulking dark shadows, next to them a double sentry: the Sherman tanks they had been searching for.

Everything happened in a matter of seconds. Two Panzerfausts roared, flames sparked forth and in a single detonation the tanks burst apart. Before the English had even realized what had happened, submachine guns and hand grenades were booming in the night. The assault troop made their getaway under the protection of their weapons. Everything jumped to life behind them; the whole sector had been alerted. Flares were climbing high into the sky; bursts of machine-gun fire were hissing wildly into the dark of night. Inside this witch's kettle, the small pocket of German Fallschirmjäger pulled back. A group of Englishmen tried to cut off their path of retreat. In a brief moment of bitterly fought close combat, they crushed the enemy group. But the assault troop, who were carrying a seriously wounded comrade with them, were not out of danger yet; enemy fire pelted down on them from all sides. It felt almost like a miracle that they made it through to the canal. In the dawning of the coming day, they succeeded in crossing the canal.

During the campaign in Belgium and Holland, the men of FJR 6 were seldom deployed in battalions. Most of the time they were acting as semi-independent battlegroups of platoon strength. When motor transport was not available, forced marches were the only way to travel, and a couple of minutes of rest here and there usually took place by the roadside.

Heavy street skirmishes with the Brits lasted in Gheel until 16 September. During this time, the 15th (Scottish) Division had been released from the front and a fresh armored division had been thrown into battle. The Fallschirmjäger did not have resources like this. In addition, further British reinforcements advanced on Gheel from the bridgehead at Beeringen. On 17 September, II./FJR 6 pulled back towards La Colonie.

On 11 September, British recon units

of the Guards Armoured Division were reported near Neerpelt on the Maas–Scheldt Canal. They had proceeded from the area around Beeringen via Hechelt practically without meeting any resistance; they were building up a new point of concentration. On an order from the 1st Fallschirm Army, 6th Fallschirmjäger Regiment broke away from the enemy on the following day and relocated all their battalions to Neerpelt, in order to attack the bridgehead that the enemies were building there from the northwest. Once more the regiment's inadequate motorization proved to be an insurmountable stumbling block. Civilian vehicles were seized on the way to Neerpelt, including a ladder-truck from a fire department, but these improved the situation only minimally.

Parts of General Chill's 85th Infantry Division, a fighting unit built quickly from the remains of decimated regiments and battlegroups, were sent to Postel in support of FJR 6, in order to block the Maas–Scheldt Canal north of Lommel. The army's 559th Anti-Tank Division was a welcome support for the Fallschirmjäger; the division brought 25 tracked vehicles, including Sturmgeschütz III Ausf D and Jagdpanther tank-destroyers, and an anti-aircraft battery to provide some protection from fighter-bombers. General von Zanger, commander of the 15th Army, described FJR 6 in those days as the most valuable part of his army, because of their expertise in battle.

The deployment of FJR 6 allowed the 85th Infantry Division to relocate behind the canal to build a new main line of resistance; yet the enemy still managed to build and fortify their bridgehead. After thorough artillery preparation, the Brits sent further forces across the canal and advanced with tank units.

In compliance with orders, FJR 6 attacked the enemy in line alongside the 85th Infantry Division. Without any noteworthy artillery support or flank security, the attack quickly ran aground in the La Colonie area. The Fallschirmjäger suffered serious losses again, in particular from enemy artillery and air attacks. However, FJR 6 held its position long enough to allow two battalions from the Waffen-SS 'Frundsberg' Division to move into position along the Hechelt–Valkenswaard–Nijmegen road. With this reinforcement, the regiment sealed off the bridgehead to the west on 15 September.

Meanwhile, the Allies made preparations for Operation Market Garden. In a combined Anglo-US campaign, airborne troops planned to take the strategically important bridges between Beeringen and Arnhem in a surprise attack, and to carve out a corridor to the Rhine for the powerful XXX Corps. The goal was to cut off the German troops in Holland from the Reich and penetrate into the northern German landscape, which was well suited to tanks, and so make a deep cut into the Ruhr region. If the operation succeeded, the Allies reckoned that the war would be over by November 1944 at the latest. Expectations were high, because they predicted only minimal resistance from the second-class German replacement troops. They planned for the tank troops and motorized units of XXX Corps to establish contact quickly with the paratroopers so the 2nd British Army could follow.

In terms of daring, this operation matched the Fallschirmjäger's conquering of Crete in May 1941. Due to the bad weather that was rolling in, the troops involved only had a small window of time for support from their own air force. The 'Screaming Eagles' of the 101st US Airborne Division were supposed to land in the area of Eindhoven near Veghel, while the 'All Americans' of the 82nd Airborne Division were landing in Nijmegen, and the 1st British Airborne Division was landing to the northwest of Arnhem, the most northerly extremity of the operation. A later landing of an exiled Polish paratrooper brigade was also planned.

Around midday on 17 September, the men of FJR 6 observed an enemy air armada flying overhead towards the north. Allied bomber forces prepared the landing zones by carpet bombing the areas thoroughly. The left wing of the regiment, as well as the Waffen-SS units lying on the other side of the large road running Hechelt–Valkenswaard–Eindhoven, were affected by the bombing. After the hail of bombs, massive artillery fire followed, then at around 1400hrs the first enemy tanks moved out towards Valkenswaard. Alfons Krüsch, at the time an Obergefreiter in the 11th Company, remembers the Allied advance:

The opponents' tanks that had broken through on the main road headed towards Valkenswaard, and they stood in visibility range in front of us. Suddenly they turned to and bore down on the positions in which we were lying entrenched. They crushed the first foxholes, destroying the anti-tank defences. The fight was hopeless for us. With only infantry weapons – we lacked Panzerfausts and heavy weapons – we couldn't accomplish anything against the steel colossi.

Suddenly the order came through 'Save yourself if you can!' The tanks had closed in and were about 10 metres away. The MG42 was useless. My machine-gunner was already out of his foxhole, but a machine-gun volley from the tank struck him down. The tanks followed us like they were hunting rabbits. Another machine-gun volley caught my platoon leader in the back. Every rescue attempt was crushed by the fire from the tank crews, who knew no mercy. Everything that appeared in their field of vision was mowed down. By 1730hrs I had survived the race against death that had seemed to last an eternity. My strength was almost gone. I had used up every possibility for cover; each respective jump from one foxhole to another required my greatest efforts. A small hedge offered me protection from the opponent's line of sight. For the first time, I paused here and caught my breath. As darkness fell, I searched for my comrades, unfortunately without any luck. At the battalion's command post I found my section leader, Oberjäger Brand. Of the 3rd platoon of the 11th Company we were the only ones who had made it out in one piece. The other comrades were crushed by the tanks, fallen, wounded or missing. Oberjäger Brand and I took up positions on the Dommel Creek. It began to rain; on the street towards Valkenswaard, the English tanks and trucks rolled onward; we watched them from a distance of 200 metres.

On the evening of 9 September 1944, the 11th Company still had an authorized strength of 35 men.

Dispatch rider Erwin Kreidemann resting on his motorcycle. Communications between the far-flung battlegroups relied heavily on runners and dispatch riders. This trooper is well protected against the autumn rain with a rubberized coat. Note the camouflage pattern on his jump helmet, which does not cover the Luftwaffe eagle decal.

In the Battlegroup 'Walther', which was also subordinated to FJR 6, communications broke down within minutes, so a unified course of attack was not possible. The 6th Luftwaffe-Bewärhungsbattalion z.b.V. (Luftwaffe Probation Battalion for Special Use), which had been defensively deployed in Neerpelt, was unable to offer the British spearheads any noteworthy resistance, and they pulled out of the action. The enemy tank forces broke through the middle of Battlegroup 'Walther' onto the large road, and reached the outer districts of Valkenswaard. FJR 6 lost contact with the other division units and occupied a wooded area that offered good possibilities for defence. The Fallschirmjäger were able to fight off the attacks carried out by enemy scouting troops, and they even managed to take prisoners. Oberstleutnant von der Heydte sent out his own recon troops towards Eindhoven and to the west, in order to get an overview of the situation.

Units of the 85th Infantry Division had pulled together east of Postel and set up a defensive wall. In a nighttime march, FJR 6 relocated to Postel itself, in order to meet up with the division. On the way, Oberstleutnant von der Heydte collected and incorporated men who had been scattered and belonged to the Luftwaffe Probation Battalion, as well as a battalion from Hoffmann's Fallschirmjäger regiment. 'The ineffective leaders of these two battalions were pushed out and replaced by officers of 6th Fallschirmjäger Regiment', Oberstleutnant von der Heydte remembered later. In Postel they could receive neither thorough information about the situation nor sensible orders.

> Air landings were reported everywhere; lines of communications and the supply situation appeared to be, to the most extent, greatly damaged. According to the messages that reached through to the regiment, it appeared that the only defence that had been organized in a short time against the landed British paratroopers had taken place in Arnhem and had been personally led by Generaloberst Student. Everywhere else where the Allies had landed, complete chaos seemed to rule; this was the impression that the regiment got in those days.

Even without leadership from their superiors, FJR 6 seized the initiative again, and began nuisance raids on the Allied supply units en route on the main road to Arnhem. It was clear to von der Heydte that the air-landing operations would only be successful if the connection between the heavy units and the paratrooper units was quickly established via the land routes, and if the supplies reached the fighting men on the

Using the shadows of the trees to screen them from view, FJR 6 marches single-file to Schijndel to attack the American paratroopers that have landed there as part of Operation Market Garden.

frontlines. Because the Fallschirmjäger lacked the materials to build roadblocks, they destroyed the first ten trucks of the supply column with and thus blocked the street for hours. On the evening of 19 September, FJR 6received new combat orders: all attacks were to be stopped immediately and the regiment was to relocate to Boxtel, south of s'Hertogenbosch.

That same night, the regiment reached the city of Eindhoven, where recon troops spotted the positions of strong units of the 101st US Airborne Division. In order not to give away the presence of the regiment, the Fallschirmjäger went around Eindhoven and followed the southern Wilhelm's Canal to Schijndel. There FJR 6 fell into position with their front towards the southeast. They set up combat outposts near St Oedenrode and blocked the roads with tried and tested tactics. On the attack, FJR 6 aimed for the bridge at Veghel. American paratroopers were occupying an entrenched position near the Eerde locality. From this position they had already fought back an attack by the 59th Infantry Division on 19 September.

Now FJR 6 was supposed to move on both sides of the rail line between Boxtel and Goch, attack the American positions south of the bridge, and take the bridge. This would cut off the enemy forces around Eindhoven from those units near Nijmegen. The tank troops moving forward from the Maas River against the enemy positions north of Veghel would support the regiment's attack. Oberstleutnant von der Heydte did not see much chance of success in this plan, especially considering that II./FJR 6 had to be thrown precipitously into the sector of the 245th Infantry Division in order to close up a break in the defensive lines there.

In the early morning hours on 23 September, the 1st and 3rd Battalions occupied the staging area. Recon troops scouting out the designated battlefield and reported sobering news: the right wing of the regiment had to proceed through a wide, open area, while the left wing had to negotiate thick bushes. The men of the 3rd Battalion could therefore only advance very slowly, and often by crawling on their stomachs; meanwhile bursts of fire from enemy machine guns whistled over their heads. The defensive fire intensified until FJR 6's advance came to a standstill in a small forest around midday. Numerous dead and wounded lay on the plain; they could only be recovered after darkness had fallen. The 1st Battalion made slow progress in the practically impenetrable bushy landscape; they gained ground even more slowly than the 3rd Battalion, and their casualties were significant. Out of necessity, the Fallschirmjäger swerved into the section held by their comrades in the 3rd Battalion, and they also came to a standstill there.

The promised tank support failed to materialize; the Fallschirmjäger did not even hear combat noise from the direction that the tanks were supposed to be advancing. Around 1300hrs, Oberstleutnant von der Heydte, who had been leading at the forefront of the 3rd Battalion, called off the attack, and ordered that the line they had reached be made ready for defence.

The success of this operation, which had incurred heavy losses, only became clear two nights later. In order to hold their point of main effort near Eerde, the American

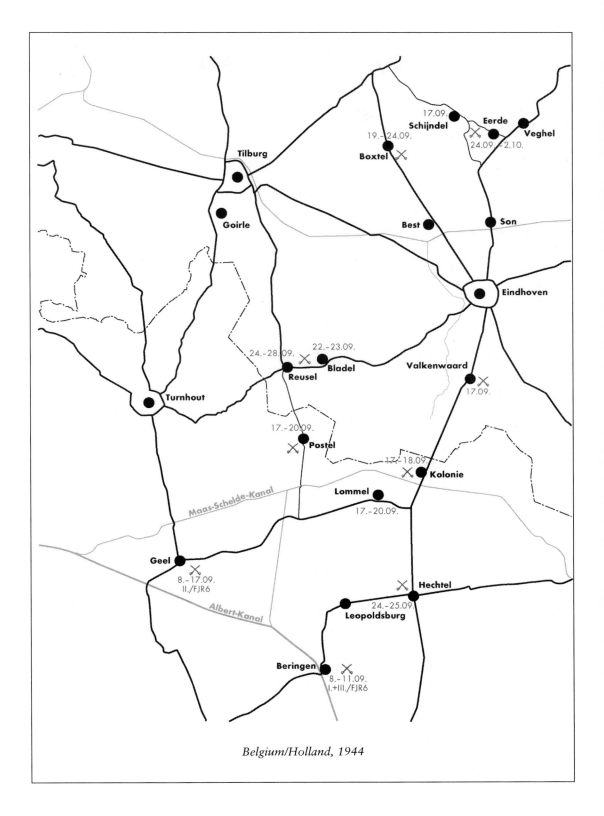

Belgium/Holland, 1944

During Operation Market Garden, these men have captured a .30-cal Browning machine gun, most likely from troopers of the US 101st Airborne Division, and use it against the Americans. The other Fallschirmjäger is guarding the flank of the machine-gun crew. Note that he is not wearing an ammunition bandolier, but regular ammunition pouches on his belt.

units pulled out of the area around St Oedenrode and relocated to positions in Eerde itself. Parts of the Fallschirmjäger Battalion 'Jungwirth' took advantage of the weakening of the rear positions to advance along the Eindhoven–Nijmegen road. In support of Battalion 'Jungwirth,' the 9th and 10th Companies of FJR 6 similarly advanced and were able to stop a jeep containing Allied liaison officers, who hadn't perceived the break in their lines, and take the vehicle's occupants prisoner. The task force also commandeered two English tanks as well as some other vehicles that were integrated into the regimental vehicle fleet immediately.

On 26 September, powerful British armoured units were able to throw the Fallschirmjäger out of their positions in the road ditches. The enemy's superior numbers and forces were too great; against them the Fallschirmjäger were unable to hold the forward deployed line of battle. FJR 6 pulled back into prepared rear positions south and west of Schijndel and transitioned into defending this new location. In his report, Oberstleutnant von der Heydte portrayed the deployment of his regiment in the context of the Allied air-landing operations:

The attack by 6th Fallschirmjäger Regiment against the positions of the American paratroopers near Eerde was the last serious attempt by the Germans to eliminate the corridor that the Allied air-landing operations created on 17 September on the Rhine. After this German attack also failed, the Germans came to terms with the way things were, and focused their attention on cordoning off the corridor in order to prevent any threats on the bridge of Saltbommel and the lifeline to the 15th Army, which was stationed south of the Maas.

Despite this negative assessment of the situation, we should, however, note the fact that the individual undertakings of the units deployed along the allied paths of advance, including FJR 6, contributed to the failure of Operation Market Garden. Because of them, XXX Corps was unable to proceed according to plan and pass through the sections held by the air-landing task forces, and thus the relief designated for the British paratroopers trapped in Arnhem was prevented from getting through.

FJR 6 only had a little bit of time to reorganize and regroup. Around Schijndel and the areas of Bladel and Reusel, severe fighting was developing, in which the regiment, in particular the 2nd Battalion, was involved. House-to-house combat demanded much of the Fallschirmjäger, as Willy Renner, at the time an Oberjäger in the company headquarters section, remembers:

Gefreiter, later Oberjäger, Willy Renner.

Hand grenades were thrown up into the living spaces or down into the cellars. Our assault team consisted of about 15 men and had the order to clear a residential street. This meant throwing the enemy out of his positions with every means we had. Of course, the best method is to beat him into retreat rather than having to kill him. But if he didn't want to flee, one had to use violence and, in war, that meant shooting him. So we had to fire on the enemy and throw hand grenades at him and there were losses on both sides. On the return trip we came across an English soldier who had suffered a stomach wound in combat. I assume that he had been hit from the street and that his people had left him lying in the house because they couldn't take him with them.

We ran towards a house when shots

came from all the cellar windows. A few metres to the left of me a comrade was hit in the throat. Blood was spurting out of his throat – it was horrible. Another comrade received a chest wound. In his breast pocket he had a photo of his girlfriend and the bullet went right through the picture. Another comrade was hit in the hip. Three casualties in rapid succession, and it became clear that there were other people in the house shooting at us from the cellar. We took cover and ran to the right, around the house so the English soldiers couldn't see us. We kicked the cellar windows in on the backside of the house and threw in hand grenades. There was a horrible explosion. It is terrible when a hand grenade explodes in such a tight space – I had experienced that before myself. The Englishmen appeared. A few of them were wounded, some had been killed. Four of them came out and I took them back with us. Shortly thereafter, we shot at some English soldiers who were trying to escape over a turnip field. They knew how to behave in this situation: throw yourself down, jump up, run, throw yourself down again, and so on.

The actual firefight was over now, and we scoured the house to see if there was still anybody in it. Finally we had to take care of our own wounded and deceased. We took the papers and valuables from the dead, their watches and their dog tags, and carefully wrapped up the things. Then we buried the dead and took the wounded back to the main first aid station. I received the order to bring back the four prisoners. It was going without a problem until I realized that the captives apparently were afraid of being executed. They relaxed a bit when we exchanged cigarettes. They were young boys and they were still suffering from the mental strain of urban warfare, the feeling of guilt of having killed somebody and the shock caused by exploded grenades.

Albert Sturm also remembers this engagement:

Everything was unknown. Where was the opponent? It slowly became evening and the darkness took away the visibility. We didn't find any bridges to destroy, but instead we found a single house on the edge of a forest area. We neither saw nor heard a single person. We made ourselves comfortable, and even found a bottle of young jenever liquor that we tried right away. One could almost forget that a war raged outside; until our guards came rushing into the house yelling, 'Go, go! The Tommies are coming!' Our comfortable circle was broken up too quickly. We were pissed about it, so the Tommies got a lot of our lead at first until they decided to take cover. We, too, made our escape secretly, softly.

Then our 7th Company had to comb through a village. Did the enemy occupy it or not? Our group arrived at a hedge, behind which there was an open field and further rows of houses behind that. I gave the sign to halt; I wanted to sit tight with my group, because one thing was clear to me: if Tommy was hiding out in the village, then he was sitting in the houses over there and already had us in his sight. The commanding lieutenant, a man from the ground personnel of the Luftwaffe, was a great guy, but had too little experience on the front. He gave the order to proceed. My eyes probed the area as we advanced, but there was no natural cover to be seen, except for a small ditch farther to the right running parallel to the houses. While I was silently hoping that my fears were misplaced, hot iron flew over our ears and I ran towards the ditch with my comrades following me. The ditch lay somewhat out of the line of fire and offered a little protection. One of our men did not make it. He lay on the open field and didn't move, but we didn't have any time to think any further about it, because a British tank advanced behind the houses, headed towards the ditch. We didn't have any Panzerfausts with us, and so we could only try to save our skin by quickly disengaging. After we had thrown our hand grenades at the tank, we headed back. The fountains of earth kicked up by the bursts of machine-gun fire sprayed around our legs until we reached the protective hedge. With a sustained roll forward, we dove over it. Out of breath I lay flat and looked around me: two comrades must have believed in it.

A few days later the Fallschirmjäger ran around with fat cigars, pretending to be hot shots... The 5th Company was stationed by a cigar factory and so the 2nd Battalion was provided with nicotine for the next few days.

During the fighting around Bladel I had to cross through a cemetery in order to replace a fallen forward-deployed post. Doing so I came into the line of a fire of an English machine gun, which forced me to claw my way into the earth. The burial mounds offered some protection. But when I tried to jump up during a break in the firing, the machine gun started banging away again. The bullets hit my belt, literally shredding it off my coveralls. Another stroke of luck, I thought, and in this moment I received fire support from my comrades. With hand grenades they destroyed the machine-gun nest and I could leave this inhospitable site. Somewhat later I found an English backpack in a conquered position. What poor buggers, the Brits: the Tommies only had a piece of soap and a bit of chewed-on emergency rations with them. When I thought about all the fantastic things we had found on the Americans in Normandy... In another bag I found a brand new leather belt with a brass buckle; I put it on right away so my overalls would lie tight on my body.

On the next evening we were supposed to be establishing a new position. We were marching on the left and right of a trail through the heath. A fine drizzle set in and brought down our mood. From up front, we received the order to halt. Overcome with exhaustion ... we leaned against trees. Even the drizzle and the cool night air could not keep us awake; we all more or less fell into a light slumber. Whispered orders startled us awake, and we were suddenly alert. The English were also slinking through this area. So we built a 'hedgehog defence' [multiple positions providing all-around defence] and stayed wide-awake until morning. The rain soaked through our clothing, our mood had completely plummeted and the soldiers cursed. In the morning it stopped raining and the sun came out. There was no sign of the enemy and the Fallschirmjäger were once again upbeat soldiers, who would not let anything shake them so quickly. Last night was forgotten, jokes were told.

The 7th Company had entrenched themselves as well as they could at the edge of the forest; after about 30–40 centimetres of digging they were hitting groundwater. We could have saved ourselves the work because around midday we were already moving on. Near Oostelbeers we were caught up in intense fighting. That evening I was called to the company commander; he had a special assignment for me. I was supposed to bring a Feldwebel to the battalion's command post. He was from ground personnel and was not accustomed to the hard fighting; he was talking nonsense. His order was easier said than done. Despite the fact that my comrade was always running off in a different direction than we were, and yelling things loud enough for the enemy to hear from miles away, I cunningly succeeded in delivering the good man in one piece to the battalion.

On the return trip I came across a small burnt-out wooden bridge. Some of the beams were still glowing, and in the night one could believe that they were the eyes of a stalking beast of prey. Then I caught a whiff of barnyard smell and saw before me a farmhouse. I couldn't help myself, and I stuck my head inside the stall door. The cattle were resting and I saw a corner full of feeding hay. It occurred to me that I could just take a quick rest there, and by the time the thought crossed my mind I was already stretched out on the hay. A comfortable warmth surrounded me and I was gone. I was awoken by the milkmaids clattering their pails. For the first time in a long time, I had the opportunity to wash, and then I took up a milking pail and started milking; a girl watched, giggling. I knew what I was doing; I had learned it too. After the pail was full, I pulled the straining cloth over it and headed back to the 7th Company, who rushed to get their hands on the fresh milk.

In the Dissel–Bladel area we had to force our way through an area of forest; then in the early afternoon we received an order to attack. The British offered little resistance and pulled back while snowing us under with their mortars. Not only iron, but also wood splinters were flying around our ears. In order to avoid further losses, our group tried to move in on the mortar. It was a success! Eight men were now hot on the Tommies' heels. We saw them dashing away amongst the trees and we took up the chase. On the other side of a clearing the forest began again. We waited here for our people, fanning out on the edge of the woods. We discovered two enemy foxholes, in one of them lay a dead English soldier. When our people closed the lines, we advanced farther and tried to cross the clearing at a run. After only about 50 metres, shots whipped out from the other edge of the forest, and we had casualties right away, most of them headshots. Damn it all! They had sharpshooters in the trees. Two men and I covered our comrades' retreat with our submachine guns, and they managed to run back to the security of the forest. We three made it to the English foxholes – one of them saved himself by jumping into the hole with the dead British soldier, and my neighbour and I jumped headfirst into the other one. Now a long wait began. Whenever we thought about leaving the holes, and held up an object over the parapet, a dry roar came from the other side of the forest and the object was blasted away. We could only hope that our comrades were scouring the forest and that they would shoot or drive away the sharpshooters from the trees. But that didn't seem to be happening. On top of all this, we could hear the noises of tanks from the other side, then high-explosive shells buzzed over our heads into the forest behind us. The comrade next to us lost his nerve and called out that he was getting out of there. He took his chance; the short, hard crack of a sharpshooter's rifle, and then not a single word more. It didn't look good. It was getting dark and we heard German voices getting closer. It was our people, going into position on the edge of the forest. We signified our presence, and they covered us, while we sprinted out of the hole and dashed back to the forest. The comrade next to us was hanging half out of the foxhole; it had been a clean headshot from behind. His eyeball was hanging half out of his eye socket, not a pretty sight. And so it went day after day, night after night. We were pushed hard. Almost every day we saw the white of the enemy's eyes.

In Reusel, the enemy could only be thrown out of his position in violent close-quarters combat. The situation regarding who had possession of certain parts of the village changed from day to day, and even sometimes from hour to hour. Almost all the houses around the church were on fire: the Brits held the church and the Fallschirmjäger held the rectory. Albert Sturm remembers how events developed:

In the morning hours of 24 September 1944, the English in Reusel attacked us; we had to push back to regroup for a counterattack. The house-to-house combat was carried out by both sides with the utmost tenacity and relentless energy. The population had moved to safety in the deep vaults of a cloistered school, and they had to endure everything going on around them. In the night I was on the move with a small recon unit, where we learned, for one, that the nights were really damn cold. On the next day we had to clear a residential street. While doing so, I saw a grey turtleneck sweater in a house that we had just stormed. As I rushed by, I grabbed it and stuck the item of warm clothing in my uniform. The urban warfare continued – over the next fence, along the wall of the house, covering and securing the area, while my comrades stormed the house. After 36 hours, we had split the small city, and a bit of calm settled in, as if both sides were weighing up if Reusel hadn't already cost them enough blood. With three men I took up position over a small outward road from the second floor of a corner house. We had a good view from there. I used the lull in battle to put on the sweater I'd snatched; now I'd solved the problem of the temperatures at night. A Fallschirmjäger discovered something – 'Over there, Albert, in the garden of the fourth house, something's not quite right.' Through the glass I discovered a well-camouflaged British Army personnel truck with a short front end. The driver leaned restlessly against the vehicle, and then he disappeared into the cab and couldn't be seen anymore.

We had Panzerfausts with us and I lined one up in position, waiting to see what would happen. In the next hour, nothing occurred. Then fierce battle sounds reached us and from the left 12 to 15 Englishmen came running in a wild dash. They were carrying wounded with them. I could see their strained and scared faces, all young guys, not much older than us. They climbed into the truck; the driver had left the motor running. I grabbed for the Panzerfaust, flipped up the sight, and sized them up. And suddenly there was a block in me. Fighting a tank, cold steel, the enemy firing wildly as it ran us down, or storming into close combat or shooting at targets farther away, all of this I had experienced so many times, but now I suddenly froze. The opponent was fleeing; I had seen their faces so clearly. They had wounded men in the truck. I could not just blow them all into the air with this horrible weapon. Why? My comrades noticed that something was wrong with me; they fired at the fleeing truck with their machine guns. Then suddenly, as quickly as it came, the spook was gone. I put the Panzerfaust off to one side, and an older Obergefreiter patted me on the shoulder and said: 'Yeah, Albert, war is shit.' And that was it, we didn't say anything else about the matter.

That evening our main line of resistance, which ran right through Reusel, was fired on by mortars. The next morning, 26 September, we attacked. The 7th Company advanced towards the church and rectory, and the ferocious house-to-house fighting began again. The Tommies' resistance became more and more intense as we moved closer to the church. To our right was the cemetery; in front of us was an open garden, on the back of which the rectory stood. Behind it, we could see the bulky church; it was its own fortress. The first platoon of the 7th Company hounded over the open terrain towards the rectory and we succeeded in taking the house from the English in close combat. They retreated into the church, which they covered with heavy machine-gun fire. But now we were stuck. If we tried to make it to the front towards the church, which was at most 20 metres away, a hellish machine-gun and submachine-gun fire opened up on us. On the left towards a gable wall, where a street opened up, we could also get no further. The English had control of the street junction and another assault to this side would be pure suicide. So we sat tight for a while and prepared ourselves for defence. Half of the platoon remained on the ground floor, while the rest split up in the second and third floors. From the attic we managed to throw hand grenades over to the church, but they had no effect. It looked as though the neighbouring groups had also run aground, somehow a standstill in the battle prevailed over everything, and it became quiet except for a few single shots. One of us had found a stone pot with eggs in it that we quickly turned into scrambled eggs, and then served as a second breakfast with a lot of hoopla.

Despite all this inactivity, the war eventually resumed and we tried again to approach the church. The attempt cost us two wounded. Around midday the Tommies turned the tables on us and attacked. We took casualties, but we managed to hold out until late in the afternoon. Then we ran into danger of getting boxed in. The order came to prepare to break through. We had to leave behind three severely wounded; one of them had double penetrating gunshot wounds to the lungs. The breakthrough was successful: firing from every position, we rushed back and reached our positions without further losses. The night passed; both sides sent out recon troops, spying on each other and feeling out the situation, so that no one could rest.

Fighting continued on 27 September. Already in the early afternoon, the 7th was entangled in intense combat with the Tommies – all this for one important street intersection. During these fights, a comrade was severely wounded. He was screaming horribly, but we couldn't retrieve him from the intersection. Tommy was shooting at everything that approached. Then the wounded man fell still and I thought of the English soldiers whom I'd had in the crosshairs of my Panzerfaust two days ago, and whom I still hadn't shot at, because they were carrying their wounded in the truck... Around evening we took position in the cloister school; our command post was set up across the way in a cellar. In searching the cloistered school, we came across two men in dark monks' robes. We tried to make it clear that it would be better for them to take shelter in the vaulted cellars of the church. The school had a large court garden, which was surrounded by a high, sturdy wall, on the inner side of which was a covered path. A small garden gate in the back wall led to an open field.

Around 1900hrs, the enemy began to bombard us with intense mortar fire. The strong walls offered us protection. The fire became ever more intense and we suspected that the English were trying to take our position from the rear. Then I received the order: 'Albert, you secure the garden gate with a machine gun.' I took along the tall blond from Prague, Gunner 1, and his Gunner 2 assistant, and went into position at the garden gate. Relief: the mortar impacts were farther back. I probed the foreground while the two machine-gunners brought their guns into position. When I came back, Shooter 2 already was lying behind his MG42, ready to fire. The tall man from Prague stood leaning on the wall with a blanket over his shoulders. He smiled at me, wanted to say something, then we heard the mortars directly above us. You never heard the shells from the mortars coming, you only heard the howling right before they impacted. I tried to get down, but saw a red burst of flame directly in front of me; then my lights went out. I neither felt the explosion nor the fact that the pressure flung me into the air. When I came back to myself, I thought for a moment that I had dreamt everything, but then the pain set in. I tried to jump up, but just lay there flat. My reasoning starting working again and I tried to figure out where I had been hit.

The one thing that I could move without pain was my right arm. There was blood everywhere else, it had hit me the worst in my leg. My right combat boot was shredded from my leg, the bone showing through. The left knee joint was swollen, full of shrapnel. Both thighs were full of iron, everything was just blood and mangled flesh. A large piece of shrapnel stuck in my left upper arm and pain wrenched my chest – I had two broken ribs, one on each side. My face and my mouth were full of blood. It took me a few minutes to determine all this. I asked myself how long I had been lying there and how much blood I had lost since then. Where were my machine-gunners? The tall one was nowhere to be seen; no one could help Shooter 2 anymore – there was now nothing in the place where his head had been. That put me over the edge and I panicked: 'Medic! Medic! Medic!' I don't know how long I was screaming for. Then I realized that my comrades were still being held back by the mortars and couldn't help me at that moment. The fear of bleeding to death pushed me, despite my overwhelming pain, to pull myself towards our position with my good arm. I unbuckled my belt with all its heavy ballast and slowly but surely made my way forward. Pain overcame me and then night fell over me again.

I awoke at the combat post. Our medic was taking care of me, but there wasn't much he could do. He covered up the large wounds and told me that two comrades had pulled me out during a lull in battle. Because I was being taken away from the combat, they had taken my hand grenades and Pistol 08 out of my combi-suit; when they realized that shrapnel had made them unusable, they had put them back. Maybe the pistol saved my life; it caught the shrapnel above my heart. I was laid out on a stretcher and brought to a house where the serious casualties were being kept. Around the morning we were picked up by the medics and driven to the main first aid station.

On 27 September at 0600hrs, Battlegroup 'Chill' reported:

In the area of the 245th Infantry Division recon activity on both sides [with] weak artillery distraction fire. II./FJR 6 slowly winning ground in the difficult urban warfare taking place in Reusel. Skirmishes still ongoing. Plans for finally clearing out the area in the early morning hours after renewed deployment. In the 59th Infantry Division sector enemy artillery and bazooka fire at the previous points of main effort, especially at the railroad intersection 1km south of Schijndel. On 9 September 1944 around 2000hrs, strong enemy fighter-bomber attacks in the area of Liempde–Orland–Schijndel. Enemy breaks through our main line of resistance 750 metres southwest of Boschkant, cordoned off in a counterattack. Plan to win back the former main line of resistance in the early morning hours. The ordered reorganization running according to plan in Battlegroup 'Chill'.

Around 1600hrs General Chill sent his evening report:

At 1015hrs forced back the enemy who broke through our main line of resistance west of Reusel, [our forces] using three tanks and six machine-gun carriers. At 1400hrs observed the enemy at strength of about two companies at the southeastern exit of Reusel with artillery fire. At 1230hrs, attacks with our own mortars on the area of forest in Broekeindsche Heath, enemy losses noted, one personnel carrier caught fire from shells.

Strong enemy artillery attacks in the area Oirschot–main life of defence north of Steenweg–Liempde–Olland and railroad intersection near Het Hoefte. There and in the Liempde–Olland area fire from at least two artillery divisions. Fire around the intersection took on the intensity of drumfire. Around 1230hrs enemy attack fought back from the direction Boschkant. The enemy lost about 35 dead. In the Liempde–Olland area lively fighter-bomber activity.

In the area Schijndel–Weibosch and the railroad intersection south of Schijndel lively enemy artillery fire. Through the course of the day about 4,000 shots of heavy and light calibre.

After hard fighting, the Reusel area fell completely into German hands on 29 September 1944. A British counterattack on the following day was fought off bloodily. II./FJR 6

Hauptmann Rolf Mager, commander of the 2nd Battalion, receives the German Cross in gold from the hand of the 'Father of the German Fallschirm troops', General Student, as recognition for his exemplary achievements. Hauptmann Mager was wounded in December in the fighting in the Eifel, and a few days later he succumbed to his wounds. For his final actions, he posthumously received the Knight's Cross.

received the following order on 30 September: 'Secret [order] to the Fallschirmjäger: II./FJR 6 to depart right away in truck transport to Baarle-Nassau. Report here to the divisional headquarters of 719th Infantry Division. Speed is requested.'

Despite their exhaustion from the battles in Reusel, Hauptmann Mager's battalion received the order to clean up a deep break in the lines of the 719th Infantry Division. One more time the Fallschirmjäger found themselves at the centre of the fighting, and they were supposed to fulfil assignments at which other troops had failed. In a tough struggle, the Fallschirmjäger managed to seal up the break and bring the enemy's attacks to a standstill.

In the first days of October, the Fallschirmjäger received gratifying news: FJR 6 was to be relieved from the front. At a stocking factory in Schijndel, the regiment prepared for the relocation in the early morning hours of 5 October 1944. In the factory's storage areas there were still large amounts of socks, so the Fallschirmjäger were able to supplement their footwear. Around 0900hrs they decamped, heading to Goirle via Boxtel, Moergestel and the loading station at Tilburg. But instead of rest and recovery, a new deployment order awaited FJR 6. In Goirle there were strong enemy tank units, and so the Fallschirmjäger went into position south of the town. The regiment was supposed to attack along the Goirle–Poppel road and take the village of Poppel. The 10th Company under Leutnant Georg le Coutre was tasked with taking the village.

Two exiled Polish tank divisions put themselves in FJR 6's path and attacked across a wide front. Oberstleutnant von der Heydte remembers this assault:

The Poles sent their tanks first and let the infantry follow under the protection of the tanks. I was directed to work together with an 8.8cm anti-aircraft battery, who were

While digging in along a roadside behind thick bushes, a squad leader conducts a visual recon the area. Note how little he stands out against the vegetation in his camouflaged jump smock and covered jump helmet.

to be found in the area around Goirle in position in a camouflaged wooded area. My own infantry entrenched themselves south of Goirle near the Belgian–Dutch border. They had the order to let the tanks roll past them in their foxholes. Our plan was successful: the Polish tanks drove towards the anti-aircraft battery and suffered heavy losses; the Polish infantry was practically destroyed by our riflemen.

The regiment immediately received new orders to go into position south of Bergen op Zoom, by Mattemburgh. British units had crossed over the Scheldt and built a bridgehead in the Hoogerheide–Woensdrecht area. If the Allies managed to expand this bridgehead, it would be a strategically important entrance to Oosterschelde and thus cut off the 15th Army's retreat path from the Breskens bridgehead.

The march from Bergen op Zoom to Hoogerheide and Woensdrecht was unexpectedly delayed, this time not due to a lack of transport. Oberstleutnant von der Heydte notes what occurred:

> The German occupation troops had heavily mined the border region as well as the stretch of coast, but hadn't drawn up any minefield records. We only realized that it was mined when the first Fallschirmjäger stepped on a mine and lost his life. Discovering this unnecessary and inappropriate mining did not improve my mood. I asked Generaloberst Student to step in and to get the bunglers who'd planted the mines to clear them out. My request was successful, yet we lost a lot of valuable time due to this stupidity, but what weighed more heavily was the loss of life.

Near Mattemburgh, in the so-called 'White House', Oberstleutnant von der Heydte set up the regimental command post. While the companies north of Hoogerheide and Woensdrecht went into position along the railway line at Krekkakdam, von der Heydte once again took a personal recon trip with a motorcycle sidecar. The enemy position was too unknown and the experienced Fallschirmjäger officer no longer relied upon the findings from his superior command headquarters.

Hoogerheide he found to be almost empty of people. Von der Heydte stopped in front of the bakery 'Schuurbiers' to buy baked goods. When he came back out on the street, he noticed soldiers from the Black Watch Regiment of Canada; so the place was at least partially occupied by the enemy. The Canadians recognized him at the same moment he saw them and lifted their weapons. The Fallschirmjäger threw his purchases in the sidecar, hopped on the motorcycle and drove in a wild race towards his own positions.

Elements of the 85th Infantry Division joined up with FJR 6 to their left. Behind the Fallschirmjäger were stationed units of the 346th Infantry Division, troops who had no real battle value any more due to their severe losses in the past few weeks – they represented a potential breakthrough point for the Canadians. The right wing of the regiment was held by one of the so-called Magendivision (lit. 'stomach divisions'):

soldiers who had been released from sick bay to do light service, but who, because of their wounds, needed a special diet in order to function.

Due to this array for units, it was once again clear to the Fallschirmjäger that they would have to take responsibility for the outcome. The neighbouring units were not as reliable as they needed to be. The most they could probably offer the enemy in an emergency was a delaying resistance. But despite the unlimited trust that the high command put in Oberstleutnant von der Heydte and his men, the Fallschirmjäger had a host of other problems besides the enemy. The supply of rations and materials from Bergen op Zoom was arriving sluggishly. They lacked ammunition for the heavy weapons; at some points since Reusel, the Fallschirmjäger had had to go into battle with no rifles, only armed with pistols and hand grenades.

FJR 6 had barely gone into position when the Canadians attacked across a wide front in Hoogerheide and Woensdrecht, aiming to take the isthmus by storm. According to their information, the Allies believed that on the German side the only defences were coastal protection units and convalescing soldiers lacking replacements. Oberstleutnant von der Heydte commented on this misbelief:

> For the Canadian leadership it was an ugly surprise that, after their successful crossing of the Scheldt, they faced a powerful, strengthened German Fallschirm-

At dawn the Fallschirmjäger arrive at their new main line of resistance at Krekkakdam, north of Hoogerheide and Woensdrecht. Without losing any time, the men go into position.

jäger regiment ready for battle. When their first attack failed due to the Fallschirmjäger's resistance, the Canadians tried again three hours later, apparently with renewed forces; this attack, too, was stopped directly in front of our main line of resistance. I decided for a counterattack with a limited target that would lead us up to the northern parts of the villages Woensdrecht and Hoogerheide. The Canadians fought – as a German I have to say this – superbly. The officers, up and including the brigadier-general, stood next to and with their soldiers in the first row.

The Canadians suffered appreciable losses during their assaults. Furthermore, the Fallschirmjäger succeeded in taking out a dozen enemy tanks and an armoured machine-gun carrier.

The fight for Woensdrecht and Hoogerheide proved to be undecided for the most part. The two side exchanged attacks and counterattacks, and fought particularly hard over the villages, as Eugen Griesser remembers:

Under the leadership of a Leutnant, this group of Fallschirmjäger push into the village of Hoogerheide. While two men keep the Canadians' heads down with their fire, the rest of the combat team climb over an embankment and move on to attack a building.

In Hoogerheide and Woensdrecht we encountered the Canadians. One could recognize them well by the uniforms that were greener and not as brown as those of the Tommies. The fight for the villages was bitter; often enough we weren't even fighting house-by-house, but room-by-room. Once we lay in a fully shot-up bedroom, the chinstraps on our helmets undone, pilot's shirts open, smocks buttoned open to our belts, panting from the battle. Next door in a similarly shot-up bedroom, sat the Canadians, helmets in their laps and jackets open. They would only have had to throw one hand grenade into our room, or us into theirs, but in that moment we were all too exhausted. After we all recovered our breath, we made ourselves combat-ready. We ran up the stairs to the attic, the Canadians jumped out the open window and disappeared into the neighbouring garden.

Oberstleutnant von der Heydte received the following message from a group of the 6th Company: 'In house number 19, the Canadians have taken the kitchen – bedroom still in our possession.'

During the next three weeks, the Canadians did not significantly threaten FJR 6's main line of resistance, so von der Heydte was able to do inspection tours of the positions of his men every night. The activities of the Dutch resistance, however, increased. For example, they were constantly radioing reports to the Allies about German troop movements and the locations of German commanders, including the coordinates of the regimental command post.

One evening the monitoring station in Bergen op Zoom intercepted a radio message stating that the Allied air forces were planning an air attack on the following day at 1700hrs on Mattemburgh. Oberstleutnant von der Heydte received the report at the very last moment. A few minutes before 1700hrs, the regimental staff fled the command post in the 'white house' and took cover. Because the Dutch resistance was unable to determine the new location of the headquarters, the bombing was called off.

In the absence of motorcycle dispatch riders, the traffic between the superiors in Bergen op Zoom and the Fallschirmjäger's regimental command post in the 'white house' had to be maintained via bicycle. This Oberjäger has just returned from a dispatch trip. We can see in this photograph how many NCOs in 1944 were still were not armed with submachine guns – this soldier carries has an ammunition bandolier for his Karabiner 98k rifle around his neck, and has slung his rifle across his back. On his belt his combat helmet hangs next to a map case; such was a popular way to carry the helmet behind the frontline.

Because of the activities of the Dutch resistance, FJR 6 set up mobile checkpoints in sensitive areas. Here a patrol searches the cart of a shoe-maker for hidden weapons or radios.

Wolfgang Langer, at the time an Oberjäger in the 12th Company and leader of the 2nd Mortar Platoon, remembers the action in Holland:

At night we arrived between Bergen op Zoom and Hoogerheide. There we moved into an ideal reverse slope position, about 1,000 metres away from Hoogerheide. The first and second platoons both lay in position in this small valley. The heavy machine guns were in position at the back, in front of Nieuwborgovel. The company's command post was located in a brickworks in Nieuwborgovel under the leadership of Oberfeldwebel Behne.

On the day after our arrival, we zeroed in on three artillery fire zones. We had an excellent forward observer with whom I worked well. There was a telephone connection to him and our assignment consisted of calling in barrages of fire on the Canadian attacks and fighting numerous targets of opportunity.

The first platoon had German 8cm mortars, the second platoon had Russian 8cm mortars. The difference between these two weapons was that the Russian barrel was about 25cm longer and had an 8.2cm calibre. In addition, the barrel had a weaker

THE LIONS OF CARENTAN

In the regimental command post, Oberstleutnant von der Heydte receives reports from his combat companies. While sleeping little, he kept in personal touch with his Fallschirmjäger whenever he could by visiting the foremost positions. In this way he could get a picture of the situation and assess the condition of his men. It is half-jokingly suggested that even the combat messengers assigned to him had the opportunity to earn the Close-Combat Clasp decoration.

wall thickness, but could shoot 400–500 metres farther than our mortars. The base plate was round, not square like ours. We had Russian ammunition for these mortars, but the shells were no good: misfires and short drops were standard. For this reason, we relied on German ammunition and buried the Russian ammunition somewhere in the ground. We had enormous firepower from the different mortars. A talented loader could put ten shots in the air before the first shells that had been fired exploded on the ground. These Russian weapons were especially suited for hitting point targets. They achieved a bull's eye always after the third or fourth shot. With the leadership of our forward observer, we often had the opportunity to take out tanks, machine-gun nests or other important single targets.

When we received these weapons in Tilburg, no one knew what to do with them. The guns were whole, but they had no battery emplacement books or charts. What to do? First, we set the thing up, then we adjusted its aiming mechanism, and, according to the adjusted values, fired a shot into the landscape. Then we put a tick mark on an indicative scale and shot again. We measured one impact to the next, re-adjusted and re-measured, and in this way we calculated the elevation and traverse values, and it worked particularly well!

So the days passed in this manner: shoot a mortar barrage, fight specific threats, shoot a mortar barrage again to fend off the Canadian attacks.

The American 'crows' [fighter-bombers] were always somewhere in the skies and we had to pay terribly close attention so we didn't get discovered in our positions. What would the Thunderbolts do to us if we were found? In any case, they flew several attack runs every day, but our anti-aircraft artillery kept them at bay. Once our anti-aircraft artillery hit one of these birds like a bull's eye; the plane blew apart like a bomb in the air, directly above our position. Later we found the pilot, poor guy, in the forest. His pistol had been bent in the crash, but his watch was still ticking, even though the band was ripped apart. I took his papers and valuables off him and provided for a proper burial. Through the company, the valuables went to the Red Cross.

One day a comrade came and told us that there was German ammunition to be found in a farmhouse between the two frontlines. It could be retrieved easily in the night. Because every round was precious, I decided to go and get it with a few men from my platoon. We snuck forward in the black of night and found the farmhouse, which matched his description. First we took cover in the cellar. Because we were soldiers, we were curious, so first we searched the whole cavernous basement. What a find – tons of bottles in a box under some rags. We broke off the neck of one of these bottles and carefully tried the contents. We determined that it was currant wine. First things first – we took a hearty swig. The wine was good and not without effect. Each of us helped ourselves from the supply and stuffed a few bottles into our tunics and trouser legs. Then, with bottles and ammunition, we returned to our own positions. I walked last, stuffed full with bottles, several in my coveralls and two in

Fallschirmjäger gather on a reverse slope, safe from fire before a counterattack into Woensdrecht. They are reloading and waiting for the signal to attack. The Krekkak dam here formed the backbone of FJR 6's positions and was practically an insurmountable obstacle for the Canadians.

It was not always possible to take wounded comrades back to the first aid station right away to treat their wounds, so the medics often performed first aid in the field. Such is the case here, near Woensdrecht.

each trouser leg. Our friends from the nearby army sector seemed to notice something. When I marched, heavily laden, through the courtyard, there was a sudden crash and whistling splinters – the bottle had smashed in my trouser legs and my combat boots filled with currant wine. As quickly as possible, I ran back to the cellar and fished the broken bottles out of my trousers. Of course, I replenished the lost supply from what was still in the box. Then I set out again to our own positions. Thankfully everything was quiet for once. My trouser legs had a few serious holes in them, but I got away without even a scratch. One has to be lucky.

The nights continued to be marked by shelling and infantry activity. The Canadians made good use of their divisional artillery: Bofors anti-aircraft guns would shoot a directional shot with tracer ammunition as a marker for the other numerous medium and heavy artillery pieces. Some 168 Canadian guns stood ranked up in a line measuring just 1,200m.

Werner Schütze, an Obergefreiter in FJR 6, remembers an unnerving incident:

The noise of battle resurfaced at dawn, but then soon abated. I was in my foxhole writing the usual reports about ammunition expenditure, etc., when I heard someone call out from behind me in the forest 'Who is the squad leader here?' I made out three Fallschirmjäger, who were unknown to me, with their fingers on the triggers of submachine guns. At my hand signal, they approached. The officer walking in the middle ... and I recognized him as an officer because of his cap. In a brusque tone, he asked how to connect up with the 6th Regiment. He ordered me to give him two men for security. Because the regiment was not far away, I consented and assigned Jäger Schreiber and Möckel to accompany him.

The officer departed with a handshake and promised to send the men right back. When they hadn't returned after an hour, I began to get worried. Moreover, the enemy had started in on us with his artillery. After another hour of futile waiting, the company messenger came running up and reported an immediate position switch. As the company gathered, I reported to the company commander what had happened. He looked at me thoughtfully and said, 'You, too?' Only then did I hear that Canadians in German uniforms were running around, causing disturbances in the frontlines.

Life in a foxhole was nothing new for battle-hardened Fallschirmjäger. Here a machine-gun team make themselves as comfortable as possible in their position with simple materials. Because the enemy fighter-bomber attacks were a constant danger, mere bad weather represented a lesser evil, even though the rain and cold night temperatures aggravated the Fallschirmjäger.

Alfons Krüsch, meanwhile, was involved in significant offensive and defensive actions:

As the messenger for the 11th Company, I was stationed at the regimental command post. At 1530hrs I delivered the order to attack to my company leader. The attack itself would take place at 1630hrs from a wooded area. The Canadian mortars met us. The attack moved forward haltingly, and we spent the night in a decommissioned gravel pit. In front of us a farmhouse was ablaze. On the morning of the next day, we took position to the right of the main road running towards Hoogerheide. With support from an assault gun, we carried out the next attack. The assault gun received heavy anti-tank fire and pulled back, so the attack came to a standstill and we took up positions alongside the nearest path. The day after, we dug ourselves a trench there. My machine-gunner no. 2, Heinz Fulda, said to me 'Alfons, we're digging our own grave here!' I tried to distract him from this idea, but I couldn't improve his mood. Was he having a premonition? At 1630hrs, our next attack took place. With our MG42, we took over providing fire support for the next group, who were already advancing in the ditch alongside the road. Comrade Heinz Fulda jumped out from cover, and ran over a small field towards the ditch. There was sudden small-arms

In offence and defence, the machine-gunners performed invaluable tactical services with their powerful weapons. Camouflage by natural materials and a tarpaulin, this machine-gunner is starting to shoot up attacking Canadians from his position on the crest of Krekkak dam.

fire from the Canadians – Fulda crumpled, hit. Shortly after, I rushed out from my cover and reached the ditch unharmed.

The Canadians blanketed us completely with their mortar fire. They shot damn well. Two comrades were wounded by shrapnel. A damn beast of a mortar detonated half a metre away from the road ditch. Clumps of dirt struck my lower back; shrapnel zoomed through the air. In the twilight, we advanced further and took up our position in a fruit garden.

On the other side of the street, within visibility, lay the Canadians. My comrade Werner Haubrich and I dug our foxhole together.

On the second day, in the afternoon, I needed the toilet. In a nearby house I did my business. What did I see on my return? A mortar fired from the opposite side had landed right on the edge of the foxhole. Whenever I did sentry guard, I always sat right on the edge. Miracles do happen. One just has to believe in them.

On the same evening – it was Tuesday, 10 October 1944 – Major Robert Slater, commander of B Company, The Black Watch of Canada, took a recon trip in the immediate vicinity of the Fallschirmjäger. A mortar shell hit his vehicle and wounded him severely. Alfons Krüsch describes the incident: 'Our attempts to recover and bandage him failed because the Canadians kept up their constant fire; they wouldn't let even one of us close to their comrade. On the next day we left our positions. We laid the wounded Canadian out on a stretcher and four of us carried him to the first-aid station.'

The help came too late. Some days later he succumbed to his wounds. The documents found in his vehicle were, however, very useful to Oberstleutnant von der Heydte.

The Fallschirmjäger gave up the village of Ossendrecht because of its exposed position, although not without causing the enemy, who was giving chase, serious losses. Therefore the Canadians nicknamed the Ossendrecht–Hoogerheide road 'the Grim Road to Hoogerheide'. On 13 October – the Canadians' 'Black Friday' – the enemy failed to turn the tables and break the German main line of resistance, despite their numerical superiority and the use of tanks. They could not throw the Fallschirmjäger out of their positions, and the men of FJR 6 held every single house like a fortress, resisting with all their might. Without losing any time, the two sides exchanged attacks and counterattacks. The Fallschirmjäger managed to take numerous prisoners, whom Oberstleutnant von der Heydte personally interviewed.

On the night of 16/17 October, a message from a young lieutenant ripped Oberstleutnant von der Heydte from his sleep: the forward observers had made out unusual movement in the Canadian positions. Even though it did not look like the Canadians were about to attack, the Oberstleutnant decided to form his own impressions of the situation. In his motorcycle sidecar, he rode to the front in order to decide if measures needed to be taken or not. Fallback positions behind the lines had

This photograph illustrates perfectly the reality of urban warfare in the village Woensdrecht. Some troops are dashing across the open street, while comrades posted at the house corners keep an eye out for enemy snipers. Because of the numerous possibilities for cover in the built-up terrain, the danger of overlooking an enemy strongpoint is very high. Therefore the Fallschirmjäger move especially carefully and secure every angle.

been prepared in case of massive enemy attacks. The Fallschirmjäger would retreat to these positions, let the Canadians wear themselves out unnecessarily attacking the German main line of resistance, and then spring back in a counterattack and throw the Canadians back. This type of elastic defense had proved extremely successful before.

This time the Canadians stormed them without extensive artillery preparations; following orders, the Fallschirmjäger pulled back. Now artillery drumfire set in and pummelled what had been the German frontline. When the Canadians fell into the cleared-out positions, the Fallschirmjäger of the heavy companies open fired with mortars, according to a well-rehearsed fireplan.

Around 1000hrs, FJR 6 moved into three different positions for a counterattack. One combat team moved forward over the railway embankment west of Woensdrecht; the central combat team, personally led by Oberstleutnant von der Heydte, pushed over the smaller railway embankment northwest of Woensdrecht; and the third team advanced northeast of the city.

The plan allowed for the three combat teams to attack independently of one other,

After sneaking up to the corner of a house, this Fallschirmjäger checks to see if the enemy has hidden himself behind the corner or if this area is clear. House-to-house fighting was not only exceedingly physically demanding, but was also psychologically unnerving. The Jäger is armed with the Karabiner 98k rifle and carries the ammunition for his weapon in a bandolier called the Fallschirmjäger-Patronentragegurt. The pockets of his coveralls are filled with hand grenades, rations and personal gear.

but then reunite in the northwest part of Woensdrecht in the old positions. The counterattack was supported by some assault guns as well as tanks, and it was so fierce that the Canadians were unable to resist for long.

On this day, the 67th Army Corp reported to the high command of the Wehrmacht:

Enemy attacks (2–3 battalions and tanks) NW Hoogerheide. Enemy advanced until embankment 3km NNW Woensdrecht, breaking land connection towards Walcheren. In Woensdrecht and at the Elevation 19.8 (north of Woensdrecht) bitter fighting underway. Local breakthrough in Nederheide, attack east west of there repelled. Our own counterattack 2.5km west Esschen ran into enemy tank attacks with 20 tanks. 7 tanks destroyed. Tank foray from the west against the northern edge Nispen sealed off. Several tank advances on both sides of the Esschen–Nispen road beaten back.

On this day, 16./FJR 6 was deployed under the command of Leutnant Carl Werner 'Charlie' Wiegand to the village of Nederheide. The Fallschirmjäger were supposed to push back Canadians positions along the German supply line towards Woensdrecht. To support his 50-man strong company, Leutnant Wiegand received three assault guns of the 255th Assault Gun Company. The Fallschirmjäger managed to throw the Canadians out of their positions in bitter close combat, as well as take out their artillery, tanks and machine-gun carriers. Leutnant Wiegand and his men took a last strongpoint in a bayonet attack, because they had used up all the ammunition they brought along. As the Canadians threw a further company of the Royal Hamilton Light Infantry into the fray, the Fallschirmjäger grabbed the weapons of the fallen and captive Canadians and continued the fight with undiminished vigour. The close combat raged for a total of two hours at extremely close quarters, back and forth in Nederheide between blazing houses. When the Fallschirmjäger could no longer withstand the opponent's superior numbers and firepower, Leutnant Wiegand ordered his company, which now consisted of just 19 men, to disengage the enemy and pull back to their own fallback positions. There he gave Oberstleutnant von der Heydte his report, and received the order to advance again and clear Elevation 19.8, a tactically important point behind Nederheide, of the enemy. For this task, Oberstleutnant von der Heydte assigned him the command of the regimental platoon.

When darkness fell, the Fallschirmjäger made for Nederheide once again. The march there took place silently, under the strictest observation of the noise reduction measures, and so Wiegand's combat team managed to approach Nederheide unnoticed. In a bend in the street by the entrance to the town, the Fallschirmjäger ran into a Canadian outpost. The enemy's fire was random, because in the darkness the Canadians could not make out where the Germans were. Leutnant Wiegand detached three men to engage in the firefight, and to feign the strength of a much larger unit, in order to allow the rest of the combat team to advance without being noticed. This stratagem allowed the division to come up to 600m closer to the Elevation 19.8

The Fallschirmjäger heard snatches of English-language voices nearby, and saw the shadows of British artillery and the silhouettes of vehicles against the horizon. There was no doubt that they had infiltrated the Canadian position. At this moment a dark-skinned Canadian crawled out of a well-camouflaged bunker off to the right of the Fallschirmjäger. Because he was drowsy, he offered no resistance to them taking him prisoner, although he was physically in a position to do so – mamed Private Washington, he was well over 1.8m tall and wide-shouldered. In a coup de main, the Fallschirmjäger took the bunker and captured five more men.

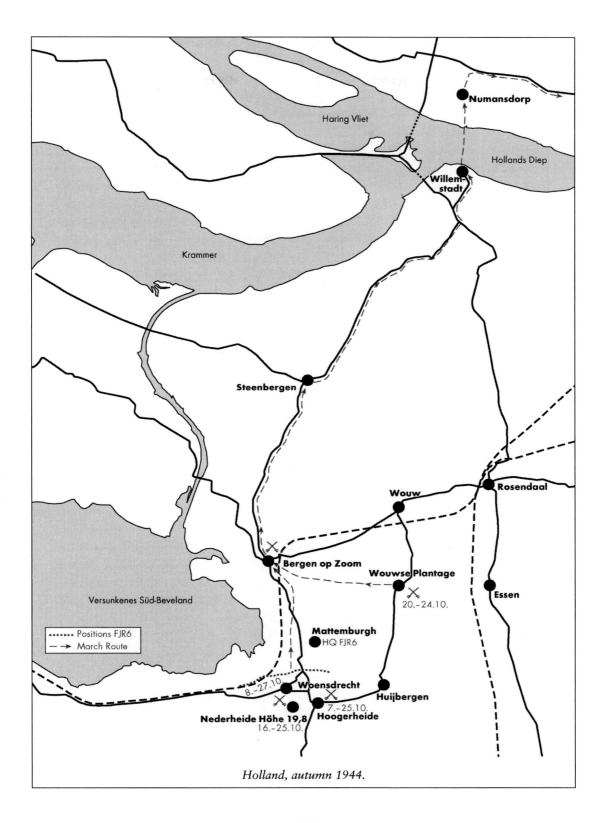

Holland, autumn 1944.

Now, however, the Canadian team in the neighbouring bunker opened fire, and the Fallschirmjäger returned it. The German troops even managed to capture a British anti-tank gun and use it against its former owners. The anti-tank artillery proved to be a well-suited bunker-cracker.

The Canadians had turned one cellar into a virtual fortress, but the Fallschirmjäger soon smoked out the nest with concentrated machine-gun fire, supported by numerous hand grenades and anti-tank weaponry, and the combat team could move forward. At one point, Leutnant Wiegand had his leg broken by a hand grenade, but was still able to lead his men onward in their mission. He was unable to walk, but he let himself be loaded onto the back of Private Washington and continued the battle from a dizzy height. Despite their greater numbers, the Canadians could not hold Elevation 19.8 against Leutnant Wiegand's men. Finally, due to a diversionary attack into the flank led by the 1st Company under Leutnant Erich Hosp, the Canadians gave up the fight and pulled back. The 16th Company brought back two Canadian officers and 60 other ranks as prisoners that evening.

In the next few days, the Canadian opponents received further reinforcements. The pressure on the Fallschirmjäger's main line of resistance increased so much that General Chill ordered them to fall back to alternative positions that had been established. This shift led to the Canadians finally taking over complete occupation of Hoogerheide and Wonesdrecht; they also threw the army's Magenbataillon (lit. 'stomach battalion'), who were in position

In Nederheide, the 16th Company under Leutnant Wiegand managed to take two Canadian officers as well as 60 other ranks prisoner. Because a British Mills grenade broke Leutnant Wiegand's leg in combat, the Fallschirmjäger officer let himself be carried back to the regimental command post on the shoulders of a prisoner, Private Washington. These figures are from the German frontline newspaper "Der Fallschirmjäger," and were drawn by Peter Wywiorski.

on the right flank of FJR 6, out of their positions. Now the Canadians held the entrance to South Beveland.

FJR 6 undertook renewed recon activities at this time, in order to unsettle the enemy and to disguise the relocation of some German troops to the north. This activity meant that the regiment came to blows and skirmishes with the Canadians several times a day. Eugen Griesser remembered the opposition:

The Canadians had fresh reinforcements. Like us, many of them were really young boys, who had just left their homes and been tossed into the chaos on the front. With my team I lay in position near the former regimental command post by Mattemburgh when a Canadian recon troop headed directly for us. They came very close to us without spotting us there. We prepared to open fire and just then the Canadian troop leader waved to us; a smile lit up his whole face and he called in English: 'I didn't know that Americans were fighting here, too!' As we were lying in position, he had only seen our helmets and faces. Apparently because of our helmets, he took us for Americans. I waved at him. With their weapons strapped over their shoulders, the Canadians came toward us to chat. By the time they recognized their mistake, it was too late to offer resistance. They cursed impressively as we took them prisoners.

This Feldwebel was leader up a recon unit near Woensdrecht. He has blackened his face with charcoal and camouflaged his uniform and equipment. His combat helmet has a wire frame that holds natural camouflage materials in place, such as grasses and moss. In combination with camouflaged coveralls, and the talent gained through years combat experience in natural terrains, these techniques make it possible for the Fallschirmjäger to blend in with his surroundings and launch ambushes on his opponents.

Oberstleutnant von der Heydte continued to work day and night and barely slept. For example, on 21 October 1944, he hand wrote a multiple-page letter to Renate Uhlig, the wife of Oberfeldwebel Alexander Uhlig, who had asked the regiment about her husband's remains:

Dear gracious lady!

My communications officer, Oberleutnant Dietrich, who has, since your husband went missing, led the 16th Company in his stead, gave me your letter from 21 September 1944.

Unfortunately, I cannot give you any information about your husband's remains. On 26 July, the regiment, along with a tank group from the SS-Panzer Division 'Das Reich', tried to break through towards the south out of the American cordon around the encircled area of Coutances. On the Coutances–Percy road the regiment encountered a powerful enemy position. The attempt to break this blockage frontally, along the road, failed. I was at the tip of the 16th Company, which was led by your husband, and tried to circumnavigate the enemy position on the left side, and then break out from the deep flank. In front of a group of farmhouses occupied by the enemy, the company split up. Your husband worked right with half of the company, and I took the other half left towards the farmhouse. The attack failed; we did not gain control of the farmhouses. Because the enemy had secured his flank with tanks and was constantly reinforcing it, I took the company back to the line of departure and sent a messenger with an order for your husband to do the same. I do now know if your husband received this order. No one came back from his combat team except for a few men who had been separated from their comrades. According to the reports of some soldiers, your husband was later seen at the line of departure, where he was looking for me. I personally never saw your husband again. Shortly after returning to the line of departure, I ordered the regiment to disengage from the enemy in order to try to break through the cordon at another point. I assigned a Fahnenjunker with the task of delivering this message to your husband and any other members of the 16th Company whom he should meet. If he succeeded in this task, I do not know. In the second breakout attempt, the bulk of the regiment was wiped out. Only two combat teams, each with 150 men, one under Hauptmann Mager and the other under me, made it out of the cordon in one piece. Many of the regiment fought their way out, alone, in pairs, or in threes. Your husband was not among them.

I regret not being able to deliver you better news. I still hope that your husband ended up in captivity. I got to know and value him as an excellent soldier, an attentive leader and an open, straightforward man. As the leader of the 16th Company, he and his men achieved impressive feats more than once.

With the best regards,
I remain loyally yours,
Signed: Heydte

At this time there was a radical change for FJR 6: On 23 October 1944, Oberstleutnant von der Heydte received two telegraphs. One instructed him that he was awarded the Oak Leaves to the Knight's Cross of the Iron Cross, and the other recalled him as regimental commander and reassigned him as commander of the newly formed Fallschirm-Armeewaffenschule (Parachute Army Weapons School) in Aalten/Holland.

Some of the experienced men of FJR 6 were also reassigned to work as a squad in the weapons school. Oberst Fritz Henke of the anti-aircraft division of the 4th Battalion succeeded von der Heydte as the regimental commander.

On 25 October, Oberstleutnant von der Heydte issued his last order of the day as regimental commander:

The Führer awarded me the Oak Leaves to the Knight's Cross of the Iron Cross on 30 September 1944. This honour does not just refer to me personally, but first and foremost to the regiment, whose leader and representative I am. It is in recognition of the regiment's achievements, above all, your achievements, my old comrades from Normandy. I owe this award to your readiness for battle, your bravery, your will for action, and your toughness. I would like to express my gratitude to you! I can only give you these thanks by regarding you with the same comradeship that you have given me, by showing you the same trust with which you have followed me into hard battles, and by committing everything to leadership and care, just as you have committed everything in battle. I especially express gratitude to the fallen and wounded soldiers of the regiment, who have made the greatest sacrifice by fulfilling their duties to the utmost. In proud grief, I commemorate the dead of the regiment, in loyal fellowship the wounded comrades! My gratification over this honour has unfortunately been significantly impaired by an order from the Fallschirm Army Superior Command, who has relieved me from the leadership of this regiment and tasked me with another assignment. I do not need to tell a single one of my old comrades, how difficult the separation is from this regimen, a regiment that I was allowed to organize, train and lead in difficult and uncertain battles. The time in which I have stood at the head of the regiment belongs to the most cherished of my military life. I was immensely proud to have led you. Soldiers, who have dutifully and energetically fulfilled every assignment, even the most difficult, as it was expected by our superiors; soldiers, who have held out toughly and tenaciously in defence, and who stormed forward wildly and fearlessly in attack. I thank you all for that which you have achieved under my leadership! Commanders and subordinate commanders, Jäger and heavy machine-gun operators, messengers, telephone and radio operators, medics, drivers – all of you who have selflessly given your last for the greater goal, and who have all contributed to the fact that the name of our regiment is respected everywhere by German troops and feared by the enemy.

I promise you, that I will continue to regard you with the comradeship that is grounded in our joint experiences in hard days of fighting. Even though I am no longer your commander, I request that you keep me in comradeship. I am convinced that you will follow your new commander as well as you followed me, that you will show him the same trust you have shown me, and that under his leadership you will fight as bravely and hold out with as much determination as always. Your new commander is also a soldier of the front, who knows what the Landser [soldier] needs, and where his shoe pinches him. Hold the regimental flag high; add new deeds to the regiment's achievements in Normandy and in southern Holland, deeds that correspond to the previous ones. Fight faithfully in the tradition of the regiment, and stand your ground so that you will never have to be ashamed of our deeds. Make good on the words that I called out to you in February in Wahn during the organization of the regiment:

'When everything falls apart and wave after wave crashes down upon our people, then there will still be one Fallschirmjäger of my regiment to defy fate, and one to hold the flag high above the flood in heavy storms; on this flag one word will stand in shining letters: 'Greater Germany' – and this word 'Greater Germany' he will yell into the storm's raging, and stronger than all storms that threaten us, this call will come from a Fallschirmjäger from 6th Regiment.'

For the presentation of the Oak Leaves by Reichsmarschall Göring, Oberstleutnant von der Heydte was picked up by special aircraft and flown to Göring in Berlin. After the presentation, the Reichsmarschall suggested that the high command confer a special 'Adolf Hitler' armband on the whole regiment because of their extraordinary achievements, and that they be renamed 'Fallschirmjäger Regiment Adolf Hitler'. Von der Heydte managed to talk Göring out of this idea, by convincing him that an armband was not particularly appropriate in general, but especially inappropriate in combat situations. In reality, the declining of the armband was down to Oberstleutnant von der Heydte's nonconformity and his sceptical attitude to leadership and the party. However, he gladly took Göring up on his next suggestion, which was to grant all members of the regiment the Nahkampfspange (Close-Combat Clasp) in silver for their excellent service on the Normandy front and in the subsequent missions. He knows that his men had earned the honour to wear the medal, buying it with their blood and sweat. FJR 6 was the only unit of the German Fallschirm troops to be awarded, in their entirety, the Close-Combat Clasp in silver.

While Oberstleutnant von der Heydte spent time in Berlin, FJR 6 received the order the relocate to Bergen op Zoom and take up new positions on the Zoom. The 1st and 4th Battalions remained for the time being in their existing positions, in order to delay the enemy from advancing. Because the British 49th Division was moving on Bergen op Zoom from Esschen, II./FJR 6 set out for Roosendaal with the goal of holding the British off until the positions in Bergen op Zoom were occupied. Meanwhile, in an industrial area on the Zoom, the 3rd Battalion set up the new defensive line.

At the Wouwse Plantation, the 2nd Battalion under Hauptmann Mager clashed with British troops. Under him were the 1st Battalion of the Ersatz- und Ausbildungs-Regiment (Replacement and Training Regiment) 'Hermann Göring', as well as a company of assault guns from the 280th Assault Gun Division. The brick factory, in which some of II./FJR 6 had entrenched themselves, became the key point over which both sides fought for days. Primarily, the British tried to overrun the position with infantry supported by tanks. Their Sherman tanks and their machine-gun carriers, however, ran into trouble against the well-disguised assault guns, and they suffered heavy losses. Weakened by that, the enemy infantry pulled back with significant casualties.

Some of the Canadian 4th Division arrived from the south in support of the Brits. The Canadians had access, amongst other things, to heavy Churchill tanks and the so-called 'Crocodile' tanks that, instead of an assault gun, had a high-powered, long-range flamethrower built in. These tanks became particularly problematic for the Fallschirmjäger, because the flamethrowers also represented a great danger to infantry occupying fixed positions. The remaining Panzerfausts were saved up for the flamethrower tanks, while all other Canadian armoured vehicles had to be overcome with close-combat weapons – a Fallschirmjäger would jump on the tank from behind, remove the pin of a grenade, throw the grenade through an open hatch and jump off the tank. In this way, the Fallschirmjäger managed to hold the brick factory in a bitter fight against the enemy's superior forces.

After three days, the 2nd Battalion's supplies of ammunition and especially anti-tank weapons began to dwindle. Holding off the 49th Division was a daring choice; it was practically inconceivable for one battalion to pin down two enemy divisions for more than three days. When the report arrived on 27 October 1944, explaining that a new main line of resistance was being formed, Hauptmann Mager ordered his men to disengage from the enemy in a delaying action and march to the north. One of his Fallschirmjäger, Alexander Schmidt, a youthful 19-year old, belonged to the detachment that mined the road to Bergen op Zoom. On that evening he occupied a machine-gun position with his comrade:

A Canadian tank that had broken through on the day before drove over one of our mines and flew into the air. The drivers were thrown clear, and they lay wounded on the ground. A little later, two further tanks with accompanying infantry arrived. The leading tank stopped only about 5 metres from my foxhole. For seconds, I just stared at the Canadians – I thought, if they see me now, it's over. I had a Panzerfaust, but in order to shoot it, I would have needed to stand up straight. While I considered what to do, my comrade, who was with me, shot his Panzerfaust at the Canadian tank and hit it straight on.

With my machine gun, I opened fire and the second tank withdrew, taking the infantry mounted on it. The personnel from the shot-up tank climbed out of the hatch; they had suffered burns. Now we had the personnel from two tanks and no idea what to do with them. We were a forward-deployed combat post; our main line of resistance was farther behind us. My comrade ran back to his company command post and asked what to do with the wounded, but because there were no bandages and no medic there, we decided to send them back to the Canadians.

We salvaged a Red Cross flag from the tank and went into the village where the

Canadians lay in position. We let them know about the four wounded men, and stated that we had no transport capacities, so they should pick them up themselves if they wanted to get them back. That was pretty risky for the Canadians, because they did not know how many of us were guarding the street. They didn't know that we were alone. However, an ambulance picked up the wounded. When we said goodbye, they gave us a pack of cigarettes in thanks.

On the next day, Schmidt received the order to give up the machine-gun nest and rejoin the company.

It had just become dark and I had two machine guns in the position. One of them wasn't working anymore, so I buried it, and we took the other one back to the company. There an officer asked me where I had left the second gun. I told him that I was only able to carry the one, so he sent me back to get it. It took a good half hour to get to the position. In the meantime, the Canadians had advanced, so I had to approach carefully and quietly. When I finally returned to my company command post with the second machine gun, my company had already departed. A subordinate officer of the 'Hermann Göring' Regiment told me he knew where my comrades had marched to, and that he would show me a shortcut. I just needed to line up behind him... I didn't realize what that meant until I heard the Canadians order us to put our hands over our heads. He had led us directly into enemy lines in order to surrender himself.

When the Canadians searched me, they found the Canadian cigarettes that I had received as a present, and a pistol that I had taken from one of their tank men. They wanted to know where the items came from, so I told them the whole story. It took awhile for them to confirm my story and make sure I wasn't lying to them, but then they let me go in and I got coffee. The following morning I was transferred to a collection point for prisoners.

Meanwhile, recon troops from FJR 6 were still travelling between Woensdrecht and Bergen op Zoom; they had lost contact with their battalion. One of them was Alfons Krüsch:

Later, with tanks and infantry, the Canadians managed to break through about 1–2 kilometres away from our positions. We were supposed to close up this break with tank support. I was detailed to a combat patrol. At dawn on the next day, we carried out our attack with two assault guns. The English tanks were next to a farmhouse; the infantrymen had taken positions in and around the house. The tanks as well as the Canadian artillery fired on our assault vehicles, so we pulled back. In a nearby forest, we lay in visible range of the enemy tanks and infantry. For the entire day the Canadian artillery covered the whole area with fire, including the positions of their own infantry. Around evening we figured out that their own soldiers must have have had their lungs ripped apart by the artillery fire – they lay unmoving in their foxholes. Some of them were hit and killed by strikes aimed at the farmhouse. One Canadian's lower back had been broken by a falling beam. The Canadian tank personnel held out until the last shot and then set their tanks on fire. We spent the night in the forest, without knowing that the regiment had already taken positions behind Bergen op Zoom.

Around 0400hrs, a messenger suddenly appeared, who had been searching for us for half the night. He told us that the regiment was in position near Bergen op Zoom and that a comrade had been wounded by resistance fighters, so we should keep our eyes open as we returned. We were happy about this news because it meant that we had a connection to our own unit again!

We moved through Bergen op Zoom on both sides of the main street, with the safety off on our weapons, ready at any moment to defend ourselves. The civilian population were out on the streets, dressed in their Sunday best, probably waiting for their rescuers. They greeted us amiably until they noticed that we were German Fallschirmjäger moving through Bergen op Zoom. Because of our coveralls and helmets they had probably believed us to be Allies. On their faces we saw the expression: we've got the wrong side. Unmolested we left the city, passed the train lines and the Zoom River. To the left, a factory area caught our attention. We couldn't believe our eyes – it was a liquor factory making Bols, a well-known brand. We searched the rooms thoroughly, tasting the different liquors, a sip here, a sip there. Stuffed full with bottles, our coveralls took on an usual shape. We moved on to our unit , who had taken up positions behind the train tracks as well as on the embankment of the road to Roosendaal.

In the meantime, III./FJR 6 went into position in Bergen op Zoom. One of the city's main points of defence was directly on the Zoom in a row of massive buildings: a laundry, a liquor factory, Becker's iron foundry and a factory site. Every building was built up like a fortress, the whole area a death trap of overlapping fields of fire.

Once again, it was the Canadians who followed and stormed the positions of FJR 6 in Bergen op Zoom. Because the Fallschirmjäger had destroyed the bridge over the Zoom, the river presented a serious obstacle to the Canadians. They fired on the Fallschirmjäger with mortars and artillery. The 9th Company, deployed across from the demolished bridge, attacked the Canadian engineers, who were brought in to build up a makeshift bridge, with heavy crossfire from their machine guns. The Canadians sent their special assault tanks to attack the Fallschirmjäger positions with cannon.

Eventually the Canadians succeeded in building the bridge. Canadian recon troops carefully infiltrated the industrial area. Soon heavy firefights and close-quarters engagements broke out between them and the Fallschirmjäger entrenched there. But the men of FJR 6 were facing an even greater danger from the flanks. There other Canadian units had managed to cross the Zoom and were searching the buildings for German soldiers. Because the Canadians could not bring their tanks into the densely built-up area, a tough and relentless infantry battle developed. Four companies of the Canadian Lincoln and Welland Regiment encountered the 10th Company under the order of Leutnant Georg Le Coutre. The 10th had just received a delivery of automatic assault weapons a few days earlier, which proved especially useful. In the fight for the iron foundry, the Fallschirmjäger were therefore able to produce a volume of fire that demanded the Canadians' respect.

During the battles in Bergen op Zoom, which ran through night and day, the Canadians demonstrated the superiority of their numbers. While the Fallschirmjäger were beset once again by exhaustion and a lack of ammunition, the attackers could send in fresh, rested troops constantly to grind down the Fallschirmjäger. On 28 October 1944, therefore, in response to an order from the division's headquarters, FJR 6 began

In Steenbergen, the companies that had previously been separated from each other were brought together again. The Fallschirmjäger built themselves makeshift shelters from simple materials and then tried to catch a few hours of rest. The battles of the past few weeks had taken a heavy toll on them, and their physical and metal depletion is evident.

to relocate to Steenbergen, where they were to establish a new line of defence. Already decimated, the 10th Company fell in for a counterattack one more time in the early afternoon on this day. Yet even the highest combat morale was not able to hold out against such superior force, and so Leutnant Le Coutre's men withdrew in a delaying action that made their comrades' withdrawal possible. Leutnant Le Coutre was awarded the Knight's Cross for his personal role in the battle for the iron foundry.

In Steenbergen, all the companies of FJR 6 were reunited; since the battles for Hoogerheide and Woensdrecht some of them had been scattered far afield. Wolfgang Langer remembers the move:

Around morning, when it was still dark, a Feldwebel came up to me and ordered me to dismantle our shelters and head for Malsteren then Steenbergen. He advised that I circumvent Bergen op Zoom if possible because, ever since the disengagement had begun, there had been lively partisan activity in Bergen. I went around Bergen op Zoom to the northeast and encountered our units on the path to Malsteren.

We marched beyond Steenbergen and took up quarters in a farmhouse near Dinteloord. Steenbergen had become the main line of resistance and all hell had broken loose there. Fighter-bombers were attacking nonstop, bombing the small city, which was ablaze on every corner. As night fell, we received the order to relocate towards Dintelass, where men were being ferried over to Numansdorp. Dinteloord was also on fire. We headed towards the embarkation point in Dintelass. What chaos! The boarding area lay under constant fire from heavy long-barreled artillery. Every time one of the ferries arrived, all hell broke loose anew. At least there was a position there that was fortified with concrete emplacements and shelters, so even though the losses were high, they were much less than they would have been if there hadn't been this cover. I lost some of my people there, including little Schimdt, a Berliner with fire-red hair and irrepressible humour. A piece of shrapnel hit him in the chest and killed him instantly.

As often happened, the order suddenly arrived: 2nd Mortar Platoon was to stay behind, regroup and proceed towards Willemstadt, where we were to link up with the 10th Company under Oberleutnant Fehling. The same order came for the 3rd Heavy Machine-gun Platoon. Now we had to try gathering these people together amidst such chaos! I was able to find some of them, but not others. Then I headed off with my men towards the burning town of Dinteloord. On the way, I put a severely wounded horse out of its misery. I went through Dinteloord and then back to the embarkation point. On the return trip, I encountered a machine-gunner from the 3rd Platoon with his MG42. It had become quiet on the landing pier because the operation had ended and no longer offered a worthwhile target for the enemy artillery. When I had collected my men, I counted the following equipment: 7 men, 1 base plate, 2 mortar tubes, 2 bipods, 1 sighting mechanism, as well as 80 rounds of ammunition. Not enough to let loose a whoop of joy, but still better than nothing. So after this memorable night we marched at dawn towards Willemstadt and reported there to Oberleutnant Fehling.

The heavy machine-gun platoon, well, what was left of them, was directed to a bunker. With the rest of my mortar crew, I went to a farmstead that sat on an ideal position on an embankment. In addition, I had found another MG42. We went into position and waited. On the first day nothing happened – no shots, no Canadians. The next morning, a Canadian armored recon vehicle was suddenly standing 200 metres away from the bunker in which our comrade with his heavy machine-gun was located. Our first shot was a bit short, the second landed better. Before the third shot could come, the tank quickly drove backwards and disappeared behind the houses to the left and right of the street on the embankment. Now we knew that the opponent had taken up positions across from us. With my mortar, I shot at the street and houses, and marked some important targets.

Thankfully, the machine-gunner in the bunker remained quiet, otherwise he would have really caught it. That evening I visited him once and told him it would be best if he didn't give away his position too soon. I lay in an ideal position with my mortar. The farmstead's roof overlooked the embankment a bit, so that from the roof I was well-placed to observe and guide the mortar fire. We had enough ammunition to cause them constant unrest. A few times the Canadians tried to get us with mortars, but it was a useless undertaking, because the shells all impacted far behind the farmstead. Even the shells that landed on the crest of the embankment couldn't harm us. I learned later that we took out one tank with a direct hit in the tank turret, and that we seriously damaged another.

On the third or fourth day, a runner came and gave us the order to clear out of the position by 0300hrs, and to relocate to the harbour at Willemstadt. We were to board there and be transported to Numansdorp. The Canadians had thrown down leaflets ordering us to clear out of Willemstadt, otherwise they would carpet bomb the city at 1800hrs. Punctually we evacuated the position and marched to the harbour. Engineers stood ready to transport us in assault boats. The weather was stormy, and Holland's wide Diep River caused us some anxiety; furthermore, fighter-bombers were flying overhead at a height of 300– 400 metres. Nevertheless, the operation went fairly well. One or two boats filled up with too much water and they went under with all hands; a single man managed to swim to the other shore.

In Numansdorp some of our comrades received us, and we went into position on the shore of Holland's Diep. That evening we observed from there the bombing of the unfortunate city of Willemstadt, in which not a single German soldier was left.

CHAPTER SEVEN

Deployment in the Eifel Region, 1944

On 8 November 1944, FJR 6 relocated to Gorinchem, where they received human reinforcements, although they were limited in number. From there the battalions marched toward Wesel for further replenishment. The regiment received additional reinforcements: boys without military experience taken directly from their school desks, and Luftwaffe personnel who could be spared from other positions. Unlike at Güstrow, there was no talk of a completely new reorganization this time, because the latest arrivals lacked everything; uniforms, equipment and weapons had to be supplied in inventive and sometimes adventurous ways. Nevertheless, in these days FJR 6 counted as one of the most powerful units in the German Wehrmacht.

The recuperation period did not last long for the regiment – on 24 November 1944 they were relocated via train from Wesel to the Eifel, where they were to support weakened German troops who had been taking part in lengthy ongoing battles in the Hürtgenwald region.

The regiment marched at night from Weilerswist to the assembly area near Zülpich. The Fallschirmjäger were once against sent to the hot spots: Obermaubach, Untermaubach, Bergstein, Brandenberg, Zerkall, Nideggen, Rath, Leversbach, Vossenack, Schmidt, Abenden and Boich. The defence of this huge number of positions was only possible by splitting up the regiment into independent battlegroups, some of which were only as strong as a single company.

The 1st Battalion occupied a position near Zerkall; the battalion's command post was set up in a paper factory in Zerkall itself. The companies of the 2nd Battalion went into position between Bogheim and Untermaubach; the 3rd Battalion occupied the mountain range west of Obermaubach by Brandenberg and Bergstein in Hürtgenwald.

The Fallschirmjäger had barely set themselves up in their positions, when the Americans began a renewed offensive against the German bridgeheads on the Rur River. They carried out their attacks with the support of strong armoured combat teams and heavy air attacks. The jagged forest terrain gave the Fallschirmjäger an advantage, because tanks deployed here could not push across the landscape with decisive speed. In order to advance with their tanks, the American engineers had to cut swathes through the forest, and the terrain repeatedly presented new difficulties for them.

The Americans quickly noticed that the Fallschirmjäger they were dealing with were opponents of especially high calibre. The men of FJR 6 put a lot of effort into protecting their front with minefields and improvised booby traps. They set up trip wires and tin cans filled with pebbles as a warning system along the paths, so that they would be notified early of the enemy's advance.

On 30 November, the Americans attacked the Brandenberg and Bergstein heights in order to destroy the German artillery positions there, from which they had been under constant fire during the November battles for Schmidt and Vossenack. The Burg Mountain (called Castle Hill, or Hill 400 by the Allies), which lay in the Rur Valley between Bergstein and Zerkall, was another target; positions below Bergstein were held by individuals companies of III./FJR 6, while further companies of the battalion stood ready to defend the Burg Mountain.

Supported by heavy fighter-bomber attacks, the Americans managed to throw the army units out of Brandenberg and to take over their positions. That afternoon, they continued with an attack on Bergstein, which ran aground under the collective fire of the Fallschirmjäger. During these skirmishes, the men of FJR 6 experienced a sight they had not seen for a long time. On 3 December, German fighter squadrons intervened from the air and helped fight back the Americans. While the Fallschirmjäger cheered, around 60 Messerschmitt 109s inflicted heavy losses on the enemy.

Further American forces began marching from Vossenack towards Bergstein. In

During the lulls in battle, Oberjäger Heinrich Fugmann captured his impression of the battles in the Eifel in the form of a pencil sketch. Here is a picture of his position near the forester's lodge in Bergstein, below the Burg Mountain (Hill 400).

Tiefenbach Valley, they managed to occupy the Lukas Mill, but their advance was brought to a standstill along the Hubertushöhe west of Bergstein. Bitter close combat took place here; the Hubertushöhe changed hands several times, but finally the German defenders managed to gain the upper hand.

After days of almost uninterrupted fighting, the Fallschirmjäger were also suffering under the bad weather. Barely a single man had a scrap of dry cloth on his body, and the incipient frost led to the first incidents of frostbite. Nevertheless the Fallschirmjäger held their positions against the opponent's superior forces.

Reinforced by fresh units, the Americans renewed their attacks on Bergstein and Burg Mountain on Tuesday, 5 December. Only after the Allied air forces had bombed the positions for hours, and after the village literally lay in ruins, could the Americans advance with strong tank support. The Fallschirmjäger's losses were high, and faced with the hopeless situation, the men of the 3rd Battalion pulled back under heavy delaying counterfire from Bergstein. The positions below the Burg Mountain still remained in the hands of FJR 6, and the Americans again suffered painful losses here, because the machine-gun bunker at the foot of the mountain made each of their advances a suicide mission. In this way, the Fallschirmjäger effectively prevented the Americans from quickly capturing this strategically important elevation. Furthermore, the hillsides, which snow and ice had made barely walkable and on which the defenders had entrenched themselves, presented practically impassable obstacles for those Americans who did manage to get past the machine-gun fire from the bunker.

On the following day, some of FJR 6 set out to win back Bergstein in an counterattack. They had so little tank-unit support, however, that the Fall-schirmjäger's attacks could not penetrate far enough, and the village's ruins remained in the hands of the Americans.

The battles in the Eifel region were marked by the massive deployment of Allied artillery; the whole area was transformed into a ruined landscape within a very short space of time. This Propaganda Company photograph shows Oberjäger Erwin Kreidemann, who served in the regimental staff as a dispatch rider after the battle of Normandy until the end of November 1944.

Initially, the thick undergrowth of the hillside offered the Fallschirmjäger excellent concealment, but the Americans' massive artillery fire soon changed the overgrown mountain into a bare, smoking landscape. The shelling and aerial bombing resulted in high losses on the German side, but it also constantly formed deep foxholes in the rocky terrain. The Fallschirmjäger used these to their defensive advantage well, so finally the Americans called off their air attacks, in favour of throwing the Fallschirmjäger out of their positions in close combat. If anyone was spared the crossfire of the machine guns, the Fallschirmjäger drove him back down the mountain in a quick counterattack.

The uninterrupted fighting demanded everything the Fallschirmjäger had in terms of manpower and materials. The lack of supplies, in particular of food and ammunition, and reinforcements, as well as the Americans' advances at other points of the front in the Kall Valley, were turning the battle irrevocably against the Germans.

In the meantime, the Americans sent in their 2nd Ranger Battalion to storm the Burg Mountain. An elite, battle-tried unit that was specially trained for close combat and rapid assaults, they were meant to decide the outcome of the battle. Teamed with the regular infantry and armoured units, the Rangers advanced from Bergstein towards the Burg Mountain, but at first they came to a standstill under heavy defensive fire. When the tanks attacked the German positions with direct as well as indirect fire, the Rangers finally managed to plant themselves on the mountain and set up their defences, despite heavy losses. This elite troop still could not manage to take by storm the steep, icy slopes of the mountain; they had met their match in FJR 6. The seriously depleted Fallschirmjäger undertook several counterattacks throughout the night, but could not prevail against the opponent, who fought bitterly. In order not to be cut off completely from their own forces, the Fallschirmjäger disengaged from the enemy in an aggressive, delaying action, and fell back into alternative positions in the Kall Valley. Their resistance had cost the Rangers great losses: the battalion had been ground down to only 60 men.

Alfons Krüsch remembers the action vividly:

In a barn filled with hay, packed in like sardines, removed from the thick of it by only a few kilometres, we waited for further developments. We could see the Eifel Mountains, and hear the thunder of battle. What was in store for us?

In the first days of December – it must have been the 8th or 9th – we moved into the new operational area. In the darkness we crossed a bridge and passed along the Serpentine on the mountain range, towards our new position. Artillery fire accompanied us along the way. The army unit lay to the right of our path in rank and file, ready to be relieved. In front of us, no one was in position. There was no relief from those on site, only a brief greeting.

Four of us occupied forward-deployed posts; the other comrades, a total of two groups, were positioned on the mountain range. Digging holes was especially difficult because our shovels were not well suited to the slate-heavy soil. While we were at our posts, the Americans were sawing and shovelling eagerly. After three days we came back to our squads. During this time, the Americans had felt their way forward again, trying to invade a neighbouring group. In the night we attached demolition devices of all kinds – hand grenades, etc. – to the trees, so that when the opponent attacked, we only had to pull a wire to detonate them. At night a 'hero thief' [in this case not an officer who collected stragglers for redeployment, but an enemy raiding party] tried to get some of the comrades out of their holes. Individual Americans were constantly trying to infiltrate our lines. A thin, mined forest path divided our positions. In addition to our small arms, the two groups had access to three MG42s. My weapon was an MP38.

Late in the afternoon, it must have been on around 15 December, three Americans were trying to draw out or destroy one of our machine guns with their own machine-gun fire. A comrade pointed out to me that something was moving up ahead. I let the Amis go into position by a small brushwood pile, then my submachine gun came to the ready, and I fired a complete magazine from a distance of 25 metres. I changed the magazine, pulled the trigger again and gave the medics some work to do.

In the next few days, the Americans attacked again and again, but could not manage to break through. On Christmas Eve, they attempted an assault one more time, around 1700hrs, hoping to overrun our position, and again they failed. That evening, around 1900hrs, we had something to eat for the first time in a while: an army bread loaf, a sausage and a bottle of Bols liqueur for every ten men. We had been starving back then, and taken enough hardship.

A fallen American was lying across from our position, about 40 metres away. I went to recover him in the twilight. I found chocolate on him as well as his weapon with 70 rounds of ammunition. The Amis got those back immediately on the next day from me; they must have been surprised to be shot at with their own ammunition.

The forester's house in the Kall Valley became the scene of a memorable Christmas. A combat patrol of FJR 6 was deployed in the Kall Valley with an assignment to stop enemy recon activity. The forester's house offered the men an opportunity to warm themselves up and dry out their uniforms and boots. The windows were steamed up, so they could not get a glimpse inside the house. The Fallschirmjäger therefore entered the house suddenly, with their weapons ready, and ran into an American patrol with their weapons similarly ready. The forester's wife resolutely put herself between the two fronts; in her house no blood would be spilt. She collected the Fallschirmjäger's and the Americans' weapons and carried them into the shed. The soldiers agreed to a ceasefire; friend and foe gathered around the hot oven and warmed up. One of the soldiers began to hum a Christmas song 'Silent night, holy night'. Germans as well as Americans joined in, singing the old song, each in his own language.

The Americans presented the Fallschirmjäger with cigarettes, and the Germans shared their Kommissbrot (army bread), which was so beloved by the Americans. For a few hours, Christmas really came to the Kall Valley, which was so violently fought over.

The Battlegroup 'Fugmann', part of III./FJR 6, set up position along a railway line near Kallerbend. Here, Oberjäger Fugmann also reached for his drawing pencil.

The next morning, both combat patrols left the forester's house, shook hands one last time; then they took up their weapons and returned to their units.

Willy Renner remembers one day during the Christmas period, 1944. As the leader of the company headquarters, he received the assignment to visit the company positions and check to see if everything was in order:

I had the choice to go through the hills on a trail, and from there get to our positions along a hedge, or to take a shortcut across a field. I decided to take the shortcut. Luckily, one could say. Shortly afterwards, at the corner where the hedge began, a mortar shell struck. This time I had been lucky.

The hedge, under cover of which I had advanced, divided at an opening in the forest. I stood silently there, and heard a noise. I turned to the right and saw a black soldier directly in front of me, about 30 or 40 metres away. He looked very martial; and was well wrapped-up because of the cold – it was freezing in the Eifel region. He had a long scarf around his neck, and stood in front of me; a gigantic man, seriously taller than I was, with a spade in his hand.

If I remember correctly, he smiled when he saw me, but in such situations one thinks of one's training. Whoever shoots first, lives longer. I had a submachine gun and wanted to shoot, but because of the cold and the bad weather of the past few days, I couldn't get a single shot off – the loading mechanism had jammed! Nonetheless, I was more or less sure that I had forced him to take cover; he must have hid in the hedge.

I continued my inspection round, and did not think further about this incident. Only later I realized that it had been a mistake not to run back to report the man's presence, and let the commander know that the enemy had advanced so far. Finally, I arrived at the last position in our line; here machine guns were set up in the valley where the Americans held the opposing side. It surprised me a bit that everything was so calm. Suddenly someone yelled to me 'What are you doing? Take cover or you'll be blown away!' Shots cracked in the air, and I threw myself down, taking cover next to a mound of earth. I hadn't done it correctly, though – my legs should have been flat on the ground, but they weren't completely covered by the earthwork. I felt a sudden hit. It was a strange feeling, as if someone had struck me with a heavy club. I had taken a hit in the left leg, specifically through the lower leg. Panicked, I crawled into the machine-gun position, where my comrades wrapped strips of bed sheets around my leg; they had found the sheets in the houses they were quartered in.

I lay there for an hour, and waited. After a while, however, the pain became too much and I told my comrades that I couldn't wait any longer, otherwise I could bleed to death. If I were to run out of the position, the enemy would probably shoot me. We discussed the situation. One of the comrades thought that I should stay; others said they would leave the choice up to me. Whatever the consequences, I decided to give it a try. I took a piece of the white fabric they had used to bandage me up, wrapped it around the barrel of my submachine gun, and held it up. For a long time, all was quiet. Finally, I stuck my head out of the position. It wasn't anything heroic; I just had no other choice than to try it. I managed to push out my upper body and then to stand up completely.

A few seconds later, there was a noise in the bushes and I heard an American calling out to me in German: 'Komm rüber!' [Come over!]. My whole life I will never forget these two words. In order to gain some time, I called back in German, 'I can't walk!' Then another thought gripped me – if I were to surrender, I could be accused of desertion afterwards. This was possible, and I could not allow this, because my family could be taken into custody of the state under Sippenhaft regulations [kin liability, the Nazi policy that allowed the punishment of family members of those who were accused of crimes against the state]. My only other thought at this moment was that I should try to throw myself behind the hedge, whereby the enemy would shoot after me with the machine gun, and could still hit me. Of course I didn't have enough time to think through all possibilities. I threw myself to the side, as much as that was possible with one leg, and crawled on all threes along the hedge. There was a ton of shooting behind me, but they could not see where I had crawled off. Meanwhile, the company headquarters had sent a comrade out to search for me. He found me and loaded me onto his back like a sack of coal. When he was running across a frozen turnip field with me, we came under fire and he threw himself and me to the ground, forgetting that he was carrying my additional weight, and causing injury to his knee on the hard frozen earth. Now we both had a damaged leg: his right, my left. Nonetheless, we managed to make it to the company command post.

CHAPTER EIGHT

Parachute Mission in the Ardennes, 1944

In Aalten, the former commander of FJR 6, Friedrich August Freiherr von der Heydte, now commander of the Parachute Army Weapons School, and recently promoted to Oberst, was ordered to report immediately to Generaloberst Kurt Student on 8 December 1944. Student informed von der Heydte about a massive offensive, the planning of which had been in the works for a while, and which was now ready. Student explained to von der Heydte that he had been chosen as the commander of a special Fallschirm battlegroup that would carry out a parachute mission in the context of this offensive.

At first Oberst von der Heydte assumed that this offensive would take place on the Eastern Front, in order to give that threatened front some relief, but he soon learned that the undertaking was planned for the Western Front, specifically in the Ardennes. His wish to use his former FJR 6 for this mission could not be granted. For reasons of secrecy, each Fallschirmjäger regiment located on the Western Front would provide 100 men to form this contingent. However, Student conceded the right to nominate the officers who would be involved.

Von der Heydte later described the situation:

Oberst von der Heydte.

I was horrified: a troop built from a mixture of forces and units is seldom good; at least it is never so good as a regiment that has grown close by surviving together over a half of year of heavy fighting with their commander. My fear that I would receive what soldiers called 'a pile of pigs' turned out to be unfounded. The spirit of the assembled battlegroup appeared good, and their core personnel were excellent. An important part of this core were 150 members of my former regiment, who, when they had heard that their old commander was forming a new force, managed to find their way to me. With the benevolent indulgence of their regimental aide-de-camp, they were allowed to exceed the requested number of 100 men.

Indeed, FJR 6 made the effort of sending as many good men for the parachute mission as they could spare under the circumstances; the regiment was still fighting difficult daily battles against the Americans, who were advancing against bitter resistance.

Oberst von der Heydte divided his battlegroup into a signals communication platoon, four Jäger companies, a heavy artillery company with 12 heavy machine guns and four mortars, and a engineer company. On 11 December, all personnel who had been detached for this mission gathered in the Parachute Army Weapons School, and Oberst von der Heydte was able to fill the company leaders' positions for all Jäger companies with officers from FJR 6: Leutnants Köhne, Wagner, Le Coutre and Wiegand. Still without equipment, machines or, most importantly, parachutes, the battlegroup relocated on the same day to Sennelager near Paderborn, where it would meet up with the transport aircraft division allocated for this mission.

Around 0300hrs, the troops entered the camp, but found it fully occupied with other duties and the commander of the drill ground uninformed about the situation. After they learnt that the air force administrative command headquarters in Münster was also not prepared, and unable to offer help, Oberst von der Heydte took the initiative and decided to move his battlegroup to Oerlingshausen, where an acquaintance lived, the pharmacist Dr Wachsmuth. With his assistance, they managed to find quarters in Oerlinghausen for the battlegroup, which was 1,200 men strong.

Over the next few days, Oerlinghausen remained the battlegroup's home base. Oberst von der Heydte had all shipments rerouted there – weapons, kit and parachute equipment – so that the soldiers could be made ready for deployment. For this important mission, the combat team received fresh, unworn uniforms, new equipment and unused parachutes.

On the evening of 12 December, Oberst von der Heydte met with Major Erdmann, the commander of the air force unit of 120 Junkers Ju 52s. In course of the conversation, it transpired that the pilots were all young, inexperienced fliers, who had never before flown Fallschirmjäger in a parachute mission. On the following day, Oberst von der Heydte and Major Erdmann were ordered to Taunus, where they would receive further information about the upcoming mission. On the way back, von der Heydte and Major Erdmann visited the headquarters of Generalfeldmarschall Model in Euskirchen to voice

In Oerlinghausen, the Oberjäger of Fallschirm Battlegroup 'von der Heydte' gather for a souvenir photo.

their reservations about the plan. Originally the battlegroup was scheduled to jump as the advance guard for the 6th Panzer Army, as part of the powerful offensive in the Ardennes. Then they were to fight their way through two strategically important passes. In a second revision of the deployment plan, they were to occupy a street junction in the High Fens, as well as a pass and heights at Mont Rigi and Hockai. Despite the Fallschirmjäger's reservations, Model decided that the parachute drop was indispensable, and he sent the two officers to the commander-in-chief of the 6th Panzer Army, SS-Oberstgruppenführer Josef 'Sepp' Dietrich.

Dietrich was against the parachute operation from the outset, because in his opinion 'everything was crap that came from the Luftwaffe'. But he deferred to Model's order. Oberst von der Heydte received the following combat objectives from Dietrich: take the strategically important Melmedy–Eupen/Malmedy–Verviers road intersection, which lay behind enemy lines near the Baraque Michel in the High Fens; hold it until the tank forces from the 6th Panzer Army arrived. The drop would take place under cover of darkness shortly after a concentrated artillery bombardment.

The information about the landing zone was limited. The drop would take place over an inhospitable terrain featuring bogs, coniferous forests, a raw climate and stormy weather. There was great uncertainty about the enemy's positions – the aerial images and maps that were available were sketchy at best.

Oberst von der Heydte requested from Dietrich a jump-ready, forward-deployed artillery observer to direct the fire from the supporting artillery, as well as messenger pigeons. He received the artillery observer, but Dietrich categorically refused him the messenger pigeons. 'If I've been leading a whole army without any messenger pigeons, then you should be able to lead your few men without messenger pigeons!'

Oberst von der Heydte received better support from the commander of the Kampfflieger West (Bomber Flight West), General Pelz. Batteries of spotlights would form a path of light to assist the Ju 52s' take-off. A quarter of an hour before the jump, a Ju 88 flying ahead would drop four incendiaries to mark the landing zone. Furthermore, the drop zone would be lit up with light markers (called 'Christmas trees' in German) for two and a half hours after the drop, in order to make it easier for the landed troops to gather. At the same time, to the north and west of the battlegroup, dolls would be dropped by parachutes in a mock assault, to divert Allied efforts. Despite the efforts, however, Oberst von der Heydte still gave Operation Stösser only a 10 per cent chance of succeeding. The drop was planned for the night of 16/17 December 1944. The battlegroup relocated to the airfields in Paderborn and Lippspringe. Oberst von der Heydte here describes the opening phase of the action:

This Jäger is wearing his full jump gear. His knees are covered with kneepads, he is wearing his combat gloves and the parachute is on his back. As machine-gunner no. 1, he is carrying the accessories kit for the machine gun on his belt, as well as a pistol as his close-quarters weapon. The machine gun is packed into a special holder for jumps so that it could be carried on the body. After the mission in Crete, the Luftwaffe developed different packing material for the Fallschirmjäger's weapons, so that personal weapons no longer had to be thrown down with containers, leaving the Fallschirmjäger practically defenceless on the ground until they recovered the containers.

I was flying in the first plane, because I was convinced that as the leader of such an attack, I had to jump first. It was less important that I show a good example, but rather getting on the ground first meant I could quickly gather impressions of the terrain and the enemy situation, and then would have to organize and order the troops that followed. Inside the dark interior of the plane, all were quiet as a mouse, after we had sung during take-off the last verse of 'Red Shines the Sun'. Every man was alone with his thoughts. Time passed endlessly slowly. Under us was the lit-up runway, the airfield of Hangelar that had been illuminated for us, and then to the front – a flash from the artillery positions, burning houses. I looked at the light on my watch. So, what was that? According to the calculations of the pilot, based on the weather reports, we should have already been over the drop zone. Had we flown too far?

Finally! A quarter hour later than planned, the order: 'Make ready to jump!' A moment at the door, and then the sign to jump. I jumped, my wounded arm, which had not completely healed, and which I wore in a splint, was pressed firmly against my body. Something wasn't right. I was jumping with a parachute that was unknown to me, a triangular Russian model that was supposed to function without much oscillation. Yet still I was being ripped back and forth in the wind; I finally landed on the ground at a bad angle and was dragged quite a way. Apparently our weather reporters had seriously miscalculated: instead of the 4–6m/sec surface wind that was predicted at the drop zone, there was a proper storm with driving snow and a surface wind of at least 12–15m/sec. This also explained why the planes were late, because they had been fighting against the storm.

The images that greeted me at the drop zone were ghostly beautiful. Above me were the fireflies of the aircraft running lights. Like a curtain of pearls, the tracer bullets from the American light anti-aircraft artillery seeking out planes. Behind dark trees, like the fingers of a dead hand, the beams of American spotlights searched back and forth. To one side, the red light of a slowly dying blaze – a fire-bombed field. In this light, a parachute hanging from a tree looked like a spectre flickering back and forth in the wind, suddenly brightly lit, suddenly dark, seemingly alive. And then the 'Christmas tree', a torch over the area. From a distance, the flares of the German and American artillery positions; the muffled roars of an awakening artillery battle, blending with the noise of the low-flying aircraft to form an unusual harmony. I unbuckled myself, stood up, and stretched with a wonderful feeling in my heart: the feeling that only one who has jumped as a Fallschirmjäger against the enemy can know – the feeling of power, the joy of being grounded again, the expectation of adventure and the lust for action. At first I was alone. I oriented myself by the smouldering fire-bombed fields and made for the fork in the road that was the designated meeting point.

Here Oberst von der Heydte determined that during the drop, a bullet had injured him on his right forearm.

Only a few men from the battlegroup found their way with Oberst von der Heydte to the meeting point. Some aircraft had been shot down during the descent into the landing zone, but that did not fully explain why so many of the troops were missing. Later von der Heydte learnt that due to enemy anti-aircraft fire and the pilots' inexperience, the squadron had been scattered during the descent, and a few groups had mistakenly been dropped behind Bonn.

On the morning of 17 December, von der Heydte managed to gather 125 troops around him, including the forward-deployed artillery observer of the Waffen-SS and the radio section. In familiar fashion, weapons, ammunition, rations and equipment were in short supply, because the Fallschirmjäger were limited to jumping with only what they could carry. Oberst von der Heydte sent out recon troops to recover the air-dropped supply containers, but only five or six could be found. The rest were either never dropped, or had sunk in the bog. Of the heavy weapons, the Fallschirmjäger could only get their hands on one mortar, and the radio set was irreparably damaged. Things were not looking good for Operation Stösser.

Even before day broke, the Fallschirmjäger heard the sound of motors – American trucks driving by them in the semi-darkness. Once more the Fallschirmjäger, wearing camouflage coveralls and rimless combat helmets, were taken for Americans; the drivers waved amiably and passed by the troops, who were lying under cover in a ditch along the road. As it became light, Oberst von der Heydte ordered an all-round defence of the

Oberstleutnant Kayser (middle) reports on the situation to Oberst von der Heydte. The latter's already damaged right arm had been wounded again during the jump over the High Fens, and he was suffering from wound fever. Because the decisive breakthrough of the 6th Panzer Army never occurred, Oberst von der Heydte decided to lead his battlegroup back to their own lines, in order to salvage what could be saved.

fork in the forest road, and sent recon troops to learn the whereabouts of the enemy positions and to seek out contact with other German troops.

The scouts brought back valuable information about the American troop movements, assembly areas and artillery positions. Yet they had been unable to establish contact with the forces of the 6th Panzer Army, so the information they gained could neither be passed on nor productively used. On the following day, the advance guard of Sepp Dietrich's forces also failed to show up. Oberst von der Heydte sent out volunteer runners with the most important information from their recon work, including the corps orders from the US Army XVIII Corps, which had been taken from an American messenger. The runners were intercepted by the Americans, however.

On the afternoon of 18 December, an American armored recon vehicle encountered the Fallschirmjäger. A hit from a Panzerfaust did not manage to destroy the vehicle, but it at least sent it fleeing. Oberst von der Heydte recognized that the Americans by now were aware of the presence of German Fallschirmjäger behind their own lines. Because there was no more hope that members of his battlegroup would find their way to the meeting point, he gave the order to relocate farther northeast into the forest, and to go into position before the enemy recon troops could return. In the forest, his small troop met up with another 150 men under the leadership of Oberleutnant Kayser. While this addition doubled their manpower, it also increased the problems of limited ammunition and rations.

The Fallschirmjäger from Oberst von der Heydte's battlegroup managed to take numerous American prisoners, but they had to let them all go, because the situation did not allow for bringing them along.

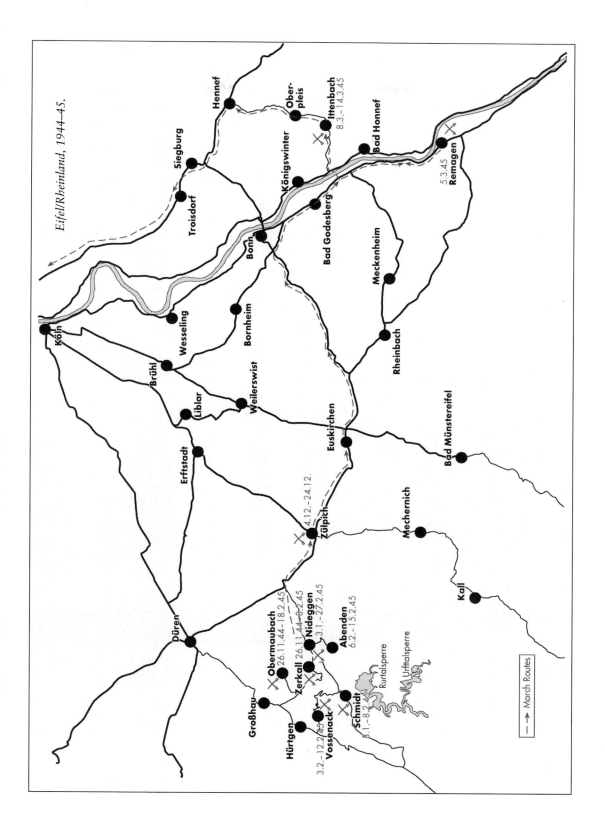

Eifel/Rheinland, 1944–45.

Hennef

Ober-
pleis

Ittenbach
8.3.–14.3.45

Königswinter

Bad Honnef

Siegburg

5.3.45
Remagen

Troisdorf

Bad Godesberg

Bonn

Meckenheim

Wesseling

Bornheim

Rheinbach

Köln

Brühl

Weilerswist

Liblar

Euskirchen

Bad Münstereifel

Erftstadt

4.12.–24.12.

Zülpich

Mechernich

Kall

Düren

Obermaubach
26.11.44–18.2.45

Nideggen
3.1.–27.2.45

Zerkall 26.11.44–8.2.45

Abenden
6.2.–15.2.45

Rurtalsperre

Urfttalsperre

Großhau

Schmidt

Hürtgen

Vossenack
3.1.–8.2.45

3.2.–12.2.45

— → March Routes

That evening, a recon unit of Fallschirmjäger brought back a dozen American prisoners. Little information was gained from these men, who were reinforcements, and because the Fallschirmjäger could not take back the prisoners, von der Heydte sent the Americans back towards the fork in the road once darkness came. He gave them a Fallschirmjäger to take along; his ankles had been injured, so he could no longer walk. He also sent along a letter written in English asking the Americans to provide for the Fallschirmjäger's medical care.

Another recon troop reported a powerful enemy patrol moving through the drop zone and the old positions. The presence of company-strength American search parties caused the battlegroup to switch their positions daily. Oberst von der Heydte continued to carry out his own energetic recon activities, but the planned advance of the 6th Panzer Army still failed to appear. The recon troops now had frequent contact with the enemy and entered into short but fierce firefights. They took prisoners again, who also eventually had to be released.

Meanwhile, the rations situation was serious. The emergency rations that the

Oberst von der Heydte sent out recon troops to gather information about enemy activities. This Fallschirmjäger is writing a short report for the Oberst. His combat pack lies on the ground, along with a grenade close at hand. He is wearing camouflaged coveralls (the third model) and has camouflaged his helmet with twigs. An ammunition bandolier is hanging around his neck for his weapon, a Karabiner 98k rifle.

Fallschirmjäger had carried with them on the drop had long been used up, and ammunition was low. While a Ju 88 threw down a supply container near them, it only held drinking water and wet cigarettes, nothing that the battlegroup really needed; there was no lack of drinking water in the snowy Eifel region.

On 20 December, Oberst von der Heydte decided to call off the operation and lead the battlegroup back to their own lines. His scouts reported that strong American forces with armoured support were conducting search parties in all directions. It was only a matter of time before the Fallschirmjäger were discovered and forced into an engagement with an enemy who greatly outnumbered them.

Indeed there were numerous enemy battalions taking part in combing through the High Fens. The American leadership suspected that at least a complete German Fallschirmjäger division was involved in the deployment. Even more US battalions were detailed to secure the supply depots and command posts. In this way, the German battlegroup, just by their presence, diverted a large number of US troops who were desperately needed at the front.

After a short but intense firefight with American troops on 21 December, Oberst von der Heydte dissolved his battlegroup into small teams no larger than three men each; they were to make their own way back to their lines in the east. He figured that small teams had a much higher chance of making it through than the combined force. Alone with his adjutant and one combat messenger, he and his two men set off, as he recounts:

> On the way another group of young Fallschirmjäger tried to join up with us; they thought that I was the surest way for them to reach the German front. They did not understand it when I rejected them harshly and curtly forbade them to follow me. They did not see the tears that welled up against my will as I watched them walk away after this last gruff dressing-down that I had to give them.

Feldwebel Wolfgang Langer near Steenbergen. He does not carry heavy equipment, not even a breadbag, messkit or canteen. The magazine pouches on his belt are worn without the support of Y-straps.

On the night of 23 December, Oberst von der Heydte – tired, hungry, physically depleted and suffering from a high fever –

reached Monschau, the place where the 6th Panzer Army was supposed to have started their offensive on the first day. It appeared that the city was still (or once again) in American hands. The group split up and everyone sought out shelter and food for himself. Oberst von der Heydte knocked on the door of a remote house occupied by a secondary school teacher named Bouschery. The teacher and his family took him in and gave him care, food and shelter for the night. The stress of the last few days, the lack of sustenance and the sleep deprivation had all driven von der Heydte into a fever and a state of complete physical collapse. During the night, his fever climbed even higher, making it impossible for him to march any further the following day. In order not to endanger the teacher and his family any further, von der Heydte wrote the following letter to the military leadership in Monschau. The son of the Bouschery family carried the letter to the Hotel Horchem, where American officers were staying:

Dear Sirs!

I was attempting to reach the German troops near Monschau. Because I have not found any German soldiers here, I am surrendering myself, because I am wounded and at the end of my physical strength. Please be so kind as to send me a doctor and an ambulance, as I am unable to walk. I can be found in bed at Herr Bouschery's house, where I await your help and orders.

Respectfully yours,
Freiherr von der Heydte
Oberst
Commander of the German Fallschirmjäger troops in the Eupen-Malmedy area.

The Americans surrounded the house with a full company of soldiers and took Oberst von der Heydte prisoner. He was taken to a nearby hotel, where he received medical treatment. Only when he was in a prisoner-of-war camp in England did von der Heydte learn that a large portion of his battlegroup had made it back to their own lines unharmed.

CHAPTER NINE

The Final Battle in the Homeland, 1945

While Operation Stösser was underway, FJR 6 was embroiled in combat with the Americans. Even though the offensive in the Ardennes was carried out with great panache, it only marginally took the pressure off them. It became clear that the Americans were trying to circumnavigate and cut off the Fallschirmjäger' positions from the north and south, yet the Fallschirmjäger were able to fight off every American attack on their positions in the Kall Valley.

II./FJR 6 valiantly held their ground at the Maubach bridgehead, even though their losses increased daily. Hauptmann Rolf Mager, the seasoned commander of the 2nd Battalion, counted among the fallen. When the bridgehead was relocated to its original position in the last days of December, the rest of the battalion, in battlegroups, went into positions at Froitscheid, Vossenack and Abenden. The 3rd Battalion followed on the eastern shore of the Rur River from Untermaubach to Abenden.

On 10 January 1945, the Americans renewed their attacks in the Kall Valley. They managed to take a few German bunkers at Raffelsbrand and Ochsenkopf. Yet they came to a standstill when faced by the strongly reinforced Fallschirmjäger positions in the forest on the southern slope of the Kall Valley. With utmost effort, the Americans then managed to take the remaining positions in Ochsenkopf inch by inch. The fight in the

At the end of December 1944, battlegroups of the 3rd Battalion were still holding down their defensive positions in this mountain range near Nideggen and Obermaubach.

snow-locked Eifel region was difficult for the US troops. In contrast to the German defenders, who could rely on their experience of winter warfare in Russia, the Americans attacks often ground to a halt purely on account of the extreme weather. The temperatures of around -20°C inflicted cold-weather casualties upon the Americans.

Some of FJR 6 relocated to positions on the Schwammenauel River dam to reinforce army units deployed there, because as part of a spring offensive the Americans were advancing with armour-reinforced divisions. Here the Fallschirmjäger also managed to fight off the American attacks.

Manfred Vogt was deployed during these days as a dispatch rider:

I could no longer march because of my leg wound sustained in the Holland campaign, but I could still work as a driver and dispatch rider. Every trip as a messenger was truly a suicide mission, because, from their positions, the Americans had an overview of whole sectors. I would have barely arrived and they would start shooting with heavy-calibre weapons. The Americans did not hold back with their artillery in the Eifel region. With every trip I took at night, I was happy if I was not attacked by fighter-bombers. During the day, I was frequently followed by the aircraft, but at least I could jump off the motorcycle quickly and throw myself in a ditch by the road to survive the attack.

As they had the previous November, the Americans tried again at the beginning of February to take the Schmidt area. The attempt to advance from Vossenack to Schmidt had failed bloodily; now the Americans advanced again through the evacuated Kall Valley.

In Schmidt, combat teams of II./FJR 6, amongst others, were lying in well-fortified positions. Despite the Americans adopting new tactics, therefore, the attack on Schmidt proved to be a difficult undertaking, and the Americans suffered heavy losses. Even the first step, an advance via Strauch and Hechelscheidt, did not go according to plan, and there were many casualties incurred against the elastic German defence. The Germans also managed to hold Steckenborn down to their last cartridge, which in turn took a heavy toll in blood on the American forces. All such fighting and losses happened before US troops had even reached Schmidt, the objective of their operation. Finally, American artillery and air attacks leveled Steckenborn. Other American units were advancing at the time on Kommerscheidt; they reached the edge of Schmidt on the evening of 5 February.

After their forward-deployed recon troops became caught and held by fierce machine-gun crossfire, the Americans pulled back to the nearby edge of a forest. Overnight further reinforcements arrived, including tank units, and the Americans began their assault anew in the morning.

Schmidt became a death trap for the Americans. The Fallschirmjäger of the 2nd Battalion had experience in Carentan and Hoogerheide/Woensdrecht that made them old hands at urban warfare . They had built up their positions well, creating overlapping fields of fire in town squares and alleys, making it practically impossible for the Americans to advance. Enemy tanks fell into Fallschirmjäger traps and had to be taken out with close-combat weapons, because the Fallschirmjäger had few Panzerfausts left. The Americans had to take Schmidt house-by-house, while suffering heavy losses. Once again the lions of Carentan proved themselves to be tough and talented fighters, who demanded a high price in manpower from the enemy before they surrendered their positions.

The battle raged for five days, with the Americans repeatedly sending fresh and well-equipped troops with tank support into battle, a luxury that the German defenders could not afford. After a fierce struggle, the Germans finally retreated from Schmidt on the afternoon of 10 February. The survivors of II./FJR 6 were the last to disengage from the enemy, as they covered the retreat of their own troops.

Experiencing heavy losses, the Americans took the German positions at Schwammenauel over the next few days. Nonetheless, an engineer team managed to blow an bottom outlet pipe on the reservoir dam, as well as the pressure pipes of the Heimbach powerplant. These actions, coupled with the high water at the Rur River dam and at the artificial Urft Lake due to snow melt, caused the water level of the Rur to rise by a whole metre, and flooded the Auen. In this way, the Germans managed to delay the American advance across the Rur to the Rhine area by at least two weeks. This American push to the Rhine was planned as the beginning of a large-scale offensive codenamed Operation Grenade.

In order to avoid being surrounded, FJR 6 pulled back via Nideggen and Berg to the line Wollersheim–Embken. Here Oberst Henke called together all remaining regimental battlegroups and formed them into the Regimental Battlegroup FJR 6, made from the survivors of the battles in the Eifel; they could not even form a complete battalion.

Now subordinated to the FJR 3, the regiment went into position in Wollersheim and defended their sector against the Americans with great bravery. When the US forces attacked Wollersheim with three reinforced divisions, however, the Fallschirmjäger had to pull back on 1 March, and retreat in a delaying action via Zülpich and Euskirchen to Bad Godesberg on the Rhine.

This retreat was not really a unified effort, because individual combat teams from FJR 6 remained at this time to form a rearguard, and offer protection on the flanks. Scattered members of the regiment were also trying, individually and in small groups, to find their way back to their battalion, as Heinrich Fugmann remembers:

Because we were in danger of being trapped by American tank units, I fled in the night with an Oberjäger medic towards Füssenich, through a forested area that the Americans already occupied. There I was stopped by a higher officer and ordered to defend the area together with 8.8cm anti-aircraft units who were trying to prevent the Americans' advance to the Rhine and on Cologne. Because here, too, we were in danger of being encircled, I tried to escape towards Zülpich. In the darkness, I came to a village and discovered a dampened light from the cellar windows. After quietly knocking on the window, an old man opened the house door to me. He stared wide-eyed at me and waved me in without hesitating. He asked where I was from, because the Americans were also in this area. Frozen through and hungry, I sat down in his cellar. First I changed into dry clothes and then the man gave me army bread with treacle to appease my great hunger.

I asked him where I was and how I could make it back to the German units at the front. After a few hours of sleep, I wanted to try to escape through this occupied area at dawn. It had snowed a bit in the night, giving me a better view over the terrain. I made it through to the city of Zülpich and reached a railway embankment there. I had just climbed over this to reach the other side along some freight cars, when I must have been recognized and explosives flew every which way around me. Under constant fire I reached the railway embankment on the other side. Peering over the embankment, I saw the outlines of a tank. There was no way through here for me. The Americans must have thought that they were dealing with a combat patrol, because they kept shooting in my direction. It took a full half hour before some soldiers approached me and I walked out from behind the embankment with hands held high.

Because the Americans had firmly established their bridgehead at Remagen, FJR 6 was deployed to attack the positions they held there. One more time the remaining companies moved decisively to storm their opponents, but they were beaten back by the American firepower, who had superior numbers on their side. With their remaining, weak forces, FJR 6 was unable to complete the task of containing the bridgehead, and they withdrew towards Bad Godesberg.

Reduced to just a few companies, and almost without heavy weapons, FJR 6 crossed the Rhine by Niederdolldendorf and took up lodging for the night in Oberpleis. The following day the regiment went into position in the Margarenthenhöhe in Ittenbach. This was the highest point of the mountain range across from Königswinter, and formed a natural fortress with its steep slopes, forests, thick undergrowth and jagged ravines.

Oberst Henke's regimental command post was in a quarry that made up the centre of the Fallschirmjäger positions. It was not really possible to build extensive trenches because the ground was still mostly frozen through; however, the area could be utilized well as a natural system of defence.

Four American infantry battalions swarmed from Königswinter towards Ittenbach. Tanks climbed the single road up the mountain, but were blocked by an abatis and then incapacitated by the Fallschirmjäger's heavy defensive fire. For several days, the Americans stormed the heights without managing to break through the German lines; the American infantry was unable to throw the Fallschirmjäger out of their position.

Eugen Griesser remembers the US assault:

It was hard enough for the Americans to make it up the steep mountain. In some parts they had to sling their weapons around their necks and climb the slope on all fours. Our foxholes were so well covered in the thick undergrowth that the Americans usually needed to be only one or two steps away just to be able to spot us. From that short distance, they were too surprised to exchange fire with us, and so in this way we drove the Americans back down the mountain. When they realized that they couldn't take our positions this way, they began to shoot at us with heavy-calibre weapons from the opposite shore of the Rhine. Even more dangerous than the artillery fire were the mortars that were blasting us from Königswinter, especially when the shells would explode in trees above us, causing splinters of wood to mix in with the shrapnel flying through the air, so-called Baumkrepierer [tree explosions].

In addition, the Allied air forces were still flying bombing raids over our position, so that after a few days the upper ridge was practically completely caved up. On 13 March, enemy fire increased and the Americans sent their infantry up the hill again. This time they came in such huge numbers that it was difficult to beat off their attack. On this day I took shrapnel in my right forearm and was sent to the main first aid station in Ittenbach. There I found rows and rows of wounded. The doctors, medics and nurses weren't able to move quickly enough to deal with all the wounded coming in.

Meanwhile on the Margarethenhöhe a bitter fight developed, sometimes with only weapons, shovels and fists. The Fallschirmjäger fought fiercely against the enemy, but on 14 March the Americans captured Oberst Henke, the regimental staff and most of the surviving Fallschirmjäger. Eugen Griesser here reflects on the moment of surrender:

From outside we heard the sounds of motors and voices, apparently Americans. I looked out the window and saw that the school had been surrounded by Americans. That meant that our position on the Margarethenhöhe must have fallen, because otherwise the Americans would not have been able to get up the mountain pass from Königswinter to Ittenbach. I still had my submachine gun, a few hand grenades and my 08, and a few others were armed, too, but it would have been insanity to defend the whole first aid station, and to try to shoot our way out would have been pure suicide. A staff doctor who spoke English collected our weapons and went out. A little while later the Americans moved into the school and took us prisoners.

Those in the FJR 6 who remained deployed – the men who had escaped capture – went around Ittenbach and withdrew to the old positions of FJR 9 on the Öl Mountain by Oberpleis. In Oberpleis the Fallschirmjäger encountered a regimental column, a motor vehicle unit, a maintenance troop and a WuG troop. In compliance with their last order, the regiment fell back to Haiger. In a soap factory there, the remaining men of FJR 6 took shelter. They quickly took off again, however, when they realized that an arms factory was located directly next door. Surely it would soon become a target for the air attacks. Only two days later both the soap factory and arms factory lay in rubble.

The Battlegroup FJR 6 received the order to relocate via Gummersbach to the Ruhr district, because the remaining Fallschirmjäger were being gathered for a defensive battle against the Allies. Following orders, FJR 6 withdrew to the Ruhr pocket. Every day the situation became more and more confused, and individual members of FJR 6 were caught up in the chaos of the last few weeks of the war. Reinhold Schmidt, deployed at the time as a driver for the regimental staff, drove in a captured American vehicle back and forth across Germany, from the headquarters on the front to one unit and then to the next. His trip took him through the forests in Thuringia to Halle on the Saale River. In his vehicle, he had war diaries and personal documents from the regiment. In Halle he was assigned to a personnel replacement transfer battalion and was then sent into combat, this time on the Eastern Front, which was closing tighter around Germany. In the confusion of those days, the documents went missing.

Once more in March 1945, the Luftwaffe tried to form a new FJR 6 from the surviving men and the members of the Fallschirmjäger Convalescence Battalion. General Student was personally involved in the reorganization – this photo shows him inspecting the Fallschirmjäger Convalescence Battalion in Stendal. Despite the efforts of the High Command, they did not manage to rebuild a regiment capable of battle.

After the last firefights, which caused further losses to the FJR 6 battlegroup, the few remaining Fallschirmjäger gathered on 16 April 1945 in a farmhouse near Velbert. The barn offered a comfortable place to spend the night, and the farmer gave them something to eat and fresh milk. Everybody knew that the end was nigh. Obergefreiter Wübbold buried the WuG weapons that were no longer needed at the edge of a field, so that they wouldn't fall into enemy hands.

In the morning, the Fallschirmjäger heard the rattle of tracks: American tanks approaching the farmhouse, and infantry with them in half-track vehicles. The Americans surrounded the farmhouse; later the Fallschirmjäger found out that a traitor from the area had tipped off the Americans to their presence in the barn. In the face of the numerical superiority of the US troops, the Fallschirmjäger offered no more resistance. Enough blood had been spilt.

Thus, on 17 April 1945, the last force of FJR 6 went into American captivity. In an act of desperation, there was talk in March 1945 of reforming FJR 6 from those injured men from the Fallschirmjäger Convalescence Battalion who had recovered enough to re-enter battle. But during a visit to the new camp in Stendal, General Student decided that there were not enough combat-ready Fallschirmjäger for this undertaking.

Until 8 May 1945, scattered members of FJR 6, or those who had been released from the hospital, continued to fight on German ground. Some of them were thrown into battle on the Eastern Front in different Fallschirmjäger regiments, or deployed in the defence of the capital, Berlin.

CHAPTER TEN

Peace

The story of FJR 6 does not end on 17 April 1945 in Velbert. In June 1978, after a trip to their former deployment area in Normandy organized by Herbert Hasenclever, the survivors of the regiment founded the Fellowship of the 6th Fallschirmjäger Regiment. Under the motto 'Come along and don't hesitate!', the former regimental commander, now Brigadegeneral der Reserve (Brigade General of the Reserves), Professor August Freiherr von der Heydte, gave the celebratory speech for the founding of the Fellowship:

The present is not meant for thinking too much of memories, living in the past, looking backwards. It demands that one turn his gaze to what is ahead of him, it demands engagement in the here and now. All of us, regardless of how old we are, must live for the future, and not for the past. The founding of this fellowship of our regiment also falls under this dictate. We are not a league or an association; we are not here to found a new union in addition to the many others out there, nor a club nor a weekly discussion table, where we sit and do nothing else but exchange memories and tell ourselves the same stories over and over.

Surely, we want to keep our memories, we do not want to forget the selfless actions of young men. We will never forget or be silent when it comes to the sacrifices of our best comrades. Yet when we think back on that difficult time that bound us together as a unit in comradeship, then we want to draw conclusions for today and tomorrow from that which we have experienced. In order to do this together, we meet again in the company of our old regiment...

To be a Fallschirmjäger once means to be a Fallschirmjäger for life. The Fallschirmjäger remains duty-bound until his death, and in his fulfilment of duty he also remains a volunteer until death. This willingness to take troubles and hardship upon himself and give his life for others, this belongs to the inner core of a Fallschirmjäger. In his training, the Fallschirmjäger was not forced to jump, in the war he was not forced into battle. He who has led Fallschirmjäger in missions knows that they did not need to be ordered to follow the example of their military leader.

To be a Fallschirmjäger means to be a volunteer, in the deepest sense of the word [Freiwilliger in German, 'one of free will']. Without volunteerism – exercising free will – there can be no freedom. It is no coincidence that we have come together on June 17th to found our regimental fellowship. Twenty-five years ago in another part of Germany, young workers stood up to fight for their freedom from oppression! [A workers' uprising against communist rule in East Germany, crushed by Soviet forces.] ...

We Fallschirmjäger know the meaning of freedom, perhaps better than some others. We know that freedom has nothing to do with a lack of bonds, and nothing to do with chance or arbitrariness. Freedom is self-determination, is the free choice of a goal and of the way of shaping one's life. It is the determination to follow this goal and to have the power over one's own existence.

Freedom is, on the other hand, responsibility for oneself, for the goal one chose and for the means one used to reach that goal. We know about the nature of freedom, because we were once volunteers, and because we will remain so. Freedom stands and falls with free will. And when there are no more volunteers, no more people with the independence to sacrifice their lives for freedom, then there will soon no longer be any freedom. This is the true lesson of 17 June 1953, and 25 years later we should not forget that. If we do, then the freedom that we enjoy here will be a freedom that exists only for a limited time.

'So to be a Fallschirmjäger means to be one with free will. It means to be ready to sacrifice everything without hesitation, including one's own life. But sacrifices should only go to values that one recognizes, and not for goods that one values more than that which one is ready to sacrifice. To be a Fallschirmjäger means to recognize these values and to stand with them. This is the heart of the question about why we are founding a fellowship of our regiment.

Surely, at first we would like to see each other, to hear how the men are doing, men with whom we lay down together in the mud, with whom we froze in Russia, with whom we baked under the North African sun, with whom we experienced the rolling barrage of the Americans above us in Normandy, and with whom we tried to stop the advance of British tanks in southern Holland. We want to exchange our memories of the bitter and the happy times. We want to renew previous comradeship, which we all need in order to find strength and optimism. Because to give his life meaning, man needs other men, similarly minded men around him; he needs assurance that he does not stand alone. We want to give each other this assurance.

We want to commemorate our dead comrades and stand by the side of their relatives when they need us! We want all of this, but there's more that we want, too!

First and foremost, we want to cultivate and pass on the spirit that filled us and drove us when we still wore uniforms, the spirit of our unit, the spirit of the Fallschirmjäger – the willingness to sacrifice and to commit ourselves to higher values. The great European Charles de Gaulle described this spirit: 'For the Fallschirmjäger, war means danger, daring and loneliness. They all head out, and are left to their own devices behind enemy lines. So they lose their dead and they reap their fame. May everything that lies beneath be silent. They look up to the heavens without blanching, and they look down to earth without blushing.'

The Fallschirmjäger spirit could not be better described. We want to keep this spirit alive in our fellowship and pass it on to the youth who will follow us and who will need role models. Because preserving this Fallschirmjäger spirit means being a role model, today in peace just as it did during wartime. Being a role model for youth who yearn for this spirit and have to resort to following idols, because they are lacking ideals. Behind this ideal stands an ethos; behind the idol only emptiness.

A Fallschirmjäger ethos exists and we want to cultivate this in our fellowship. It will take over the task of 'inner leadership'. We want to foster this spirit, even though others may shake their heads, criticize or even insult us. We have always gone our own way without looking to the right and left, and we want do keep doing so! Come along, comrade, and do not hesitate, come along!

The men of FJR 6 not only participated in reconstruction work in post-war Germany as skilled workers, civil servants, engineers and teachers; their valuable military experience also contributed to the founding of the Bundeswehr. Former officers and NCOs formed the pool for the new airborne troops of the Bundeswehr. As noted above, the previous commander of the regiment, Oberst von der Heydte, was promoted to Brigadegeneral der Reserve, and sent on a special mission to Egypt by the foreign minister Heinrich Brentano, to build up and train the paratroopers there in the German model.

Since 17 June 1978, the Fellowship has held annual meetings in Germany as well as trips to the former war zones and combat areas. In France and Holland, they are always warmly welcomed as guests, and well respected. Under the mottoes 'Out of enemies become friends' and 'For peace in freedom', they fellowship has also maintained contact with the veterans groups of their former opponents, in particular to that of the US 90th Infantry Division. Since 1979 the men of FJR 6 and their former American opponents have cultivated a friendly relationship through exchange visits.

As an expression of their aspirations for peace and understanding among nations, the Fellowship of the 6th Fallschirmjäger Regiment dedicated a young tree in the peace park of the war cemetery at La Cambe in Normandy. Furthermore, the Fellowship regularly visits the graves of their fallen comrades – in Marigny, La Cambe, Orglandes, Mont-de-Huisnes, Recogne-Bastogne, Lommel, Isselstein and Ittenbach. Countless fallen Fallschirmjäger remained as unknown soldiers in scattered cemeteries, or in Italy or Russia; these men, too, are not forgotten.

In June 2004, the Fellowship took another trip to Normandy to remember past times, visit their fallen comrades and renew their friendships with former opponents. They stayed in the same hotel as the veterans of the US 101st Airborne Division, the men with whom they had fought over the city of Carentan. They were invited to provide the funeral escort for the body of one of their comrades, which had only recently been uncovered near St Lô. He was buried in La Cambe. At the personal invitation of the

French president Jacques Chirac, 18 members of the Fellowship took part in the official commemoration service with the German chancellor Gerhard Schröder on 6 June in Caen. On 7 June, they met again with their comrades from the US 90th Infantry Division, and both sides laid commemorative wreaths to the fallen on the memorial for the division on the battlefield of Sèves Island. Members of the Traditionskompanie FJR 6 (Traditions Company FJR 6; a re-enactment group, but also a group that participates in the Fellowship) from Germany, the United States and Greece stood honour guard at the memorial stone. Once more, perhaps for the last time in their lives, the Fallschirmjäger met the former enemies as friends.

Colonel Edward Hamilton, who was the company commander in the 90th Infantry Division, and today is the leader of their division's fellowship, said on 7 June 2004: 'We never hated you. You were hard and tough opponents. But you fought fairly and that's why enemies can become friends.'

Even though these days, death has ripped many holes in the ranks of the comrades, due to sickness and age, the men of FJR 6 continue to this day to walk the path described by their former commander on 17 June 1978, in the spirit of the Fallschirmjäger:

> If one of us becomes tired,
> The other keeps watch for him!
> If one of us should doubt,
> The other smiles faithfully!
> If one of us should fall,
> The other stands for two!
> For God has attached to every warrior,
> His comrade!
>
> Loyalty for Loyalty!

Appendices

Fallschirmjäger Ranks and their Allied Equivalents

Reichsmarschall	No equivalent
Generalfeldmarschall	General (5 star)
Generaloberst	General
General der Flieger (etc)	Lieutenant General
Generalleutnant	Major General
Generalmajor	Brigadier General
Oberst	Colonel
Oberstleutnant	Lieutenant Colonel
Major	Major
Hauptmann	Captain
Oberleutnant	1st Lieutenant
Leutnant	2nd Lieutenant
Stabsfeldwebel	Sergeant Major
Oberfähnrich	Warrant Officer First Class
Oberfeldwebel	Master sergeant
Feldwebel	Senior sergeant
Fähnrich	Warrant Officer Second Class
Unterfeldwebel	Sergeant
Oberjäger	Corporal
Hauptgefreiter	No equivalent
Obergefreiter	No equivalent
Gefreiter	Private First Class
Jäger	Private

Staffing
FJR 6 in spring 1943

Regimental staff and support companies

Regimental Commander:	Major Liebach
	(occasionally Oberstleutnant Meder-Eggbert)
Adjutant:	Hauptmann Eisenbarth
Aide-de-camp:	Oberleutnant Graf
IVa Divisionsintendant	Stabzahlmeister Hesse
(Division Director):	
WuG (Weapons and Equipment):	Oberleutnant Franke
Vehicles Officer:	Oberleutnant Hofmann
13th Company	Hauptmann Faller
	Oberleutnant Harjes
	Oberleutnant Schmidt
	Oberleutnant Beier
	Leutnant Wedding
	Leutnant Doll
14th Company	Hauptmann Gantzer
	Hauptmann Leyerer

I./FJR 6

Battalion Commander:	Hauptmann Tannert
	Hauptmann Matheas
	Hauptmann Finzel
Adjutant:	Oberleutnant Billion
	Oberleutnant Eikmeier
IVa Division Director:	Oberzahlmeister Appel
Doctor:	Dr Dobra
	Dr Müller
1st Company:	Oberleutnant Donner
	Oberleutnant Wörner
2nd Company:	Oberleutnant Hamer
	Leutnant Bittkowski
	Leutnant Buschmeyer
	Leutnant Regenbrecht
	Oberfeldwebel Harbig

3rd Company:

Oberleutnant Finzel
Oberleutnant Billion
Oberleutnant Donner
Oberleutnant Westphal
Leutnant Kaup
Leutnant Schlömann

4th Company:

Hauptmann Sauter
Hauptmann Finzel
Oberleutnant Schaufelberger
Hauptfeldwebel Schick

II./FJR 6

Battalion Commander: Major Gericke
Adjutant: Leutnant Angele
WuG: Leutnant Falk
Aide-de-camp: Leutnant Christiansen
IVa Division Director: Head Inspector Stork
Signal Communications Platoon: Leutnant Schindler
Doctor: Staff Dr Zänkler
                                   Staff Dr Gockel

5th Company:

Oberleutnant Loerzer
Oberleutnant Knaus
Leutnant Düwell

6th Company:

Oberleutnant Nietzschke
Oberleutnant Brehde
Leutnant Späing
Leutnant Kiewitz

7th Company:

Oberleutnant Thomsen
Leutnant Angele
Leutnant Simon

9th Company:

Oberleutnant Engelhardt
Oberleutnant Weiß
Leutnant Kummer
Leutnant Schöffler

III./FJR 6

Battalion Commander:	Major Pelz
	Hauptmann Krammling
Adjutant:	Oberleutnant Gruber
	Leutnant Neumann
Aide-de-camp:	Leutnant Mohrmann
IVa Division Director:	Staff Paymaster Eckhardt
Signal Communications Platoon:	Leutnant Meier
Doctor:	Staff Doctor Weber

9th Company:

Oberleutnant Metheder
Leutnant Kleiner
Leutnant Lucke
Oberleutnant Schulz
Leutnant Botterweck

10th Company:

Hauptmann Sprockhoff
Oberleutnant Hofmann
Leutnant Ebell
Hauptfeldwebel Schierle

11th Company:

Oberleutnant Kaths
Leutnant Kaup
Leutnant Karcher
Leutnant Linnert
Hauptfeldwebel Schlicht

12th Company:

Oberleutnant Heck
Hauptmann Herterich
Hauptmann Voss
Oberleutnant Grosse
Leutnant Hessel

FJR 6 in Russia 1943–44

Battalion Commander:	Hauptmann Finzel
	Hauptmann Matheas
	Hauptmann Hamer
Adjutant:	Hauptmann Eikmeier
	Hauptfeldwebel Kühne
IVa Division Director:	Oberzahlmeister Appel
Doctor:	Dr Dobra
	Assistant Dr Müller
1st Company:	Oberleutnant Wörner
	Oberleutnant Auerbach
	Hauptfeldwebel Wagner
2nd Company:	Oberleutnant Hamer
	Leutnant Buschmeyer
	Leutnant Regenbrecht
	Leutnant Bittkowski
	Oberfeldwebel Harbig
3rd Company:	Hauptmann Donner
	Leutnant Höpfner
	Leutnant Kaup
	Hauptfeldwebel Kühne
4th Company:	Oberleutnant Schaufelberger
	Leutnant Höhne
	Oberfeldwebel Helpa
	Oberfeldwebel Linnig
	Oberfeldwebel Schulz

FJR 6 from February 1944 to April 1945

Regimental staff

Regimental Commander:	Major von der Heydte
	Oberst Henke
Adjutant:	Hauptmann Peiser
	Oberleutnant Schlichting
	Oberleutnant Kayser
Hauptmann beim Stabe (Staff Captain):	Major Lembach
Aide-de-camp:	Hauptmann Schulte
	Oberleutnant Mundt
K-Offizier:	Oberleutnant Aringer
	Feldwebel Gaujahn
Ia 1st General Staff Officer:	Feldwebel Breu
Ib 2nd General Staff Officer:	Feldwebel Kugel
	Feldwebel Wern
IVa Division Director:	Stabszahlmeister Schmidt
	Oberzahlmeister Braunschweig
WuG:	Oberinspektor Wern
Signal Communications Platoon:	Oberleutnant Dietrich
	Fahnenjunker-Feldwebel Mertens
Staff Company:	Feldwebel Rumbach
Reconaissance Platoon:	Leutnant von Cube
Doctor:	Staff Dr Ross
	Staff Dr Thalheim
Baggage Train Leader:	Feldwebel Mellefahrt

I./FJR 6

Battalion Commander:	Hauptmann Preikschat
	Hauptmann Zierer
	Hauptmann Bartmetler
	Hauptmann Peiser
Adjutant:	Oberleutnant Reese
	Leutnant Waschke
Aide-de-camp:	Hauptmann Seeliger
IVa Division Director:	Zahlmeister Frotzem
Doctor:	Staff Dr Ferl
	Assistant Doctor Kienzlen
1st Company:	Oberleutnant Preikschat
	Oberleutnant Billion

Leutnant Meyer
Leutnant Gradler
Oberfeldwebel Elsner
Oberfeldwebel Niemann
Leutnant Hosp

2nd Company:

Oberleutnant Schulz
Leutnant Kaul
Oberfähnrich Ortland
Oberleutnant Beck
Leutnant Stenzel
Leutnant Hörr
Leutnant Schünemann
Leutnant von Venroy

3rd Company:

Hauptmann Bucher
Leutnant Then
Leutnant Stenzel
Oberleutnant Kreßmann
Fähnrich Hagemann
Oberleutnant Knaussed
Oberleutnant Lange
Leutnant Müller

4th Company:

Leutnant Scherer
Leutnant Hossfeld
Leutnant Krüger
Leutnant Kretschmer
Oberfeldwebel Uhlig
Leutnant Hartmann
Leutnant Merbach

II./FJR 6
Battalion Commander:

Hauptmann Mager
Hauptmann Reimer
Hauptmann Mlak
Hauptmann von Hütz

Adjutant:

Hauptmann Schulte
Oberleutnant Schlichting

Aide-de-camp:

Hauptmann Hasenclever
Hauptmann Schernbeck

Battalion Battledress:	Feldwebel Kogel
Doctor:	Feldwebel Huskotte
	Staff Dr Holtz
	Dr Beißel
	Assistant Dr Blisee
5th Company:	Hauptmann Hermann
	Leutnant Holtz
	Fähnrich Köhne
	Oberleutnant Bette
6th Company:	Leutnant Brunnklaus
	Leutnant Thym
	Leutnant Holtz
	Leutnant Runge
	Leutnant Hanig
	Leutnant Schlagen
7th Company:	Leutnant von Socha-Borzestowski
	Oberleutnant Endres
	Leutnant Gänzle
	Feldwebel Netzel
	Leutnant Keilwagen
	Leutnant Niermann
8th Company:	Oberleutnant Count Bethusy-Hoc
	Leutnant Naupert
	Leutnant Köhne
	Oberfeldwebel Uhlig
	Leutnant Niermann
	Leutnant Köhne

III./FJR 6

Battalion Commander:	Hauptmann Trebes
	Hauptmann Dobbeler
	Oberleutnant Ulmer
Adjutant:	Leutnant Treuherz
	Leutnant Doppelstein
	Leutnant Wagner
Aide-de-camp:	Oberleutnant Ulmer
	Leutnant Treuherz

IVa Division Director:	Zahlmeister Stucke
	Oberzahlmeister Braunschweig
Signal Communications Platoon:	Oberleutnant Seibert
	Leutnant Mühlberger
Baggage Train Leader:	Hauptmann Wagner
Doctor:	Dr Schad
9th Company:	Oberleutnant Wagner
	Leutnant Röpnack
	Oberleutnant Trumbach
	Leutnant Schenkenhofer
	Leutnant Schröder
10th Company:	Oberleutnant Priebe
	Leutnant Carmesin
	Leutnant Klug
	Leutnant Le Coutre
	Leutnant Lansing
11th Company:	Oberleutnant Märk
	Leutnant Bickhauser
	Leutnant Eisermann
	Leutnant von Venroy
	Leutnant Hoffmann
12th Company:	Oberleutnant Pöppel
	Leutnant Schrader
	Oberfeldwebel Peters
	Oberfeldwebel Deutsch
	Feldwebel Ohm
	Oberfähnrich Doppelstein
	Feldwebel Behne

IV./FJR 6

Battalion Commander:	Hauptmann Dobbeler
13th Company:	Oberleutnant Nahde
	Leutnant Cleemann
	Leutnant Degen
	Feldwebel Köner
	Oberfeldwebel Schilling

14th Company:	Leutnant Geck
	Leutnant Bauer
	Leutnant Meckel
15th Company:	Hauptmann Hauck
	Leutnant Degenkolbe
	Leutnant Adams
	Feldwebel Völz
16th Company:	Leutnant von Cube
	Feldwebel Ahrenholz
	Feldwebel Radlhammer
	Oberfeldwebel Geiß
	Oberfeldwebel Uhlig
	Oberfeldwebel Dietrich
	Leutnant Wiegand
17th Company:	Major Henke

Military Postal Codes Index
FJR 6 from February to September 1944

Regimental Staff:	L 49 323
Staffs Company:	L 49 323
1a Convoy:	L 49 323
Combat Platoon:	L 49 323
Pioneer Platoon:	L 62 056
Signal Communications Platoon:	L 49 323

I./FJR 6

Battalion Staff:	L 49 057 A
Signal Communications Platoon:	L 49 057 A
1st Company:	L 49 057 B
2nd Company:	L 49 057 C
3rd Company:	L 49 057 D
4th Company:	L 49 057 E

II./FJR 6

Battalion Staff:	L 55 056 A
Signal Communications Platoon:	L 55 056 A

5th Company:	L 55 056 B
6th Company:	L 55 056 C
7th Company:	L 56 056 D
8th Company:	L 55 056 E

III./FJR 6

Battalion Staff:	L 50 370 A
Signal Communications Platoon:	L 50 370 A
9th Company:	L 50 370 B
10th Company:	L 50 370 C
11th Company:	L 50 370 D
12th Company:	L 50 370 E

IV./FJR 6

Battalion Staff:	unknown
Signal Communications Platoon:	unknown
13th Company:	L 50 023
14th Company:	L 52 556
15th Company:	L 62 056
16th Company:	L 49 323

Identification Tags/Dog Tag MOB Numbers Index

Regimental Staff:	256 165
Staff Company:	256 165
1a Convoy:	256 165
Combat Platoon:	256 165 C
Pioneer Platoon:	256 165 B
Signal Communications Platoon:	256 165 A

I./FJR 6

Battalion Staff:	256 168
Signal Communications Platoon:	256 168
1st Company:	256 169
2d Company:	256 170
3d Company:	256 171
4th Company:	256 172

II./FJR 6

Battalion Staff:	256 173
Signal Communications Platoon:	256 173

5th Company:	256 174
6th Company:	256 175
7th Company:	256 176
8th Company:	256 177

III./FJR 6

Battalion Staff:	256 178
Signal Communications Platoon:	256 178
9th Company:	256 179
10th Company:	256 180
11th Company:	256 181
12th Company:	256 182

IV./FJR 6

Battalion Staff:	unknown
Signal Communications Platoon:	unknown
13th Company:	256 166
14th Company:	256 167
15th Company:	256 165 B
16th Company:	256 165 C

Bearer of Oak Leaves to the Knight's Cross of the Iron Cross for service in the FJR 6:

von der Heydte, Friedrich August; Oberstleutnant, FJR 6, 19 October 1944

Bearers of the Iron Cross for service in FJR 6

Engelhardt, Johann; Oberleutnant, 8./FJR 6, 29 February 1944
Uhlig, Alexander; Oberfeldwebel, 16./FJR 6, 29 October 1944
Peitsch, Herbert; Gefreiter, 7./FJR 6, 29 October 1944
Mager, Rolf; Hauptmann, II./FJR 6, 31 October 1944
Köhne, Heinz; Fahnenjunker, 5./FJR 6, 31 October 1944
le Coutre, Georg; Leutnant, 10./FJR 6, 7 February 1945

Note: Bearers of the Knights Cross who earned their distinction in service before they joined FJR 6 are not listed here.

Battle Dates

Date	Location	FJR 6 Participants
8/9/1943–10/9/1943	Rome	1st and 3rd Battalions, Staff 1st and 3rd Battalions Regimental Staff Signal Communications Platoon
9/9/1943–11/9/1943	Monterotondo	2nd Battalion Staff 2nd Battalion Signal Communications Platoon
3/11/1943–16/11/1943	Reinhard Line	3rd Battalion Staff 3rd Battalion Signal Communications Platoon
17/11/1943–31/12/1943	Adria Line	3rd Battalion Regimental Staff 13th and 14th Companies Signal Communications Platoon
5/12/1943–7/12/1943	Radomyschl	1st Battalion Staff 1st Battalion Signal Communications Platoon
1/12/1943	Jelnitsch	3rd Company
16/12/1943–23/12/1943	Nowgordoka	1st Battalion
23/12/1943–27/12/1943	Elevation 159.9	1st Battalion Staff 1st Battalion Signal Communications Platoon
28/12/1943–7/1/1944	Kirowograd	1st Battalion Staff 1st Battalion Signal Communications Platoon
1/3/1944–6/3/1944	Olchowez	1st Battalion Staff 1st Battalion Signal Communications Platoon

Date	Location	FJR 6 Participants</TCH>
7/3/1944	Gussakowo	1st Battalion Staff 1st Battalion Signal Communications Platoon
8/3/1944	Talnoje	1st Battalion Staff 1st Battalion Signal Communications Platoon
9/3/1944	Kamenetschje	1st Battalion Staff 1st Battalion Signal Communications Platoon
10/3/1944	Nowo Archangelsk	1st Battalion Staff 1st Battalion Signal Communications Platoon
10/3/1944–14/3/1944	Nowosseliki	1st Battalion Staff 1st Battalion Signal Communications Platoon
16/3/1944–18/3/1944	Kuzaja Balka	1st Battalion Staff 1st Battalion Signal Communications Platoon
19/3/1944–9/4/1944	Bug-Bogen	1st Battalion Staff 1st Battalion Signal Communications Platoon
10/5/1944–11/5/1944	Stahlhelmhöhe	1st Battalion Staff 1st Battalion Signal Communications Platoon
6/6/1944	St-Georges-de-Bohon	3rd Battalion
6/6/1944	'Utah' Beach	1st Battalion Staff 1st Battalion

Date	Location	FJR 6 Participants
6/6/1944–7/6/1944	St-Mère-Eglise	2nd Battalion Staff 2nd Battalion Signal Communications Platoon
6/6/1944–7/6/1944	St-Côme-du-Mont	3rd Battalion
7/6/1944–12/6/1944	Carentan	2nd and 3rd Battalions Staff 2nd and 3rd Battalions Regimental Staff Signal Communications Platoon
13/6/1944–21/7/1944	Périers	2nd and 3rd Battalions Staff 2nd and 3rd Battalions
26/7/1944–9/8/1944	St Lô	2nd and 3rd Battalions Staff 2nd and 3rd Battalions Signal Communications Platoon
8/9/1944–11/9/1944	Beeringen	1st and 3rd Battalions Staff 1st and 3rd Battalions
8/9/1944–17/9/1944	Gheel	2nd Battalion Staff 2nd Battalion
17/9/1944–20/9/1944	Lommel	6th and 8th Companies Staff 3rd Battalion
17/9/1944–20/9/1944	Postel	5th and 6th Companies Staff 2nd Battalion
17/9/1944–18/9/1944	La Colonie	6th, 11th and 12th Companies
17/9/1944	Valkenswaard	11th Company
19/9/1944	Poppel	9th Company
19/9/1944–24/9/1944	Boxtel	9th, 10th, 12th and 15th Companies

Date	Location	FJR 6 Participants
22/9/1944–23/9/1944	Bladel	6th Company
24/9/1944–25/9/1944	Hechtel	1st and 4th Companies
24/9/1944–28/9/1944	Reusel	5th, 6th and 7th Companies
24/9/1944–2/10/1944	Eerde	1st, 9th, 10th, 13th and 16th Companies Regimental Staff Staff 3rd Battalion
25/9/1944–3/10/1944	Schijndel	3rd Battalion
1/10/1944–5/10/1944	Baarle-Nassau	2nd Battalion Signal Communications Platoon
5/10/1944–9/10/1944	Goirle	4th, 9th, 10th, 11th, 12th, 13th, 15th and 16th Companies
7/10/1944–25/10/1944	Hoogerheide	10th and 12th Companies Staff 3rd Battalion
8/10/1944–27/10/1944	Woensdrecht	1st, 3rd, 9th, 15th and 16th Companies Regimental Staff
13/10/1944–31/10/1944	Bergen op Zoom	2nd, 4th, 5th, 6th, 7th, 9th, 10th, 11th, 12th, 13th, 15th, 16th and 17th Companies Staff 2nd Battalion Signal Communications Platoon
16/10/1944–25/10/1944	Nederheide	1st, 13th, 15th and 16th Companies Signal Communications Platoon
20/10/1944–24/10/1944	Wouwse Plantation	5th, 8th, 11th and 15th Companies Staff 2nd Battalion

Date	Location	FJR 6 Participants</TCH>
26/11/1944–20/2/1945	Untermaubach	5th, 6th, 7th, 8th, 13th and 15th Companies Signal Communications Platoon
26/11/1944–31/12/1944	Bergheim	6th, 8th and 15th Companies Staff 2nd Battalion Signal Communications Platoon
26/11/1944–18/2/1945	Obermaubach	9th, 10th, 11th, 12th, 13th, 14th, 15th and 16th Companies Replacement Training Battalion Signal Communications Platoon
26/11/1944–8/2/1945	Zerkall	1st Battalion
4/12/1944–24/12/1944	Zülpich	1st, 13th, 15th, 16th and 17th Companies Regimental Staff
16/12/1944–20/12/1944	Bogheim	15th and 16th Companies
17/12/1944	Soller	7th Company
17/12/1944–21/12/1944	High Fens	Fallschirm Battlegroup von der Heydte
3/1/1945–27/2/1945	Nideggen	1st, 2nd, 4th, 9th, 11th, 12th, 13th and 17th Companies Staff 3rd Battalion Regimental Staff
3/1/1945–28/2/1945	Froitzscheidt	5th, 6th and 7th Companies Staff 2nd Battalion Signal Communications Platoon
3/1/1945–8/2/1945	Schmidt	3rd, 5th and 8th Companies Staff 2nd Battalion Signal Communications Platoon

Date	Location	FJR 6 Participants
4/1/1945–14/2/1945	Berg	10th and 12th Companies Regimental Staff Signal Communications Platoon
25/1/1945–31/1/1945	Wallerscheidt	16th Company
3/2/1945–12/2/1945	Vossenack	5th and 7th Companies
4/2/1945–9/2/1945	Haarscheidt	6th and 8th Company Staff 2nd Battalion
4/2/1945–9/2/1945	Hasenfeld	5th Company Staff 2nd Battalion
6/2/1945–7/2/1945	Kommerscheidt	8th Company Staff 2nd Battalion
6/2/1945–15/2/1945	Abenden	6th Company Staff 2nd Battalion Signal Communications Platoon
28/2/1945–1/3/1945	Wollersheim	Regimental Battlegroup FJR 6
5/3/1945	Remagen	Regimental Battlegroup FJR 6
8/3/1945–3/14/1945	Ittenbach	Regimental Battlegroup FJR 6

Photographic Appendix

Wedding photograph of Feldwebel Alois Grotzki and his wife, Lissi. Feldwebel Grotzki was the platoon leader of the 2nd Platoon, 1st Company.

Hauptfeldwebel Karl Hentschel of the 1st Company, and Oberleutnant Preikschat.

*Feldwebel G. Kabussa, I./FJR 6, here seen
as a Gefreiter with the Fallschirmschütze
insignia of the army.*

Right: This *Jäger* is wearing combat gloves in brown leather, the second model of coveralls (made from olive-green cloth), and his combat helmet. The helmet has a coat of matte-coloured, rough camouflage paint, which has fine wood shavings or sand mixed into it to cancel out light reflection.

Left: This *Gefreiter* is a survivor of the Russian campaign. On his pilot's blouse he is wearing a ribbon for the Eastern Front Medal, as well as the *Fallschirmschütze* insignia (the Ground Combat insignia of the Luftwaffe) and the Sports insignia. This portrait demonstrates the fashion of *Fallschirmjäger* for wearing coloured neck scarves, in this case a white silk scarf.

Left: *For his portrait, this Jäger is wearing the harness for his parachute, in addition to his coveralls and combat helmet. The harness belongs to the Fallschirmjäger's full parade uniform. In the left hand, he is holding the snap hook of his ripcord, which was hooked onto the static line inside the aircraft.*

Right: *This Oberjäger is also wearing the parachute harness, as well as the combat gloves and helmet for the photograph.*

Left: This Jäger is wearing third-model coveralls in the Splittertarn pattern. He is also wearing a coloured neck scarf. Further Fallschirmjäger gear here includes the brimless combat helmet and the combat gloves with their long, elastic cuffs – these were particularly appreciated by the Fallschirmjäger. He is also carrying his Pistol 08 Luge in a dark leather holster on his belt.

Right: This Oberjäger is wearing his pilot's blouse and a shirt and tie for his photograph. On his left breast is the Fallschirmschütze insignia of the Luftwaffe and the ribbon of the Iron Cross 2nd Class. The peaked cap seen here was seldom worn by the Fallschirmjäger outside of the barracks, but the pilot's cap was very popular.

Left: For his photograph, this Obergefreiter has put on his full formal uniform. The picture shows clearly the short pilot's blouse, which the Fallschirmjäger preferred over the service tunic. His distinctions include: the Fallschirmschütze insignia, the Iron Cross 1st Class and 2nd Class, as well as the Wound Badge in silver. On his belt he carries a bayonet with the company tassel.

Right: Gefreiter Kurt Joachim has a stitched version of the Fallschirmschütze insignia as well as the Wound Badge in silver and the Ground Combat insignia of the Luftwaffe. The 'Afrika' armband shows that he was a former member of the Africa Corps.

From left to right: Oberleutnant Reese,
Hauptmann Preikschat and Leutnant Waschke,
1944, in Wahn.

Obergefreiter Rudorf, 1st Battalion IIb, and
Gefreiter Geritzlehner of the 1st Battalion WuG
Troop on the steps of the Cologne cathedral in
1944. During the training period in Wahn, men
were frequently detached to clean-up crews
dealing the aftermath of Allied bomb attacks.

Portrait of Gefreiter Werner Eul and his jump
licence issued in Stendal in 1942. The swastika in
the insignia was removed after the war.

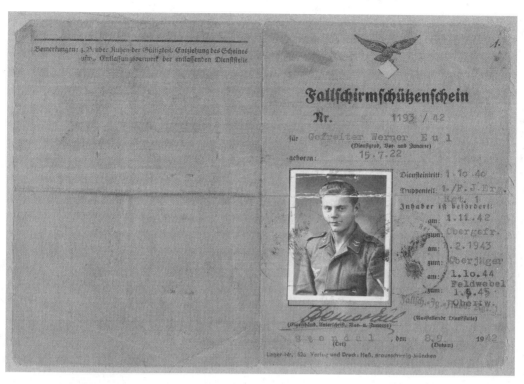

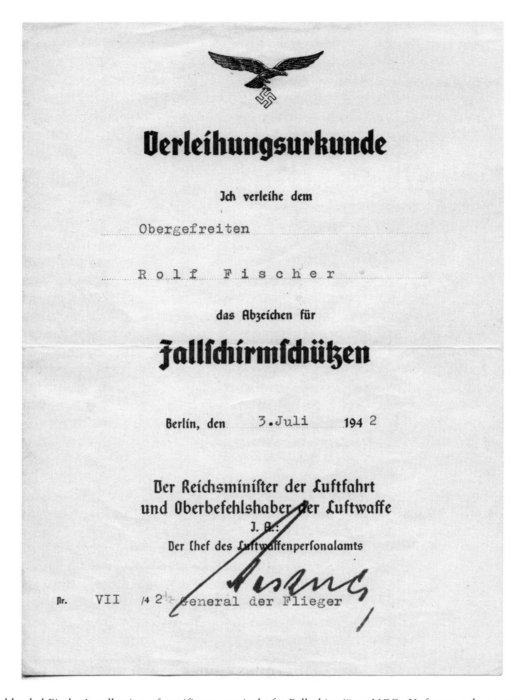

Feldwebel Fischer's collection of certificates, typical of a Fallschirmjäger NCO. Unfortunately, no more is known about Feldwebel Fischer. These documents come from C. Mason's collection. Translator's note: the first document is the Fallschirmschütze insignia; the second is for an Iron Cross 2nd Class; the third is a certificate for a Wound Badge in silver; the fourth is for an Iron Cross 1st Class.

IM NAMEN DES FÜHRERS
UND OBERSTEN BEFEHLSHABERS
DER WEHRMACHT
VERLEIHE ICH
DEM

Feldwebel

Rolf Fischer

Fallsch.Jg.Rgt. 6

DAS
EISERNE KREUZ
1. KLASSE

Gef.Stand _____ . 18.Dezbr. 19 44

Fallschirm-Armee-Oberkommando
Der Oberbefehlshaber
m.d.W.d.G.b.

(DIENSTSIEGEL)

General der Fallschirmtruppe.
(DIENSTGRAD UND DIENSTSTELLUNG)

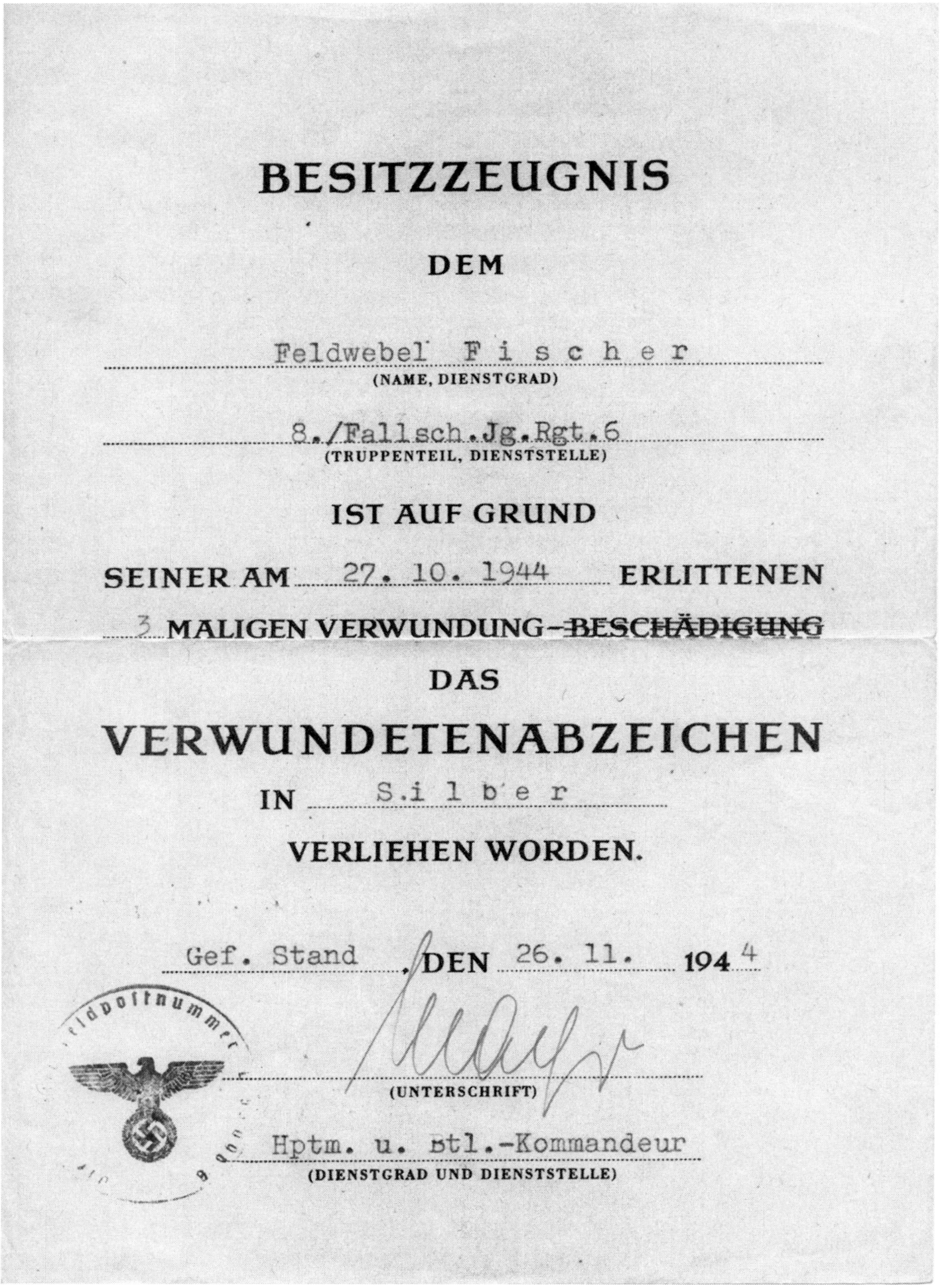

BESITZZEUGNIS

DEM

Feldwebel Fischer

(NAME, DIENSTGRAD)

8./Fallsch.Jg.Rgt.6

(TRUPPENTEIL, DIENSTSTELLE)

IST AUF GRUND

SEINER AM 27. 10. 1944 ERLITTENEN

3 MALIGEN VERWUNDUNG ~~BESCHÄDIGUNG~~

DAS

VERWUNDETENABZEICHEN

IN S i l b e r

VERLIEHEN WORDEN.

Gef. Stand , DEN 26. 11. 194 4

(UNTERSCHRIFT)

Hptm. u. Btl.-Kommandeur

(DIENSTGRAD UND DIENSTSTELLE)

IM NAMEN DES FÜHRERS UND OBERSTEN BEFEHLSHABERS DER WEHRMACHT

VERLEIHE ICH

DEM

Oberjäger

Rolf Fischer

DAS

EISERNE KREUZ 2. KLASSE

Gefechts-Stand, 18. Januar 19 44

(DIENSTSIEGEL)

Generalleutnant und Kommandeur
der 2. Fallschirm-Division

(DIENSTGRAD UND DIENSTSTELLUNG)

The photographs on this page and the following pages come from a picture collection entitled Unsere Luftwaffe. It was sold, amongst other places, in the enlisted men's clubs at the barracks. Photojournalists took the pictures, which show the different stages of the Fallschirmjäger training. Some, too, show the future Oberfeldwebel Alexander Uhlig.